DUQUESNE STUDIES

Philological Series

1

JOHN MILTON

A BIBLIOGRAPHICAL SUPPLEMENT

1929 - 1957

DUQUESNE STUDIES

Philological Series

1

JOHN MILTON

A BIBLIOGRAPHICAL SUPPLEMENT

1929 - 1957

COMPILED BY
CALVIN HUCKABAY
ASSOCIATE PROFESSOR OF ENGLISH
MISSISSIPPI STATE UNIVERSITY

AMS PRESS, INC.
NEW YORK ● 1967

Reprinted with permission of the original publisher

AMS PRESS, INC.
New York, N.Y. 10003
1967

Library of Congress Catalog Card Number: 60-11948

Manufactured in the United States of America

PREFACE

In 1930 Professor David H. Stevens published his *Reference Guide to Milton.* This was a compilation of Milton items published between 1800 and 1928. Professor Harris F. Fletcher issued in 1931 his *Contributions to a Milton Bibliography, 1800-1930* as a supplement to Stevens' ground-breaking work. The present bibliography is intended to supplement these two reference guides. Although Fletcher collected data for 1929-1930, I have included material published in those years so that students of Milton may conventiently check only one bibliography for items which have appeared since 1928.

My purpose has been to bring together significant books and articles in the field of Milton scholarship. Like Stevens and Fletcher, I am aware of the incomplete nature of my work. However, the present volume is not intended to be an allusion book. I have omitted casual references and much of the background material and have not been so diligent as Stevens in listing school editions of the works unless they contained rather extensive notes or critical commentary. Master's theses and doctoral dissertations have been included whenever published lists were available. Foreign studies occupy a significant place in this bibliography, but it has been difficult to locate many of them, especially those published in a number of European countries since the war.

In compiling the entries, I have generally followed the organization of Stevens. Classification of the items has been a problem because some deal with more than one aspect of Milton criticism. The only solution has been to list these items wherever they are relevant.

Whenever possible, I have examined every entry, but I have been forced to rely on the compilers of the annual bibliographies for a number of the annotations. Some of the entries are more fully annotated than others. Often the title of a work is an adequate annotation in itself, but in any case the annotations are intended as guides only and not as critical evaluations. In listing the critical works, I have departed from Stevens' chronological-alphabetical order of compilation for the more convenient alphabetical order. On the other hand, the editions and translations of Milton's works are listed chronologically under their respective classifications. When listing reviews that appeared in *The Year's Work in English Studies,* I have omitted volume numbers unless the entry was reviewed in a year other than that in which it was published.

The increasing number of Milton items published each year since 1928 records an intense interest in Milton the man and artist. If the early twentieth-century critics removed him from the shaky eminence of Victorian idolatry, the more recent critics have no less surely placed him on another pedestal with a firmer basis. Scholars have explored almost every possible facet of Milton's life and works. A variorum commentary on his poems is in progress, not to mention the Yale edition of his prose. Professor William R. Parker is writing a definitive biography.

Many individuals have aided me in the preparation of this bibliography. The trustees of the Southern Fellowships Fund made the undertaking possible by supplying financial assistance. Professors Esmond L. Marilla of Louisiana State University and Robert B. Holland of Mississippi State University offered encouragement and advice on a number of occasions. The reference librarians at the Library of Congress and those at the Sterling Memorial Library, Yale University, were helpful in locating volumes and in suggesting new avenues of reseach. My wife offered invaluable service in gathering and checking the entries. One of my students, Mr. Reuben A. Triplett, typed the manuscript.

I hope that this supplement will be of use to older scholars and to those who are only beginning their study of Milton. Corrections and additions will be appreciated.

Calvin Huckabay

Mississippi State University
January, 1959

VI

LIST OF ABBREVIATIONS

AB	American Bookman
AHR	American Historical Review
AJP	American Journal of Philology
AL	American Literature
AM	American Mercury
Ang.	Anglia
Ang. Bbl.	Anglia Beiblatt
Archiv	Archiv für das Studium der neueren Sprachen und Literaturen
BA	Books Abroad
BHM	Bulletin of the History of Medicine
BMLA	Bulletin of the Medical Library Association
BNYPL	Bulletin of the New York Public Library
BS	Bibliotheca sacra
Camb. Jour.	Cambridge Journal
CE	College English
CHR	Catholic Historical Review
CJ	Classical Journal
Class. Bull.	Classical Bulletin
Class. Rev.	Classical Review
CL	Comparative Literature
Com. Rev.	Comparative Review
CP	Classical Philology
CQR	Church Quarterly Review
CR	Contemporary Review
Crit.	Criterion
CW	Catholic World
DA	Dissertation Abstracts
DL	Deutsche Literaturzeitung (Berlin)
DR	Dalhousie Review
DUJ	Durham University Journal
EA	Études Anglaises
EHR	English Historical Review
EIC	Essays in Criticism
EJ	English Journal
ELH	A Journal of English Literary History
Eng.	English
ER	English Review
Eras.	Erasmus

ES	English Studies
E&S	Essays and Studies
ESt.	Englische Studien
Expl.	The Explicator
FR	Fortnightly Review
FS	Franciscan Studies
GRM	Germanisch-romanische Monatsschrift
HJ	Hibbert Journal
HLB	Huntington Library Bulletin
HLQ	Huntington Library Quarterly
HR	Hopkins Review
HTR	Harvard Theological Review
Ital.	Italica
JAAC	Journal of Aesthetics and Art Criticism
JEGP	Journal of English and Germanic Philology
JEH	Journal of Ecclesiastical History
JHI	Journal of the History of Ideas
JMH	Journal of Modern History
JR	**Journal of Religion**
KR	Kenyon Review
LGRP	Literaturblatt für germanische und romanische Philologie
Libr.	The Library
LL	Life and Letters
L&P	Literature and Psychology (New York)
LQHR	London Quarterly and Holborn Review
MA	Microfilm Abstracts
MB	More Books, Bulletin of the Boston Public Library
Merc.	(London) Mercury
MGW	Manchester Guardian Weekly
MHRA	Modern Humanities Research Association
ML	Music and Letters
MLJ	Modern Language Journal
MLN	Modern Language Notes
MLQ	Modern Language Quarterly
MLR	Modern Language Review
MP	Modern Philology
Nat.	The Nation (New York)
Nat. and Athen.	The Nation and Athenaeum
NB	New Books
NC	Nineteenth Century

Neophil.	Neophilologus
NEQ	New England Quarterly
NER	Nation and English Review
NLB	Newberry Library Bulletin
NQ	Notes and Queries
NR	New Republic
NSN	New Statesman and Nation
NYHTBR	New York Herald Tribune Book Review
NYTBR	New York Times Book Review
Obs.	The Observer
Oxf. Mag.	Oxford Magazine
PAPS	Proceedings of the American Philosophical Society
PBSA	Proceedings of the Bibliographical Society of America
Pers.	Personalist
PMLA	Publications of the Modern Language Association of America
PQ	Philological Quarterly
PR	Partisan Review
PRv.	Philosophical Review
PULC	Princeton University Library Chronicle
QJS	Quarterly Journal of Speech
QQ	Queen's Quarterly
QR	Quarterly Review
RA-A	Revue Anglo-Americaine
RC	Revue Critique
RES	Review of English Studies
RIP	Rice Institute Pamphlet
RLC	Revue de litterature comparée
RN	Renaissance News
RR	Romanic Review
SAB	South Atlantic Bulletin
SAQ	South Atlantic Quarterly
Sat. Rev.	Saturday Review (London)
SCN	Seventeenth Century News
Scr.	Scrutiny
SEER	Slavonic and Eastern European Review
SFQ	Southern Folklore Quarterly
SN	Studia Neophilologica
SP	Studies in Philology

Spec.	Speculum
Spect.	Spectator
SR	Sewanee Review
SRL	Saturday Review of Literature (New York)
Sun. Times	(London) Sunday Times
SWR	Southwest Review
Th.	Thought
TLS	(London) Times Literary Supplement
TRSC	Transactions of the Royal Society of Canada
TT	Time and Tide
UEIES	Uppsala English Institute Essays and Studies
UM	University Microfilms
UTQ	University of Toronto Quarterly
UTSE	University of Texas Studies in English
VQR	Virginia Quarterly Review
WHR	Western Humanities Review
WR	Western Review
YR	Yale Review
YWES	The Year's Work in English Studies

CONTENTS

BIBLIOGRAPHY

1 ARMS, GEORGE, and JOSEPH M. KUNTZ, Poetry Explication: A Checklist of Interpretation since 1925 of British and American Poems, Past and Present. New York: Swallow, 1950.

2 BATESON, F. W., ed. The Cambridge Bibliography of English Literature. Cambridge: Cambridge University Press; New York: Macmillan, 1941. 4 vols.
John Milton (1608-1674), by D. H. Stevens, 1, 463-73. Supplement, 1957, pp. 225-37, by W. Arthur Turner, Alberta T. Turner, and W. Edson Richmond.

3 BOND, RICHMOND P., and D. MACMILLAN. Recent Publications: Studies in the Seventeenth and Eighteenth Centuries. SP, 29, 1932, 505-13.

4 BAUGH, ALBERT C., et al. American Bibliography, 1922—. PMLA, 37, 1922, 10-11; 38, 1923, 10-11; 39. 1924, 12-13; 40, 1925, 12; 41, 1926, 13-14; 42, 1927, 28-9; 43, 1928, 27-8; 44, 1929, 33-4; 45, 1930, 37; 46, 1931, 27-8; 47, 1932, 1235-6; 48, 1933, 1326-7; 49, 1934, 1229-30; 50, 1935, 1264-6; 51, 1936, 1237-8; 52, 1937, 1254-6; 53, 1938, 1247-8; 54, 1939, 1240-2; 55, 1940, 1254-6; 56, 1941, 1245-8; 57, 1942, 1251-3; 58, 1943, 1221-3; 59, 1944, 1213-14; 60, 1945, 1223-5; 61, 1946, 1255-7. Until 1946, these bibliographies were published in supplements and are bibliographies of the year indicated. There was no list published in 1947. The following volumes contain the American bibliography for the previous year: PMLA, 63, 1948, 51-2; 64, 1949, 31-2; 65, 1950, 54-5; 66, 1951, 63-4; 67, 1952, 34-5; 68, 1953, 119-20; 69, 1954, 103-4; 70, 1955, 138-40; 71, 1956, 141-2; 72, 1957, 210-11; 73, 1958, 166-7.

5 BUSH, DOUGLAS. English Literature in the Earlier Seventeenth Century. Oxford History of English Literature, Vol. 5. Oxford: Oxford University Press, 1945.
Chronological Tables and Bibliography, pp. 359-98; Milton Bibliography, pp. 567-71.

6 Canadian Graduate Theses in the Humanities and Social Sciences. Ottawa: Edmond, Cloutier, 1951.

7 (CANDY, HUGH C. H.). John Milton. A Catalogue of Works by or Relating to John Milton, Largely Comprising the Library of the Well-Known Milton Scholar, the Late Professor Hugh C. H. Candy. London: Maggs Bros., 1936. 56pp.

1

A Bibliographical Supplement

8 ENGLISH ASSOCIATION. The Year's Work in English Studies, 1920—. Oxford: Oxford University Press, issued annually. Author of Milton sections: L. C. Martin, Arnold Davenport, et al. 1. 1919-20, 81-4; 2. 1920-1, 103-8; 3, 1922, 111-19; 4, 1923, 137-41; 5, 1924, 163-70; 6, 1925, 195-201, 208-9; 7, 1926, 187-92; 8, 1927, 199-205; 9, 1928, 201-4; 10, 1929, 234-8; 11, 1930, 219-30; 12, 1931, 202-3, 206-9; 13, 1932, 205-12, 219-21; 14, 1933, 249-53; 15, 1934, 234-41; 16, 1935, 248-57, 264; 17, 1936, 187-91; 18, 1937, 180-6; 19, 1938, 174-9; 20, 1939, 112-17; 21, 1940, 167-75; 22, 1941, 158-64; 23, 1942, 157-65; 24, 1943, 147-59; 25, 1944, 139-45; 26, 1945, 140-50; 27, 1946, 169-75; 28, 1947, 184-93; 29, 1948, 186, 191-7; 30, 1949, 162-71; 31, 1950, 169, 173-82; 32, 1951, 184-92; 33, 1952, 177-86; 34, 1953, 199-210; 35, 1954, 137-44; 36, 1955, 158-65.

9 FISHER, JOHN H. Serial Bibliographies in the Modern Langues and Literatures. PMLA, **66**, 1951, 138-56.

10 FLETCHER, HARRIS FRANCIS. Contributions to a Milton Bibliography, 1800-1930, Being a List of Addenda to Stevens's Reference Guide to Milton. University of Illinois Stud. in Lang. and Lit., 16. Urbana: University of Illinois Press, 1931. 166pp.
Rev: Paul Chauvet, RA-A, 9, 1931, 150-1; S. B. Liljegren, Ang. Bbl., 43, 1932, 369-71; A. Koszul, RC, 65, 1932, 571; Neophil., 17, 1932, 309; D. Saurat, MLN, 48, 1933, 413-14.

11 GREGORY, RUTH W. American Criticism of Milton, 1800-1938, A Contribution to a Bibliography. Type-written, Library School, University of Wisconsin, 1938.

12 HANFORD, JAMES H. A Milton Handbook. Fourth Edition, Revised. New York: Crofts, 1946.
Bibliography, pp. 421-47.

13 HENRY E. HUNTINGTON LIBRARY AND ART GALLERY. An Exhibition of William Blake's Water-color Drawings of Milton's Paradise Lost, May 12-July 31, 1936. San Marino: Huntington Library, 1936. 15pp.

14 HUGHES, MERRITT Y., ed. John Milton. Complete Poems and Major Prose. With Notes and Introds. New York: Odyssey Press, 1957. xix, 1059pp.
In the notes, the introductions, and the bibliographies at the end of the introductions, Hughes brings together much of the significant scholarship on Milton since 1930.

15 - - - - - -. Paradise Lost. New York: Odyssey Press, 1935.
Bibliography, pp. liii-lvi.

2

16 - - - - - -. Paradise Regained, the Minor Poems, and Samson Agonistes. New York: Odyssey Press, 1937. Bibliography, pp. lvi-lxiii.

17 - - - - - -. Prose Selections. New York: Odyssey Press, 1947. Bibliography, pp. cxxv-cxlvii.

18 HUNTER, WILLIAM B., JR., ed. Bibliography of J. Milton French. I. John Milton. II. Other Seventeenth-Century English Literature. Milton Society of America, Annual Dinner Booklet, 1956.

19 - - - - - -. Work in Progress, 1957. Milton Society of America, Annual Dinner Booklet, 1957, pp. 8-11.

20 ILLINOIS, UNIVERSITY OF. Collections of First Editions of Milton's Works, University of Illinois Library. An Exhibition, October 1-31, 1953. Introd. and notes prepared by Harris F. Fletcher. Urbana: University of Illinois Press, 1953. 24pp.

21 Index Translationum. Paris: International Institute of International Cooperation, 1932-40. 31 vols. Continued in 1948 under the auspices of UNESCO.

22 LIBRARY OF CONGRESS. Catalogue Division. A List of American Doctoral Dissertations Printed. Washington: Government Printing Office, 1912-40. 27 vols.

23 List of Theses, 1917-1937. SAB, 4, No. 1, 1938, 2-15. A list published annually since 1938.

24 MODERN HUMANITIES RESEARCH ASSOCIA-TION. Annual Bibliography of English Language and Literature. Ed. (1956) by Angus MacDonald and Henry J. Pettit, Jr. Cambridge: Bowes and Bowes, Cambridge University Press, 1920—.
1, 1920, 23-4; 2, 1921, 73-4; 3, 1922, 112-14; 4, 1923, 108-10; 5, 1924, 75-7; 6, 1925, 77-9; 7, 1926, 83-5; 8, 1927, 95-7; 9, 1928, 113-14; 10, 1929, 117-18; 11, 1930, 114-16; 12, 1931, 133-6; 13, 1932, 128-31; 14, 1933, 130-3; 15, 1934, 142-5; 16, 1935, 146-8; 17, 1936, 145-8; 18, 1937, 163-6; 19, 1938, 146-8; 20, 1939, 148-51; 21, 1940, 144-7; 22, 1941, 116-19; 23, 1942, 74-6; 24, 1943-4, 147-51; 25, 1945, 77-9; 26, 1946, 61-3; 27, 1947, 122-4; 28, 1948, 127-31; 29, 1949, 138-42.

25 MUMMENDEY, RICHARD. Language and Literature of the Anglo-Saxon Nations as Presented in German Doctoral Dissertations, 1885-1950. Charlottesville: Bibliographical Society of the University of Virginia; Bonn: H. Bouvier, 1954.

3

26 PINTO, VIVIAN DE SOLA. The English Renaissance: 1510-1688. Introductions to English Literature. Ed. by Bonamy Dobrée. New York: McBride, 1938.
John Milton, a Bibliography, pp. 337-52.

27 PMLA: RESEARCH IN PROGRESS. PMLA, 63, 1948, 199-201; 64, 1949, 141-2; 65, 1950, 160-1; 66, 1951, 187; 67, 1952, 168-9; 69, 1954, 240-2; 71, 1956, 290-1; 73, 1958, 60-1.

28 RECORD, P. D., and MAGDA WITHROW. Index to Theses Accepted for Higher Degrees in the Universities of Great Britain and Ireland. London: Aslib, 1953—.
Five volumes have been published: 1, 1953 for 1950-1; 2, 1955 for 1951-2; 3, 1956 for 1952-3; 4, 1957 for 1953-4; 5, 1957 for 1954-5; 6, 1958 for 1955-6; 7, 1959 for 1956-7.

29 SEARS, MINNIE E., and MARION SHAW. Essay and General Literature Index, 1900-1933: An Index to About 40,000 Essays and Articles in 2144 Volumes and Collections of Essays and Miscellaneous Works. New York: H. W. Wilson, 1934. 5 vols. Supplements published, 1935 and 1955.

30 SEVENTEENTH CENTURY NEWS. 1, 1942—. Published from 1942 until 1950 as The Seventeenth Century News Letter.
Under the editorship of J. Max Patrick, this journal has become increasingly important to the student of the seventeenth century. For the Miltonist, it contains lists of current articles, abstracts of articles and papers, and book reviews. It also records the activities of the Milton Society of America.

31 STEVENS, DAVID HARRISON. A Reference Guide to Milton from 1800 to the Present Day. Chicago: University of Chicago Press, 1930. x, 302pp.
Includes items to 1928; well annotated and usually accurate. Rev: H. J. C. Grierson and A. Melville Clark, YWES, 230; E. N. S. Thompson, PQ, 9, 1930, 317; G. Saintsbury, Bookman, 78, 1930, 161-2; TLS, Apr. 10, 1930, p. 320; NQ, 158, 1930, 450; E. C. Batho and E. J. Vaughan, MLR, 26, 1931, 203-4; D. Saurat, RES, 7, 1931, 472-4; R. S. C., MP, 28, 1931, 380-1; H. F. Fletcher, MLN, 46, 1931, 539-41; S. B. Liljegren, Ang. Bbl., 43, 1932, 369-71; F. Delatte, Rev. belge de philol. et d'hist., 12, 1933, 309-12.

32 THOMPSON, E. N. S. John Milton: A Topical Bibliography. New Haven: Yale University Press, 1916. xl, 104pp.

33 TROTIER, ARNOLD H., and MARION HARMON. Doctoral Dissertations Accepted by American Universities. New York: H. W. Wilson, 1933-55. 22 vols.

This annual list has been continued in Dissertation Abstracts, beginning with the thirteenth issue of Vol. 17, 1957, with the title, Index to American Doctoral Dissertations.

34 WELLS, WILLIAM, et al. Recent Literature of the English Renaissance. SP, 1917—.

SP, 14, 1917, 225-6; 15, 1918, 216; 16, 1919, 212-13; 17, 1920, 261-2; 18, 1921, 375; 19, 1922, 278-80; 20, 1923, 277-80; 21, 1924, 449-51; 22, 1925, 319-22; 23, 1926, 276-81; 24, 1927, 350-3; 25, 1928, 249-53; 26, 1929, 260-3; 27, 1930, 361-3; 28, 1931, 352-6; 29, 1932, 322-6; 30, 1933, 313-18; 31, 1934, 303-6; 32, 1935, 326-30; 33, 1936, 346-50; 34, 1937, 329-33; 35, 1938, 348-51; 36, 1939, 331-4; 37, 1940, 349-52; 38, 1941, 332-6; 39, 1942, 383-7; 40, 1943, 307-10; 41, 1944, 307-10; 42, 1945, 318-20; 43, 1946, 327-31; 44, 1947, 323-6; 45, 1948, 301-4; 46, 1949, 278-82; 47, 1950, 322-8; 48, 1951, 344-9; 49, 1952, 319-24; 50, 1953, 295-8; 51, 1954, 283-6; 52, 1955, 280-4; 53, 1956, 301-5; 54, 1957, 253-7; 55, 1958, 288-92.
Contains items published during the previous year.

35 (WHITING, GEORGE W.). The Published Writings of George Wesley Whiting. Compiled by Ann M. Gossman. RIP, 44, 1957, vi-viii.
Contains a list of Whiting's Milton scholarship.

36 (WHITNEY, HENRY AUSTIN, 1826-1889). The John Milton Collection Formed by Henry Austin Whitney. New York: Alexander Press, (1935). 21pp.

COLLECTED WORKS: PROSE AND POETRY

37   The Student's Milton, Being the Complete Poems of John
     Milton, with the Greater Part of His Prose Works, Now
     Printed in One Volume, together with New Translations
     into English of his Italian, Latin, and Greek Poems.
     Ed. by Frank Allen Patterson. New York: Crofts, 1930.
     ix, 1090, 41pp. Revised Edition, 1933.

     Rev: H. J. C. Grierson and A. Melville Clark, YWES, 225-6;
     E. C. Batho and E. J. Vaughan, MLR, 26, 1931, 202-3;
     D. Saurat, RES, 7, 1931, 472-4; H. F. Fletcher, JEGP, 31,
     1932, 156-8; R. D. H(avens), MLN, 69, 1934, 558; W.
     Fischer, Ang. Bbl., 47, 1936, 56-7.

38   The Works of John Milton. Gen. Ed., Frank Allen Patter-
     son. New York: Columbia University Press, 1931-38.
     18 vols. in 21.

     Vol. 1, Pt. 1: The Shorter English Poems, ed. by
     Frank Allen Patterson; The Italian Poems, ed. and trans.
     by Arthur Livingstone; The Latin and Greek Poems,
     ed. by W. P. Trent in collaboration with Thomas O.
     Mabbott, with a trans. by Charles Knapp, 1931.

     Vol. 1, Pt. 2: Samson Agonistes, ed. by Frank Allen
     Patterson, 1931. xv, 605pp.

     Vol. 2, Pt. 1: Paradise Lost, Books 1-8, ed. by Frank
     Allen Patterson, 1931.

     Vol. 2, Pt. 2: Paradise Lost, Books 9-12, ed. by Frank
     Allen Patterson, 1931. ix, 547pp.

     Vol. 3, Pt. 1: Of Prelatical Episcopacy, Animad-
     versions... against Smectynmuus, The Reason of Church
     Government, An Apology against a Pamphlet, ed. by
     Harry Morgan Ayres, 1931.

     Vol. 3, Pt. 2: The Doctrine and Discipline of Divorce,
     ed. by the Late Chilton Latham Powell and Frank Allen
     Patterson, 1931. ix, 585pp.

     Vol. 4: The Judgment of Martin Bucer, Tetrachordon,
     Colasterion, ed. by Chilton Latham Powell; Of Educa-
     tion, Areopagitica, ed. by William Haller, 1931. ix,
     368pp.

     Vol. 5: The Tenure of Kings and Magistrates,
     Eikonoklastes, ed. by William Haller, 1932. ix, 352pp.

     Vol. 6: A Treatise of Civil Power; Considerations
     touching the likeliest means to remove Hirelings out of
     the church; A letter to a Friend Concerning the Ruptures
     of the Commonwealth; The Present Means, and brief
     Delineation of a Free Commonwealth... In a Letter to
     General Monk; The Readie and Easie Way to Establish
     a Free Commonwealth; Brief Notes upon a late Sermon,

Titl'd, the Fear of God and the King, &c; Of True Religion, Heresie, Schism, Toleration; Articles of Peace... Observations; A Declaration of Letters Patent of the Election of this Present King of Poland, ed. by William Haller, 1932. xi, 371pp.

Vol. 7: Joannis Miltoni Angli Pro Populo Anglicano Defensio, ed. by Clinton W. Keyes, with a Trans. by Samuel Lee Wolff, 1932. ix, 587pp.

Vol. 8: Joannis Miltoni Angli Pro Populo Anglicano Defensio Secunda, ed. by Eugene J. Strittmatter, with the Trans. of George Burnett, London, 1809, Revised by Moses Hadas, 1933. vii, 266pp.

Vol. 9: Joannis Miltoni Angli Pro Se Defensio contra Alexandrum Morum Ecclesiasten, ed. by Eugene J. Strittmatter, with the Trans. of George Burnett, London, 1809, Revised by Moses Hadas, 1933. vii, 308pp.

Vol. 10: The History of Britain, A Brief History of Moscovia, ed. by George Philip Krapp, 1932. ix, 387pp.

Vol. 11: Artis Logicae Plenior Institutio, ed. and trans. by Allan H. Gilbert, 1935. xv, 538pp.

Vol. 12: The Familiar Letters of John Milton, ed. by Donald Lemen Clark with the Trans. of David Masson; The Prolusions of John Milton, ed. by Donald Lemen Clark with a Trans. of Bromley Smith; An Early Prolusion by John Milton and Miscellaneous Correspondence in Foreign Tongues, ed. and trans. by Thomas Ollive Mabbott and Nelson Glen McCrea; English Correspondence by John Milton, Collected and Ed. by Thomas Ollive Mabbott; Correspondence of Milton and Mylius, Collected, Ed., and Trans. by Thomas Ollive Mabbott and Nelson Glenn McCrea, 1936. xi, 415pp.

Vol. 13: The State Papers of John Milton, Collected and Ed. by Thomas Ollive Mabbott and J. Milton French, including (1) Literae Pseudo-Senatus Anglicani, 1676, with the Translation of Edward Phillips, 1694, and (2) Additional Material, with Translations by Several Hands: Letters from the Skinner Manuscript, State Papers from Various Sources, English State Papers by John Milton now first printed from the Columbia Manuscript, Major State Documents Translated by Milton, 1937. xv, 646pp.

Vol. 14: De Doctrina Christiana, Bk. 1, Chs. 1-6, ed. with the Trans. of Charles R. Sumner, D. D., by James Holly Hanford and Waldo Hilary Dunn, 1933. vii, 403pp.

Vol. 15: De Doctrina Christiana, Bk. 1, Chs. 7-20, 1933. viii, 409pp.

Vol. 16: De Doctrina Christiana, Bk. 1, Chs. 21-33, 1934. viii, 381pp.
Vol. 17: De Doctrina Christiana, Bk. 2, 1934. viii, 587pp.
Vol. 18: The Uncollected Writings of John Milton, ed. by Thomas Ollive Mabbott and J. Milton French with Trans. by Nelson Glenn McCrea and Others, including (1) Proposalls; (2) Latin Documents by Milton in the Scriptum Parlamenti, 1652; (3) Additional State Papers; (4) Milton's Commonplace Book, ed. by James Holly Hanford, with a Trans. by Nelson Glenn McCrea; (5) Additions to the Commonplace Book; (6) Outlines for Tragedies; (7) Character of the Long Parliament; (8) Toland's Additions to the History of Britain, contributed by Harris Fletcher; (9) Essays from the Columbia Manuscript; (10) Additional Correspondence; (11) Fugitive, Lost, and Projected Works; (12) Book Inscriptions; (13) Introduction to Raleigh's Cabinet Council; (14) Marginalia. Appendices: (1) New Discovered Texts of Hobson Poems, Contributed by William R. Parker; (2) Poems Ascribed to Milton; (3) Apothegmata and Records of Conversations; (4) Legal Documents; (5) Joannis Philippi Angli Responsio; (6) Supposed Collaborations; (7) Index to Pro Populo; (8) Index to History of Britain; (9) Apocryphal Prose Works; (10) Conversations with Mylius; (11) Marginalia on Malvezzi; 1938. xv, 656pp.

Rev: G. R. Elliott, AB, Sept., 1931, pp. 74-6; H. W. Garrod, Nat., 132, 1931, 681-2, 135, 1932, 175-6, and 143, 1936, 498-9; TLS, Sept. 3, 1931, p. 987, June 23, 1932, p. 461, Jan. 26, 1933, p. 54, July 4, 1935, p. 435, Mar. 20, 1937, p. 226, Apr. 23, 1938, p. 283, and Jan. 7, 1939, p. 8; A. M. Witherspoon, SRL, Aug. 8, 1931, pp. 33-5, and Dec. 24, 1938, p. 19; A. Tate, NR, 68, 1931, 266-8; D. Saurat, RES, 8, 1932, 340-3, 10, 1934, 229-31, 14, 1938, 349-52, and 16, 1940, 221; F. S. Boas, YWES, 13, 1932, 219, and 16, 1935, 264; H. Darbishire, RES, 9, 1933, 61-2, 319; H. J. C. Grierson, RES, 9, 1933, 316-19; B. A. Wright, MLR, 29, 1934, 452-8, 31, 1936, 79-83, 32, 1937, 96, 33, 1938, 432, and 35, 1940, 88-9; H. F. Fletcher, JEGP, 33, 1934, 132-44, 300-5, and 38, 1939, 147-52, 292-300; L. C. Martin, YWES, 18, 1937, 181-2, and 19, 1938, 174-5; Maurice Kelley, MLN, 51, 1936, 463-6; W. C. Abbott, AHR, 44, 1938, 101-4; NQ, 175, 1938, 394-6, and 176, 1939, 35.

39 PATTERSON, FRANK A., and FRENCH R. FOGLE. An Index to the Columbia Edition of the Works of John Milton. New York: Columbia University Press; London: Milford, 1940. 2 vols. xxviii, 1073, and xi, 2141pp.
Vol. 1: A-K; Vol. 2: L-Z.
Rev: L. C. Martin, YWES, 175; TLS, Nov. 16, 1940, p. 583;

D. F. Smith, N. Mex. Quar., 10, 1940, 187-9; H. F. Fletcher, JEGP, 40, 1941, 146-8; R. T. F., Pers., 22, 1941, 309; A. W. Witherspoon, SRL, No. 14, 1941, p. 11; A. S. P. Woodhouse, UTQ, 10, 1941, 504-5; W. C. Abbott, AHR, 46, 1941, 978-9; W. R. Parker, MLN, 57, 1942, 405-6.

40 Complete Poetry and Selected Prose of John Milton. With English Metrical Translations of the Latin, Greek, and Italian Poems. Ed. by E. H. Visiak, with a Foreword by Sir Arnold Wilson. London: Nonesuch Press; New York: Random House, 1938. xxvii, 860pp.
Rev: L. C. Martin, YWES, 180-1; K. John, NSN, N. S., 15, 1938, 698-700; John Hayward, Spect., Apr. 15, 1938, p. 680; CR, 154, 1938, 128; NQ, 175, 1938, 233-4; D. Saurat, FR, 164, 1938, 367-8, and RES, 16, 1940, 219-20.

41 Complete Poetry and Selected Prose of John Milton. New York: Modern Library, 1942. vi, 756pp.

42 Milton. Selected Poetry and Prose. Ed. by C. R. Bull. Melbourne: Melbourne University Press, 1948. x, 148pp.

43 The Portable Milton. Ed. by Douglas Bush, with an Introd. New York: Viking Press, 1949. 693pp.

44 Complete Poetry and Selected Prose of John Milton. Introd. by Cleanth Brooks. New York: Modern Library, 1950. xxiv, 756pp.

45 John Milton. Complete Poems and Major Prose. Ed. by Merritt Y. Hughes, with Notes and Introds. New York: Odyssey Press, 1957. xix, 1059pp.

46 The Complete Poems of John Milton. Printed together with New Translations into English of his Italian, Latin, and Greek Poems. Ed. by Frank Allen Patterson. New York: Crofts, 1930. ix, 439pp. Revised Edition, 1933.
Contains the poetry published in The Student's Milton.

47 The Poems of John Milton. Ed. with an Introd. by Frank Allen Patterson. Modern Readers' Series. New York: Macmillan, 1930. ix, 439pp.

48 The English Poems of John Milton, from the Edition of the Late H. C. Beeching, D. D. London: Oxford University Press, 1932. vii, 488pp.
Several editions "from Beeching" are listed in Stevens.

49 John Milton. Poems. Ed. and arranged with a Preface by H. J. C. Grierson. New York: Coward-McCann, 1933. 2 vols.

50 The Poetical Works of John Milton. Introd. by W. H. D. Rouse. Everyman's Library. New York: Dutton; London: Dent, 1933. xvi, 554pp.
A reprint of Stevens' No. 254.

51 The Poetical Works of John Milton. Ed. after the original texts by the Reverend H. C. Beeching, M. A., including William Cowper's Trans. of the Latin and Italian Poems, with an Introd. by Charles Grosvenor Osgood. New York: Oxford University Press, 1935. xxxi, 599pp.

52 The Complete Poems of John Milton with Complete Notes by Thomas Newton, D. D., Bishop of Bristol. Illustrated by Gustave Doré and Others. New York: Crown Publishers, 1936. ix, 665pp.
Rev: L. C. Martin, YWES, 187.

53 The Poems of John Milton, with an Introd. and Notes by James Holly Hanford. Nelson's English Series. New York: T. Nelson, 1936. lxxxviii, 582pp. Second Edition, 1953.

54 The Poetical Works of John Milton. Ed. after the original texts of H. C. Beeching. New edition with translations of the Italian, Latin and Greek Poems from the Columbia University edition, and a Reader's Guide by W. W. Skeat. London: Oxford University Press, 1938. xiii, 679pp.
Rev: L. C. Martin, YWES, 175; NQ, 175, 1938, 341-2; P. Meissner, DL, 60, 1939, 916-18.

55 The English Poems of John Milton. With an Introd. by Charles Williams, and a Reader's Guide to Milton Compiled by Walter Skeat. World's Classics Series. Oxford: Oxford University Press; London: Milford, 1940. xxii, 545pp.

Rev: D. C. Macgregor, RES, 17, 1940, 479-81; TLS, May 11, 1940, p. 235, July 26, 1940, p. 359, and Aug. 9, 1940, p. 385; Margaret Willy, Eng., 4, 1942, 108.

56 The Complete Poetical Works of John Milton. A New Text, ed. with an introd. and notes by Harris Francis Fletcher. New Cambridge Edition. Boston: Houghton Mifflin, 1941. xiii, 574pp.

A revision of William V. Moody's Cambridge Edition. The Life and Times of John Milton, 1608-1674, pp. 1-39.

Rev: E. N. S. T(hompson), PQ, 20, 1941, 188-92; A. S. P. Woodhouse, JEGP, 41, 1942, 99-102; W. R. Parker, MLN, 57, 1942, 686.

57 John Milton's Complete Poetical Works, Reproduced in Photographic Fascimile. Ed. by Harris Francis Fletcher. Urbana: University of Illinois Press, 1943-8. 4 vols.

Vol. 1: Poems &c. upon Several Occasions, 1673. Poems, both English and Latin, 1645. With Fugitive Printings, Manuscript Copies, and Their Collations, 1943. vi, 465pp.

Vol. 2: The First Edition of Paradise Lost, with the Plans and Lists of Epic Subjects from the Trinity College Manuscript, the Manuscript of Book I, with Transcriptions and Collations, 1945. vi, 634pp.

Vol. 3: The Second Edition of Paradise Lost, 1948. iv, 455pp.

Vol. 4: The 1671 Edition of Paradise Regained and Samson Agonistes, 1948. iv, 316pp.

Rev: TLS, July 8, 1944, p. 335, and Aug. 17, 1946, p. 390; W. W. Greg, MLR, 39, 1944, 409-17; J. Milton French, JEGP, 43, 1944, 474-8, 45, 1946, 458-64, and 48, 1949, 413-20; E. N. S. Thompson, PQ, 23, 1944, 185-6, and 25, 1946, 287-8; L. C. Martin, YWES, 26, 1945, 140-1, and 29, 1948, 191-2; Maurice Kelley, MLN, 60, 1945, 188-92, 63, 1948, 208-9, and 66, 1951, 103-6; B. A. Wright, Libr., 4th Ser., 25, 1945, 87-94; Helen Darbishire, RES, 23, 1947, 170-3, and ibid., N. S., 2, 1951, 386-9; A. H. Gilbert, SAQ, 46, 1947, 289-90; W. R. Parker, PBSA, 41, 1947, 33-52, and 43, 1949, 361-4.

58 AUDEN, W. H., and N. H. Pearson, eds. Poets of the English Language. Vol. 3: Milton to Goldsmith. New York: Viking Press, 1950.

Includes the usual short lyrics, parts of Paradise Lost, and all of Samson Agonistes, accompanied by brief and somewhat commonplace introductory comments.

Rev: Bonamy Dobrée, Spect., Sept. 5, 1952, p. 304.

59   The Poetical Works of John Milton. Ed. by Helen
     Darbishire. Oxford: Clarendon Press, 1952-5. 2 vols.
     Vol. 1: Paradise Lost, 1952. xxv, 326pp. Vol. 2: Paradise
     Regained, Samson Agonistes, Poems upon Severall Oc-
     casions Both English and Latin, 1955. xx, 376pp.
     Sets forth the case for a reformed text, 1, ix-xviii. Includes
     textual notes and commentaries.
     Rev: Arnold Davenport, YWES, 33, 1952, 182, and 36,
     1955, 161; TLS, Dec. 26, 1952, p. 854; Louis Bonnerot,
     EA, 5, 1952, 253; B. A. Wright, MLR, 47, 1952, 577-9, and
     RES, 8, 1957, 78-94; Richard Murphy, Spect., Mar. 20,
     1953, pp. 352, 354; George Watson, CR, 184, 1953, 61-2;
     H. J. C. Grierson, MLR, 48, 1953, 335-6; C. V. Wedgwood,
     TT, Sept. 3, 1955, pp. 1142-3; reply by E. C. Kitson, ibid.,
     Sept. 10, 1955, p. 1169; R. O. Evans, SCN, 14, 1956, 5-6.

60   The Complete English Poems of Milton. Ed. by John
     Gawsworth. London: Macdonald, 1953. xxxv, 513pp.
     Rev: Arnold Davenport, YWES, 201.

61   John Milton. Poems. Selected with an Introd. by L. D.
     Lerner. London: Penguin Books, 1953. 316pp.
     Rev: Arnold Davenport, YWES, 201-2; TLS, Aug. 21, 1953,
     p. 537.

62   John Milton. Poems. Ed. by B. A. Wright. Everyman's
     Library. London: Dent; New York: Dutton, 1956.
     Rev: J. B. Broadbent, MLR, 52, 1957, 626-7; Kenneth Muir,
     London Mag., 4, No. 8, 1957, 8, 70, 73, 75, 77.

63   A variorum commentary on the poems is in preparation,
     with Merritt Y. Hughes as the general editor and Geof-
     frey Bullough and Bernard A. Wright as advisory editors.
     Individual volumes are being edited by the following:
     Latin Poems, Douglas Bush; Paradise Lost, Merritt Y.
     Hughes; Samson Agonistes, William R. Parker; Paradise
     Regained, Walter Mackellar; the Italian sonnets, James
     E. Shaw. The edition will be published by the Columbia
     University Press and by Routledge and Kegan Paul as
     a supplement to the Columbia Edition.

64 John Milton: Paradise Lost, Book I. Ed. by G. E. Hollings-worth and A. F. Watt. London: University Tutorial Press, 1930.

65 The Manuscript of Paradise Lost. Book I. Ed. by Helen Darbishire. Oxford: Oxford University Press, 1931. xlvii, 38, 74pp.
   Contents: Introd., collotype facsimile of the text of the first edition of Book 1, with a transcript of the manuscript on opposite pages, and notes. The editor emphasizes the importance of the manuscript as an indication of Milton's methods of preparing his copy.
   Rev: G. B. Harrison and L. C. Martin, YWES, 202-3; TLS, Dec. 3, 1931, p. 977; G. R. Elliott, AB, 74, 1931, 457-9; MGW, 25, 1931, 295; S. B. Liljegren, Ang. Bbl., 43, 1932, 378-9; B. A. Wright, MLR, 27, 1932, 334-8; R. F. Russell, Merc., 25, 1932, 502; Paul Chauvet, RA-A, 9, 1932, 549-50; A. W. Pollard, Libr., N. S., 13, 1932, 219-21; MB, 7, 1932, 395-6; W. F. P. Stockley, TLS, Feb. 18, 1932, p. 112; R. W. Chapman, TLS, Sept. 29, 1932, p. 691; H. J. C. Grierson, RES, 9, 1933, 229-34.

66 John Milton. Paradise Lost. London: Cresset Press, 1931. 442pp.
   Rev: TLS, Dec. 24, 1931, pp. 1033-4.

67 Paradise Lost. Books I and II. By John Milton. Ed. by George C. Irwin with an Introd. by Guy Boas. London: Macmillan, 1934. v, 165pp.

68 John Milton. Paradise Lost. Ed. by A. W. Verity. Cambridge: Cambridge University Press, 1934. 2 vols.
   A reprint of Stevens' No. 755.

69 Milton's Paradise Lost, Book I. Ed. by Constance Mary Le Plastrier and J. P. Guinane, with an Introd. and Notes. Sydney: Shakespeare Head Press, 1934.

70 John Milton. Paradise Lost. Ed. by Merritt Y. Hughes. New York: Odyssey Press, 1935. lvi, 422pp.
   Penetrating introduction. Selected bibliography, liii-lvi. Basis of the text is the 1674 edition of the poem.
   Rev: B. A. Wright, MLR, 33, 1938, 432-4; W. R. Parker, MLN, 54, 1939, 75.

71 John Milton. Paradise Lost. Ed. by Merritt Y. Hughes. Garden City: Doubleday, 1935. lvi, 412pp.
   Rev: L. C. Martin, YWES, 252-3.

72 Paradise Lost and Paradise Regained, by John Milton, with an Introd. by William Rose Benét and Illus. by

Carlotta Petrina. San Francisco: J. H. Nash for Members of the Limited Editions Club, 1936. xiii, 441pp.
Rev: C. P. Rollins, SRL, Jan. 16, 1937, p. 21.

73 John Milton. Paradise Lost. Prepared for the press by J. Isaacs. London: Golden Cockerel Press, 1937.
Rev: TLS, June 26, 1937, p. 484; H. O. Wolfe, Obs., Aug. 8, 1937.

74 John Milton. Paradise Lost and Paradise Regained. London: Cresset Press, 1937.
Rev: H. O. Wolfe, Obs., Aug. 8, 1937.

75 John Milton Paradise Lost: Illus. by William Blake. Prefaces by Philip Hofer and John T. Winterich. New York: Heritage Press, 1940. xx, 311pp.
Blake's illustrations reproduced in color.

76 John Milton. Paradise Lost and Other Poems. Ed. with an Introd. by Maurice Kelley. New York: Walter J. Black, 1943. xx, 386pp.
Rev: E. L. Tinker, NYTBR, July 25, 1943, p. 25.

77 John Milton. Paradise Lost and Other Poems. Ed. by Northrop Frye. New York: Rinehart, 1951. xxxviii, 601pp.

78 ADAMS, JOHN R. The Theism of Paradise Lost. Pers., 22, 1941, 174-80.

79 ADAMS, ROBERT M. The Text of Paradise Lost: Emphatic and Unemphatic Spellings. MP, 52, 1954, 84-91.

80 ALLEN, DON C. The Legend of Noah: Renaissance Rationalism in Art, Science, and Letters. Illinois Stud. in Lang. and Lit., 33, Nos. 3-4. Urbana: University of Illinois Press, 1949, 221pp.
    Paradise Lost, passim.
    Rev: Arnold Williams, JEGP, 49, 1950, 581-3.

81 - - - - - -. Milton and Rabbi Eliezer. MLN, 63, 1948, 262-3.
    Parallels between Paradise Lost and Eliezer's Pirkê.
    Rev: L. C. Martin, YWES, 195-6.

82 - - - - - -. Milton and the Creation of Birds. MLN, 63, 1948, 263-4.
    Milton's letting the "egg come before the chicken" a common seventeenth-century idea.
    Rev: L. C. Martin, YWES, 195.

83 - - - - - -. Milton's Amarant. MLN, 72, 1957, 256-8.
    On Milton's transplanting the flower to heaven.

84 - - - - - -. Milton and the Sons of God. MLN, 61, 1946, 73-9.
    On Paradise Lost, 11, 573-87.
    Rev: L. C. Martin, YWES, 173.

85 - - - - - -. Milton's Busiris. MLN, 65, 1950, 115-16.
    On Paradise Lost, 1, 306-9.
    Rev: Arnold Davenport, YWES, 181.

86 - - - - - -. Milton's Winged Serpents. MLN, 59, 1944, 537-8.
    Paradise Lost, 7, 482-4, refers to winged serpents, not dragons.

87 - - - - - -. Paradise Lost, I, 254-255. MLN, 71, 1956, 324-6.

88 - - - - - -. The Scala Religionis in Paradise Lost. MLN, 71, 1956, 404-5.
    On Paradise Lost, 8, 253ff.

89 - - - - - -. Two Notes on Paradise Lost. MLN, 68, 1953, 360-1.
    On Paradise Lost, 3, 510-11 and 10, 327-9.

90 AUTRY, RANDALL F. Milton's Beelzebub. Master's thesis, Duke University, 1945.

91 BAKER, DONALD C. Mammon and Mulciber: An Old Chestnut. NQ, N. S., 4, 1957, 112-13.
    Insists that Mammon and Mulciber are two distinct figures.

92 - - - - - -. On Satan's Hair. NQ, N. S., 4, 1957, 69-70.
    The evil connotations of Paradise Lost, 2, 706-11.

93 BALDWIN, EDWARD C. Milton and Phineas Fletcher. JEGP, 33, 1934, 544-6.
    Milton's indebtedness in Paradise Lost, 10, 504-21.

94 - - - - - -. Some Extra-Biblical Semitic Influences upon Milton's Story of the Fall of Man. JEGP, 28, 1929, 366-401.

95 BALDWIN, T. W., ALLAN H. GILBERT, and THOMAS O. MABBOTT. A Double Janus. PMLA, 56, 1941, 583-5.
    In support of Gilbert, PMLA, 54, 1939, 1026-30.

96 BANKS, THEODORE H. The Meaning of "God" in Paradise Lost. MLN, 54, 1939, 450-4.
    Lists three senses which need to be distinguished.

97 BARKER, ARTHUR. ...And on his Crest Sat Horror: Eighteenth Century Interpretations of Milton's Sublimity and His Satan. UTQ, 11, 1942, 421-36.
    Rev: L. C. Martin, YWES, 162-3.

98 - - - - - -. Structural Pattern in Paradise Lost. PQ, 28, 1949, 16-30.
    Rev: L. C. Martin, YWES, 167.

99 BELL, MILLICENT. The Fallacy of the Fall in Paradise Lost. PMLA, 68, 1953, 863-83.
    Adam and Eve are never purely good but fallen and capable of redemption from the start.
    Rev: Arnold Davenport, YWES, 206-7.

100 BENHAM, ALLEN R. Things Unattempted Yet in Prose or Rime. MLQ, 14, 1953, 341-7.
    "The thing hitherto unattempted in the theme of the fall and restoration of man is to put the old story into a pattern derived from the ancient Greek and Latin epics."
    Rev: Arnold Davenport, YWES, 208.

101 BENNETT, JOSEPHINE W. Milton's Use of the Vision of Er. MP, 36, 1939, 351-8.
    Milton uses the passage from Plato in Paradise Lost.

102 BERGEL, LIENHARD. Milton's Paradise Lost, I, 284-95. Expl., 10, 1951, item 3.

103 BERKELEY, DAVID S. "Precieuse" Gallantry and the Seduction of Eve. NQ, 196, 1951, 337-9.

Finds support from contemporary literature in interpreting Paradise Lost, 9, 538-48, as a comment on the manners of Restoration society. Replies by H. Parsons, ibid., pp. 393-4, and W. H. W. Sabine, ibid., p. 482.

104 BERTSCHINGER, M. Man's Part in the Fall of Woman. ES, 31, 1950, 49-64.
Rev: Arnold Davenport, YWES, 180.

105 BIRRELL, T. A. The Figure of Satan in Milton and Blake. Satan (London: Sheed and Ward, 1951), pp. 379-93.
Attempts to show how Milton "keeps the figure of Satan under control—what happens to the Satan symbol."

106 BLACKER, IRWIN R. Did Milton Visit Hell? SCN, 9, 1951, 54.
"The geysers of the Larderello area near Florence may have suggested Milton's infernal topography."

107 BLISSET, WILLIAM. Caesar and Satan. JHI, 18, 1957, 221-32.
On the likenesses between the various figures of Caesar and those of Satan, especially Milton's.

108 BODKIN, MAUD. Archetypal Patterns in Poetry: Psychological Studies of the Imagination. London: Oxford University Press, 1934. 340pp.
An application of Jung's hypothesis regarding the psychological significance of poetry. Comments, i. a., on the Paradise-Hades pattern in Paradise Lost, on Plato's Phaedo myth and Paradise Lost, on the image of woman in Paradise Lost, and on Satan as devil and hero.
Rev: TLS, Jan. 10, 1935, p. 18; LL, 11, 1935, 491-3; S. H. Hooke, Folk-Lore, 46, 1935, 176-9; E. L. Walton, NYTBR, Feb. 3, 1935, p. 16; G. D. Willcock, MLR, 31, 1936, 91-2.

109 BOGGS, EARL R. Selected Precepts of Freedom to Choose in Paradise Lost. Peabody Jour. of Education, 30, 1953, 276-84.

110 BOGHOLM, N. Milton and Paradise Lost. Copenhagen: Levin and Munksgaard; London: Williams and Norgate, 1932. 132pp.
Discusses the human interest, the theology and philosophy, the style and language, and other poetical treatments of Genesis.
Rev: L. C. Martin, YWES, 209; TLS, Sept. 29, 1932, p. 694; S. B. Liljegren, Ang. Bbl., 43, 1932, 379-80; K. M. L., Oxf. Mag., June 8, 1934, p. 773.

111 BOLTWOOD, ROBERT M. Turnus and Satan as Epic Villains. CJ, 47, 1952, 183-6.

112 BOND, DONALD F. Milton's Paradise Lost, V, 100-113. Expl., 3, 1945, item 54.

113 BOONE, LALIA P. The Language of Book VI, Paradise Lost. SAMLA Studies in Milton (Gainesville: University of Florida Press, 1953), pp. 114-27.

114 BOWRA, C. M. Milton and the Destiny of Man. From Virgil to Milton (London: Macmillan, 1945), pp. 194-247.
Paradise Lost as an epic form.
Rev: L. C. Martin, YWES, 143-4; TLS, Apr. 28, 1945, p. 198; Gwyn Jones, LL, 46, 1945, 128-32; V. de S. Pinto, Eng., 5, 1945, 207-10; Bonamy Dobrée, Spect., May 25, 1945, p. 480; Rose Macaulay, NSN, May 26, 1945, p. 340; A. J. Grant, CR, 168, 1945, 318-19; H. L. T., QQ, 52, 1945, 377-8; A. S. P. Woodhouse, UTQ, 15, 1946, 200-5; Leonard Bacon, SRL, Feb. 16, 1946, 44-5; B. A. Wright, RES, 22, 1946, 330-1; A. Norman Jeffares, ES, 27, 1946, 121-3.

115 BROADBENT, J. B. Milton's Hell. ELH, 21, 1954, 161-92.
On the geography and literary background.
Rev: Arnold Davenport, YWES, 142.

116 - - - - - -. Milton's Paradise. MP, 51, 1954, 160-76.
Rev: Arnold Davenport, YWES, 142.

117 BRODRIBB, C. W. Milton and Valerius Flaccus. NQ, 175, 1938, 399.
The opening of Paradise Lost seems to correspond with that of Valerius Flaccus' Argonautica.

118 - - - - - -. Paradise Lost: I. 756: Capital v. Capitol. NQ, 179, 1940, 370-1.
Favors capitol.

119 - - - - - -. Paradise Lost: A Book a Year? NQ, 163, 1932, 417-18.
Suggests that the epic was written between 1655 and 1665, with Milton working from the autumn to the spring of each year.
Rev: L. C. Martin, YWES, 210.

120 BROOKS, CLEANTH. Eve's Awakening. Essays in Honor of W. C. Curry (Nashville: Vanderbilt University Press, 1954), pp. 281-98.
By using certain dominant images in his account of the creation of Adam and Eve, Milton implies the nature of the fall.

121 BROWN, J. R. Some Notes on the Native Elements in the Diction of Paradise Lost. NQ, 196, 1951, 424-8.
On Milton's probable indebtedness to earlier English writers, especially Spenser.

122 BRYCE, GEORGE P. The Biblical Allusions in Milton's Paradise Lost. Master's thesis, McMaster University, 1940. 161pp.
Finds 913 references from the Old Testament and 490 from the New Testament.

123 BUCKWALTER, KATHRYN M. Criticism of Paradise Lost Since 1890. Master's thesis, Duke University, 1942.

124 BUNDY, MURRAY W. Eve's Dream and the Temptation in Paradise Lost. Research Stud. of the State College of Washington, 10, 1942, 273-91.

125 - - - - - -. Milton's Prelapsarian Adam. Research Stud. of the State College of Washington, 13, 1945, 163-84.

126 BURKE, HERBERT C. The Poles of Pride and Humility in the Paradise Lost of John Milton. Doctoral diss., Stanford University, 1954. Abs., DA, 14, 1954, 1707. Ann Arbor: U. M., 1954. 250pp.

127 BUSH DOUGLAS. Paradise Lost in Our Time. Some Comments. Ithaca: Cornell University Press; London: Milford, 1945; Gloucester, Mass.: Peter Smith, 1957. iv, 117pp.
   Delivered as the Messenger Lectures, Cornell University, November, 1944. A refutation of the conception that Paradise Lost is a monument to dead ideas. Chapters: The Modern Reaction Against Milton, Religious and Ethical Principles, Characters and Drama, and The Poetical Texture.
   Rev: L. C. Martin, YWES, 145-6; E. N. S. Thompson, PQ, 24, 1945, 192; C. R. T., QQ, 52, 1945, 378-9; John Senior, Nat., Aug. 25, 1945, pp. 186-7; L. E. A. Byrns, Th., 25, 1946, 553<4; George Cookson, Eng., 6, 1946, 140; B. A. Wright, MLR, 41, 1946, 74-6; J. Milton French, JEGP, 45, 1946, 110-14; Z. S. Fink, MLN, 61, 1946, 199-200; A. S. P. Woodhouse, UTQ, 15, 1946, 200-5; TLS, Aug. 17, 1946, p. 390; L. C. Knights, MGW, 55, 1946, 150; Joan Bennett, NSN, Oct. 5, 1946, p. 250; B. M., DR, 26, 1946, 251-2; A. Norman Jeffares, ES, 27, 1946, 182-5; Kathleen Tillotson, RES, 23, 1947, 173-4; Desmond McCarthy, Sun. Times, Nov. 2, 1947, p. 3.

128 - - - - - -. Recent Criticism of Paradise Lost. PQ, 28, 1949. 31-43.
   Rev: L. C. Martin, YWES, 165.

129 BUTLER, A. Z. The Pathetic Fallacy in Paradise Lost. Essays in Honor of W. C. Curry (Nashville: Vanderbilt University Press, 1954), pp. 269-79.

130 BUXTON, CHARLES R. Milton's Paradise Lost. A Politician Plays Truant. Essays on English Literature (London: Christophers, 1929), pp. 60-82.

131 CAIRNS, E. E. The Theology of Paradise Lost. BS, 105, 1948, 478-91; 106, 1949, 106-18.
   Considers De Doctrina Christiana as a gloss on Paradise Lost.

132 CAIRNS, HUNTINGTON, ALLEN **TATE** and MARK VAN DOREN. Milton: Paradise Lost. Invitation to Learning (New York: New Home Library, 1942), pp. 307-21.
> A symposium. Transcript of a direct recording broadcast by the Columbia Broadcasting System.

133 CARLISLE, A. I. A Study of the Trinity College MS., Pages 35-41, and Certain Authors Represented in Milton's Commonplace Book, in Their Relationship to Paradise Lost and Paradise Regained. B. Litt. thesis, St. Hughes, Oxford, 1952.

134 CARNALL, GEOFFREY. Milton's Paradise Lost, III, 481-483. NQ, 197, 1952, 315-16.
> Suggests that the clue to the meaning may be found in the Sphaera (1639) of Johannes de Sacrobosco, pp. 11-13.

135 CARVER, P. L. The Angels in Paradise Lost. RES, 16, 1940, 415-31.
> Rev: L. C. Martin, YWES, 170-1.

136 CLARK, EVERT M. Milton's Abyssinian Paradise. UTSE, 29, 1950, 129-50.
> On Paradise Lost, 4. Milton indebted to Samuel Purchas and Peter Heylyn.
> Rev: Arnold Davenport, YWES, 181.

137 CLEMENTS, REX. The Angels in Paradise Lost. QR, 264, 1935, 284-93.
> "...Milton's angels are like himself—individual personalities of godlike strength. They do not fit easily into any scheme or classification."

138 COFFIN, CHARLES M. Study Questions on Milton's Paradise Lost. New York: Crofts, 1938. vi, 2pp.

139 CONDEE, RALPH W. Milton's Theories Concerning Epic Poetry: Their Sources and Their Influence on Paradise Lost. Doctoral diss., University of Illinois, 1949. Abs., Urbana: University of Illinois Press, 1949.

140 CONRATH, JOHN BERNARD. The Orthodoxy of Paradise Lost. Doctoral diss., State University of Iowa, 1946. Abs., University of Iowa, Doctoral Diss.: Abstracts and References, 6, 1953, 369-71.

141 COPE, JACKSON I. Milton's Muse in Paradise Lost. MP, 55, 1957, 6-10.
> Spiritual illumination as opposed to physical blindness.

142 CORCORAN, SISTER MARY IRMA. Milton's Paradise with Reference to the Hexameral Background. Doctoral diss., Catholic University, 1945. Washington: Catholic University of America Press, 1945. xvi, 149pp.
   Rev: L. C. Martin, YWES, 141-2; Arnold Williams, MLN, 61, 1946, 352-3; Grant McColley, JEGP, 45, 1946, 464-6; Harris Fletcher, MLQ, 7, 1946, 359-61; Sister M. Teresa, Th., 23, 1948, 340-1; Arthur Barker, MLR, 44, 1949, 110-11.

143 COWLING, GEORGE. Milton's Paradise Lost. Shelley and Other Essays (Melbourne: Melbourne University Press; London: Oxford University Press, 1936), pp. 131-56.
   Emphasizes the grand style of the epic in a manner similar to the late Victorians.

144 CRUNDELL, H. W. The Power to Reason: A Milton Paradox. NQ, 185, 1943, 113.
   Reply to Svendsen, NQ, 184, 1943, 368-70.
   Rev: L. C. Martin, YWES, 155.

145 CURRY, WALTER C. The Consistence and Qualities of Milton's Chaos. Vanderbilt Stud. in the Humanities, 1, 1951, 56-70.

146 - - - - - -. The Genesis of Milton's World. Ang., 70, 1951, 129-49.
   Outlines the order of progress from chaos to cosmos.
   Rev: Arnold Davenport, YWES, 191.

147 - - - - - -. Milton's Chaos and Old Night. JEGP, 46, 1947, 38-52.
   Defends "the hypothesis that the conception of the divinity of both Chaos and Night was in accordance with the doctrines of Neoplatonic theology in its interpretation of Orphic and Pythagorean cosmogony."
   Rev: L. C. Martin, YWES, 191.

148 - - - - - -. Milton's Scale of Nature. Stanford Stud. in Lang. and Lit., 1941, pp. 173-92.

149 - - - - - -. Some Trevels of Milton's Satan and the Road to Hell. PQ, 29, 1950, 225-35.
   Rev: Arnold Davenport, YWES, 180.

150 DAHLBERG, CHARLES. Paradise Lost V, 603, and Milton's Psalm II. MLN, 67, 1952, 23-4.
   Interprets "begot" as "invested with kingship."

151 DANIELS, EDGAR F. The Seventeenth-Century Conception of Satan with Relation to the Satan of Paradise Lost. Doctoral diss., Stanford University, 1952. Abs., Abstracts of Diss., Stanford University, 27, 1953, 217-19.

152 DANNIELLS, ROY. Humour in Paradise Lost. DR, 33, 1953, 159-66.
Rev: Arnold Davenport, YWES, 208.

153 DARBISHIRE, HELEN. Milton's Paradise Lost. Oxford: Oxford University Press, 1951. 51pp.
Delivered as the James Bryce Memorial Lecture at Somerville College. Discusses the criticism of Bentley and Johnson.
Rev: Arnold Davenport, YWES, 189.

154 DAY-LEWIS, CECIL. The Grand Manner. Nottingham: John Clough, 1952. 26pp.
Comments, i. a., on the opening lines of Paradise Lost, 3.

155 DE MAISÈRES, MAURY THIBAUT. Les Poèmes Inspirées du Début de la Genèse â l'Epoque de la Renaissance. Louvain, 1931.

156 DENNIS, LEAH. The Puzzle of Paradise Lost. University of California Chronicle, 24, 1940, 195-200.
Milton the artist and moralist vs. Satan.

157 DE PILATO, S. Un Inspiratore italiano del Paradiso Perduto di Milton: P. Serafino della Salandra. Potenza: Marchesiello, 1934. 26pp.

158 DEUTSCH, ALFRED H. Some Scholastic Elements in Paradise Lost. Doctoral diss., University of Illinois, 1945.

159 DICKSON, DAVID W. D. Milton's Son of God: A Study in Imagery and Orthodoxy. Papers Mich. Acad., 36, 1952, 275-81.

160 DIEKHOFF, JOHN S. Eve, the Devil, and Areopagitica. MLQ, 5, 1944, 429-34.
Milton is not being inconsistent in letting Eve paraphrase Areopagitica (PL, 9, 322-41).

161 - - - - - -. The Function of the Prologues in Paradise Lost. PMLA, 57, 1942, 697-704.

162 - - - - - -. Milton's Paradise Lost, a Commentary on the Argument. New York: Columbia University Press; London: Oxford University Press, 1946. 161pp.
Chapters: Milton's Theory of Poetry, Two Rhetorical Aids to Proof, The Evil of Satan, Man's Guilt, God's Justice, God's Providence and Mercy, The Way of Virtue.
Rev: L. C. Martin, YWES, 171-2; F. R. Fogle, Rev. of Religion, 12, 1947, 66-71; A. S. P. Woodhouse, UTQ, 16, 1947, 433-5; TLS, Mar. 29, 1947, p. 140; E. M. W. Tillyard, RES, 23, 1947, 363-4; Allan H. Gilbert, SAQ, 46, 1947, 289-90; E. M. Pope, MLN, 63, 1948, 444-5.

163 - - - - - -. The Trinity Manuscript and the Dictation of Paradise Lost. PQ, 28, 1949, 44-52.
On Milton's habits of composition and correction.
Rev: L. C. Martin, YWES, 167.

164 DOUGLAS, NORMAN. On Paradise Lost. LL, 58, 1948, 86-118.
Translates "a paper by a certain Zicari tracing the origin of Milton's Paradise Lost to a sacred tragedy entitled Adam Caduto... which was written by a Calabrian monk named Salandra."
Rev: L. C. Martin, YWES, 196.

165 DUNCAN, EDGAR H. The Natural History of Metals and Minerals in the Universe of Milton's Paradise Lost. Osiris, 11, 1954, 386-421.
Stresses Robert Fludd's concepts.

166 - - - - - -. Satan-Lucifer: Lightning and Thunderbolt. PQ, 30, 1951, 441-3.
Parallel between Paradise Lost, 2, 927-38 and Comenius' explanation of thunderbolts.

167 DUNCAN, JOSEPH E. Milton's Four-in-One Hell. HLQ, 20, 1957, 127-36.
Feels that Milton unites four different conceptions of hell so that it becomes "a potent symbol in which the sinner, the cause of sin, and the punishment for sin merge significantly."

168 DURR, ROBERT A. Dramatic Pattern in Paradise Lost. JAAC, 13, 1955, 520-6.

169 DUSTOOR, P. E. Legends of Lucifer in Early English and in Milton. Ang., 54, 1930, 213-68.

170 ELTON, WILLIAM. Paradise Lost and the Digby Mary Magdalene. MLQ, 9, 1948, 412-14.
A passage from the play anticipates the infernal council and temptation scenes in Paradise Lost.
Rev: L. C. Martin, YWES, 196.

171 EMERSON, EVERETT H. Milton's War in Heaven: Some Problems. MLN, 69, 1954, 399-402.
The fact that the Son is called upon to end the war reflects Milton's idea that good cannot overcome evil completely without God's help.
Rev: Arnold Davenport, YWES, 143.

172 - - - - - -. The New Criticism of Paradise Lost. SAQ, 54, 1955, 501-7.

173 EMPSON, WILLIAM. Emotion in Words Again. KR, 10, 1948, 579-601.
"All," which occurs 612 times in Paradise Lost, appears in nearly every scene of emotional pressure. Reprinted in The Structure of Complex Words (London: Chatto and Windus, 1951), pp. 101-4.

174 ERSKINE, JOHN. Paradise Lost. The Delight of Great Books (New York: Bobbs-Merrill, 1928), pp. 159-75.
Appreciative.

175 ETHEL, GARLAND. Hell's Marching Music. MLQ, 18, 1957, 295-302.
Suggests that Plutarch's Lycurgus be added to the source possibilities for Paradise Lost, 1, 549-65.

176 EVANS, ROBERT O. Milton's Use of "E're" in Paradise Lost. NQ, N. S., 1, 1954, 337-9.
Uses Milton's spellings of "ere" and "e're" as the basis of a discussion concerning Darbishire's editorial principles.

177 - - - - - -. Proofreading of Paradise Lost. NQ, N. S., 2, 1955, 383-4.
Discusses Darbishire's and R. M. Adams' opposing views on "improving" the text of the epic.

178 FARRELL, THOMAS, JR. The Classical Biblical Epic in England. Doctoral diss., University of Iowa, 1950.
Traces the acceptance of the classical biblical epic as a literary form from the Anglo-Saxon period to the seventeenth century.

179 FARRISON, W. EDWARD. The Classical Allusions in Paradise Lost, Books I and II. EJ, 22, 1933, 650-3.

180 FIORE, AMADEUS P. O. F. M. Satan Is a Problem. The Problem of Milton's "Satanic Fallacy" in Contemporary Criticism. FS, 17, 1957, 173-87.
Uses La Driere's theory of voice and address to show that Satan is a "damned fool" throughout the epic.

181 FLETCHER, HARRIS F. Milton and Ben Gerson. JEGP, 29, 1930, 41-52.
On Paradise Lost, 7.
Rev: H. J. C. Grierson and A. Melville Clark, YWES, 227.

182 FORD, JANE F. Satan as an Exemplar of Evil in Paradise Lost. Doctoral diss., University of Pittsburgh, 1934. Abs., University of Pittsburgh Bull., 10, 1934, 546-7.

183 FOX, ROBERT C. The Seven Deadly Sins in Paradise Lost. Doctoral diss., Columbia University, 1957. 225pp. Abs., DA, 17, 1957, 1328.

184 FREEDMAN, MORRIS. John Milton, Nathanael Carpenter, and Satan. NQ, N. S., 4, 1957, 293-5.
Notes similarities between Paradise Lost and Carpenter's Achitophel (1627).

185 GAGE, CLARA S. The Sources of Milton's Concepts of Angels and the Angelic World. Doctoral diss., Cornell University, 1936. Abs., Ithaca: Cornell University Press, 1936. 6pp.

186 GAMBLE, ISABEL E. Paradise Lost as Myth. Doctoral diss., Radcliffe College, 1954.

187 GARDNER, EDWARD H. Paradise Lost, I, 549-555. MLN, 62, 1947, 360.
Rev: L. C. Martin, YWES, 192-3.

188 GARDNER, HELEN. Milton's Satan and the Theme of Damnation in Elizabethan Tragedy. English Studies (E&S), N. S., 1, 1948, 46-66.
Rev: L. C. Martin, YWES, 193-4.

189 GILBERT, ALLAN H. Critics of Mr. C. S. Lewis on Milton's Satan. SAQ, 47, 1948, 216-25.
Defends Lewis in opposing the idea that Satan is heroic or noble.

190 - - - - - -. A Double Janus (Paradise Lost XI, 129). PMLA, 54, 1939, 1027-30.
Replies by T. W. Baldwin, ibid., 56, 1941, 583-4; by A. H. Gilbert, ibid., 584; by T. O. Mabbott, ibid., 584-5.

191 - - - - - -. On the Composition of Paradise Lost. A Study of the Ordering and Insertion of Material. Chapel Hill: University of North Carolina Press, 1947, viii, 185pp.
Rev: L. C. Martin, YWES, 190; E. Sirluck, MP, 45, 1948, 273-5; G. G., Pers., 29, 1948, 311-12; M. B. Seigler, SAB, 13, 1948, 3, 315-16; Harris Fletcher, JEGP, 57, 1948, 202-3; M. Y. Hughes, Ital., 25, 1948, 259-61; J. S. Diekhoff, MLN, 64, 1949, 129-30; S. B. Liljegren, SN, 21, 1949, 79-80; Kester Svendsen, MLQ, 10, 1949, 534; A. N. Jeffares, ES, 31, 1950, 185-6; B. A. Wright, RES, N. S., 1, 1950, 268-70; V. de S. Pinto, Eras., 3, 1950, 161-3.

192 - - - - - -. A Parallel between Milton and Boiardo. Ital., 20, 1943, 132-4.
In adapting passages from the Orlando Innamorato for the war in heaven, Milton retains something of the comedy of the boasters suddenly vanquished and forced to flee in terror 'bellowing.' "

193 - - - - - -. The Qualities of the Renaissance Epic. SAQ, 53, 1954, 372-8.
A paper read before the Renaissance group of the MLA, 1952. Pays particular attention to the significance of Orlando Furioso. Paradise Lost, passim.

194 - - - - - -. The Theological Basis of Satan's Rebellion and the Function of Abdiel in Paradise Lost. MP, 40, 1942, 19-42.
Finds the basis in Psalms 2 and Hebrews 1.
Rev: L. C. Martin, YWES, 161-2.

195 GILLESPIE, HELEN. The Story of Adam and Eve from Caedmon to Milton. Master's thesis, Duke University, 1937.

196 GILLIAM, J. F. Scylla and Sin. PQ, 29, 1950, 345-7.
On Paradise Lost, 2, 650-1.

197 GIOVANNINI, MARGARET. Milton's Paradise Lost, IV, 131-193. Expl., 12, 1953, item 1.
Rev: Arnold Davenport, YWES, 209.

198 GLAESENER, H. Le Voyage de Milton en Italie. Prélude au Paradis perdu. RLC, 13, 1936, 294-329.

199 GORDON, D. J. Two Milton Notes. RES, 18, 1942, 318-19.
1. Precious Bane: a Recollection of Boethius in Paradise Lost? (1, 692).
2. The Golden Chersoness. (Paradise Regained, 4, 74).

200 GOSSMAN, ANN MARY. Man Plac't in a Paradise: A Comparative Study of Milton, St. Ambrose, and Hugh St. Victor. Master's thesis, Rice Institute, 1954.

201 - - - - - -. Milton, Prudentius, and the Brood of Sin. NQ, N. S., 4, 1957, 439-40.
Suggests Prudentius' Hamartagenia as one of the sources for Milton's treatment of Sin at Hell's gates.

202 GRACE, WILLIAM J. Notes on Robert Burton and John Milton. SP, 52, 1955, 578-91.
i. a., Burton and the Limbo of Vanity and the catalogue of fallen angels.

203 - - - - - -. Orthodoxy and Aesthetic Method in Paradise Lost and the Divine Comedy. CL, 1, 1949, 173-87.

204 GREEN, CLARENCE C. The Paradox of the Fall in Paradise Lost. MLN, 53, 1938, 557-71.
Rev: L. C. Martin, YWES, 178.

205 GRÜN, RICHARD H. Das Menschenbild John Miltons in Paradise Lost: Eine Interpretation seines Epos im Lichte des Begriffes Disobedience. Frankfurter Arbeiten aus dem Gebiete des Anglistik und der Amerika-Studien, Heft 2. Heidelberg: Winter, 1956.

206 GUERLAC, HENRY. The Poets' Nitre. Isis, 45, 1954, 243-55.
Milton's references to nitre and nitrous foam are in accord with popular Renaissance ideas concerning the cause of thunderstorms and earthquakes.

207 HALL, AMY V. Milton and The City of God. Doctoral diss., University of Washington, 1941. Abs., University of Washington, Abstract of Theses, 6, 1942, 267-8.

208 HAMILTON, G. ROSTREVOR, Hero or Fool? A Study of Milton's Satan. London: Allen and Unwin, 1944. 41pp.
  Rev: TLS, Nov. 4, 1944, p. 540; A. S. P. Woodhouse, UTQ, 15, 1946, 200-5.

209 HAMMERLE, KARL. To Save Appearances (Par. L VIII 82), ein Problem der Scholastik. Ang., 62, 1938, 368-72.

210 HAMMOND, MASON. Concilia Deorum from Homer through Milton. SP, 30, 1933, 1-16.
  Rev: L. C. Martin, YWES, 252-3.

211 HANKINS, JOHN E. The Pains of the Afterworld: Fire, Wind, and Ice in Milton and Shakespeare. PMLA, 71, 1956, 482-95.

212 HARPER, GEORGE M. The World's First Love Story. Literary Appreciations (New York: Bobbs-Merrill, 1937), pp. 70-88.
  Discusses the Adam-Eve story in Paradise Lost. Calls Milton the "most seductive painter of female delights," etc.

213 HARTWELL, KATHLEEN. Lactantius and Milton. Cambridge: Harvard University Press, 1929. xv, 220pp.
  Rev: TLS, Oct. 3, 1929, p. 770; D. H. Stevens, CP, 24, 1929, 414-15; C. W. Brodribb, TLS, Oct. 10, 1929, p. 794; D. Saurat, RES, 6, 1930, 473-5; R. S. Crane, MP, 27, 1930, 361-4; H. F. Fletcher, JEGP, 29, 1930, 465-6; S. B. Liljegren, DL, 51, 1930, 1232-3; G. Kitchin, MLR, 25, 1930, 215-16; F. Delatte, Rev. belge de philol, et d'hist., 12, 1933, 309-12.

214 HAVENS, P. S. Dryden's Tagged Version of Paradise Lost. Parrott Presentation Volume (Princeton: Princeton University Press, 1935), pp. 383-97.

215 HAVILAND, THOMAS P. Milton for the Young. University of Pennsylvania Libr. Chron., 3, 1935, 46-8.
  A humorous description of a recent library acquisition, The Story of Paradise Lost for Children, by Eliza W. Bradburn, the daughter of Wesley's friend, Samuel Bradburn.

216 HERBERT, CAROLYN. Comic Elements in the Scenes of Hell of Paradise Lost. Renaissance Papers, 1956 (Columbia: University of South Carolina Press, 1956), pp. 92-101.
  "...much of the scenes in Hell revolves laughingly around the characters representing pride...."

217 HERBST, EDWARD L. Classical Mythology in Paradise Lost. CP, 29, 1934, 147-8.

218 HERBSTER, S. I. Paradise Lost: A Study for the Modern Preacher. Lutheran Church Quar., 4, 1931, 377-89.

219 HIBERNICUS. Milton: Two Verbal Parallels: Autumn Leaves. NQ, 184, 1943, 85.
   The leaves simle and Chapman's translation of Homer and Heywood's Brazen Age.

220 ------. Mulciber's A Summer Day (Paradise Lost, i, 744). NQ, 180, 1941, 27.

221 HILDEBRAND, G. D. The Power of Chastity in Paradise Lost. NQ, 197, 1952, 246.
   On Paradise Lost, 9, 309-12, 373-4, and 455-66.

222 HILL, D. M. Johnson as Moderator, NQ, N.S., 3, 1956, 517-22.
   On Johnson's method of criticizing Paradise Lost.

223 ------. Satan on the Burning Lake. NQ, N. S., 3, 1956, 157-9.
   Since the whale is the symbol of Satan in the bestiaries, Milton's long simile in Book 1 is not a digression.

224 HORRELL, JOSEPH. Milton, Limbo, and Suicide. RES, 18, 1942, 413-27.
   Rev: L. C. Martin, YWES, 162.

225 HOWARD, DONALD R. Milton's Satan and the Augustinian Tradition. Renaissance Papers, 1954 (Columbia: University of South Carolina Press, 1954), pp. 11-23.

226 HOWARD, LEON. The Invention of Milton's Great Argument: A Study of the Logic of God's Ways to Men. HLQ, 9, 1946, 149-73.
   An analysis of Milton's logic and its relationship to the meaning of Paradise Lost.
   Rev: L. C. Martin, YWES, 172.

227 HUGHES, MERRITT Y. Myself Am Hell. MP, 54, 1956, 80-94.
   Explains the symbolism of Paradise Lost, 4, 73-79.

228 HUNTER, WILLIAM B., JR. Eve's Demonic Dream. ELH, 13, 1946, 255-65.
   Rev: L. C. Martin, YWES, 173.

229 ------. Prophetic Dreams and Visions in Paradise Lost. MLQ, 9, 1948, 277-85.
   Rev: L. C. Martin, YWES, 195.

230 ------. Two Milton Notes. MLR, 44, 1949, 89-91.
   On Paradise Lost, 8, 94-7 and 12, 632-4, 642-4.

231 HUNTLEY, FRANK L. A Justification of Milton's Paradise of Fools (P. L. III, 431-499). ELH, 21, 1954, 107-13.
   Relates the passage to the rest of the poem.

232 - - - - - -. Milton, Mendoza, and the Chinese Land-Ship. MLN, 69, 1954, 404-7.
> On Paradise Lost, 3, 431-42. Mendoza credited with the account of the land ship.

233 HUTCHERSON, DUDLEY R. Milton's Epithets for Eve. University of Virginia Stud., N. S., 4, 1951, 253-260.
> In the James Southall Wilson Festschrift.

234 HUTSON, ARTHUR E. and PATRICIA McCOY, eds. Epics of the Western World. New York: Lippincott, 1954. 512pp.
> Contains an introduction to Paradise Lost, pp. 449-57, and a summary, pp. 458-97.

235 J., W. H. Paradise Lost: "Lose" or "Loose." NQ, 174, 1938, 438.
> Concerning Belial's speech in Paradise Lost, 2.

236 JACKSON, MYRTLE L. The Spirit and Faith of Milton in Paradise Regained, Samson Agonistes, and Paradise Lost. Master's thesis, Atlanta University, 1948.

237 JAMISON, SISTER M. THECLA. The Twentieth-Century Critics of Milton and the Problem of Satan in Paradise Lost. Doctoral diss., Catholic University, 1952. On microcards, Catholic University.

238 JONES, FRED L. Paradise Lost, I, 549-62. MLN, 49, 1934, 44-45.
> The description of the march of the fallen angels is from Plutarch's Life of Lycurgus.

239 JONES, PUTNAM F. Satan and the Narrative Structure of Paradise Lost. If by your art (Pittsburgh: University of Pittsburgh Press, 1948), pp. 15-26.
> The debate over Satan's role has its basis in the narrative structure of the poem.

240 JUMP, J. D. John Milton and the Arabian Wind. NQ, 196, 1951, 270-2.
> On Paradise Lost, 4, 153-66.
> Rev: Arnold Davenport, YWES, 191.

241 KEITH, A. L. Personification in Milton's Paradise Lost. EJ, 17, 1929, 399-409.

242 KELLETT, E. E. Macbeth and Satan. LQHR, July, 1939, pp. 289-99.
> On Milton's early interest in Macbeth as a subject for a poem and resemblances between Shakespeare's character and Satan.

243 - - - - - -. The Puns in Milton. LQHR, 159, 1934, 469-76.
> Considers the puns in Paradise Lost.

244 KELLEY, MAURICE W. Milton's De Doctrina Christiana as a Gloss upon Paradise Lost. Doctoral diss., Princeton University, 1934.

245 - - - - - -. Milton's Use of Begot in Paradise Lost, V, 603. SP, 38, 1941, 252-65.

246 - - - - - -. Paradise Lost, VII, 8-12, and the Zohar. MLR, 29, 1934, 322-24.

247 - - - - - -. The Theological Dogma of Paradise Lost, III, 173-202. PMLA, 52, 1935, 75-9.
The passage in accord with the Arminian views in De Doctrina Christiana.
Rev: L. C. Martin, YWES, 185.

248 - - - - - -. This Great Argument: a Study of Milton's De doctrina christiana as a Gloss upon Paradise Lost. Princeton Stud. in Eng., 22. Princeton: Princeton University Press; Oxford: Oxford University Press, 1941. xiv, 269pp.
Rev: T. B. Stroup, MLQ, 3, 1941, 327-30; A. Williams, MP, 40, 1941, 103-4; T. Maynard, CW, 155, 1941, 506-7; J. S. Diekhoff, SR, 50, 1941, 266-7; G. L. Kane, CHR, 28, 1941, 143-4; B. M., DR, 22, 1941, 249; Douglas Bush, MLN, 58, 1943, 220-2; N. H. Henry, PQ, 22, 1943, 92-3; G. C. Taylor, Shakespeare Assn. Bull., 18, 1943, 92-5; A. S. P. Woodhouse, PRv., 52, 1943, 206-8; H. J. C. Grierson, MLR, 39, 1944, 97-107.

249 KELLOGG, ALFRED L. Some Patristic Sources for Milton's Gehenna. NQ, 195, 1950, 10-13.
Jerome and Bede.
Rev: Arnold Davenport, YWES, 181.

250 KELLY, SISTER MARGARET TERESA. The Influence of Dante's Paradise upon Milton. Doctoral diss., Cornell University, 1938. Abs., Cornell University Abstracts of Theses, 1938, pp. 33-5.

251 KENRICK, EDWARD F. Paradise Lost and the Index of Prohibited Books. SP, 53, 1956, 485-500.
A translation placed on the Index, 1734.

252 KIRKCONNELL, WATSON. The Celestial Cycle: the Theme of Paradise Lost in World Literature, with Translations of the Major Analogues. Toronto: University of Toronto Press, 1952. xxvii, 701pp.
Part 1: Analogues, in whole or in part.
Part 2: Descriptive catalogue of analogues.
Rev: Arnold Davenport, YWES, 184-5; D. C. A (llen), MLN, 68, 1953, 281; E. M. W. Tillyard, RES, 4, 1953, 405; James R. Naiden, CL, 5, 1953, 375-7; C. L. B., DR, 33, 1953-4, 37; A. E. Barker, UTQ, 23, 1954, 195-8; Malcolm Ross, QQ, 60, 1953-4, 440; Edgar Mertner, Ang., 72, 1954-5, **489-92.**

253 KORETZ, GENE. Milton's Paradise Lost, IX, 910. Expl., 12, 1954, item 53.
On the meaning of "these wilde Woods forlorn."

254 KROUSE, F. Milton's Paradise Lost, IV, 349. Expl., 7, 1949, item 44.

255 LANGENFELT, GÖSTA. The OE. Paardise Lost. Ang., 55, 1931, 250-65.

256 LANGTON, EDWARD. Satan, a Portrait. A Study of the Character of Satan through All the Ages. London: Sheffington, 1946; New York: Macmillan, 1947.
A background study.

257 LE COMTE, EDWARD S. Milton's Infernal Council and Mantuan. PMLA, 69, 1954, 979-83.
Supplies addenda to Kirkconnell's list of analogues.

258 LEE, HERBERT G. The Justification Theme in Milton's Work with Special Reference to Paradise Lost. Master's thesis, University of North Carolina, 1947.

259 LEWIS, C. S. A Preface to Paradise Lost. Being the Ballard Methews Lectures Delivered at University College, North Wales, 1941, Revised and Enlarged. London: Oxford University Press, 1942. 139pp.
Reprinted several times. Topics: The distinction between the primary and the secondary epic. Milton and Virgil, the theology of Paradise Lost, Satan, Milton's angels, Adam and Eve, the Fall, flaws in the poem.
Rev: TLS, Nov. 28, 1942, p. 528, and Dec. 5, 1942, p. 595; NQ, 183, 1942, 359-60; L. C. Martin, YWES, 160-1; Jackson Knight, Spect., Nov. 13, 1942, p. 460; Denis Saurat, NSN, Nov. 14, 1942, pp. 325-6; L. C. Knights, Scr., 11, 1942, 146-8; H. J. C. Grierson, MLR, 38, 1943, 143-8; E. H. W. Meyerstein, Eng., 4, 1943, 129-30; E. W. Wagenknecht, NYTBR, May 23, 1943, p. 10; DUJ, 4, 1943, 71-2; W. R. Parker, MLN, 59, 1944, 205-6; Irene Samuel, PRv., 53, 1944, 580-90; B. A. Wright, RES, 20, 1944, 78-84; E. E. Stoll, RES, 20, 1944, 108-24.

260 LEWIS, RICHARD B. Milton's Use of Logic and Rhetoric in Paradise Lost to Develop the Character of Satan. Doctoral diss., Stanford University, 1949. Abs., Abstracts of Diss., Stanford University, 24, 1950, 155-8.

261 LEVER, J. W. Paradise Lost and the Anglo-Saxon Tradition. RES, 23, 1947, 97-106.
Argues for the influence of the Caedomonian Genesis.
Rev: R. M. Wilson, YWES, 61-2; L. C. Martin, ibid., 190-1.

262 L(OANE), G(EORGE) G. Paradise Lost: Lose or Loose. NQ, 176, 1939, 89.
Milton habitually uses "loose" for what we write "lose."

263 - - - - - -. A Phrase in Paradise Lost (Book IV, 11. 408-10). NQ, 180, 1941, 387.
Replies by E. H. V., ibid., 181, 1941, 27; by Loane, ibid., 68, by E. H. V., ibid., 95-6.

264 - - - - - -. Ridges of War. NQ, 175, 1938, 313.
On Paradise Lost, 6, 233. Suggests that "ridges" refers to spaces between masses of troops.

265 LOANE, GEORGE G. A Simile of Milton. NQ, 175, 1938, 434-5.
On Paradise Lost, 4, 159-66.

266 LOOTEN, M. C. Milton et les amours de Dieu. RA-A, 8, 1931, 345-6.
Attacks Legouis on Paradise Lost, 7, 8-12.
Rev: F. S. Boas, YWES, 207.

267 LOVEJOY, ARTHUR O. Milton and the Paradox of the Fortunate Fall. Essays in the History of Ideas (Baltimore: Johns Hopkins Press, 1948), pp. 277-95.
A reprint of ELH, 4, 1937, 161-79. Rev: L. C. Martin, YWES, 185.

268 LUMPKIN, BEN W. Fate in Paradise Lost. SP, 44, 1947, 56-68.
Contrary to the utterances of Satan, Milton, God, and the forces of God use the word to mean a divine decree or the will of God.
Rev: L. C. Martin, YWES, 191.

269 MABBOTT, THOMAS O. Milton and Nonnos. NQ, 197, 1952, 117-8.
Paradise Lost, 4, 340ff., echoes a passage in the Dionysiaca.

270 MACKELLAR, WALTER. Milton and Grotius. TLS, Dec. 15, 1932, p. 963.
Argues that in Paradise Lost, 11, 661-71, Milton is referring to Hugo Grotius.
Rev: L. C. Martin, YWES, 210.

271 MAHOOD, M. M. Poetry and Humanism. New Haven: Yale University Press; London: Jonathan Cape, 1950. 335pp.
Contains two articles of interest: Milton: the Baroque Artist, pp. 169-206, in which Mahood holds that Paradise Lost is expressive of the humanism of the metaphysical poets rather than that of the earlier Renaissance; and Milton's Heroes, pp. 207-51, in which Samson and Satan are presented as contrasting figures.

Rev: TLS, Apr. 28, 1950, p. 258; R. G. Cox, MGW, May 11, 1950, p. 11; I. Fletcher, NSN, Apr. 29, 1950, p. 494; L. L. Martz, YR, 40, 1951, 562-5; Geoffrey Walton, Scr., 17, 1951, 277-80.

272 MALONE, KEMP. Grundtvig on Paradise Lost. Renaissance Stud. in Honor of Hardin Craig (Stanford: Stanford University Press, 1941), pp. 320-3.
   The article also appears in PQ, 20, 1941, 512-15.

273 MANNING, CLARENCE A. A Russian Translation of Paradise Lost. SEER, 13, 1935, 173-6.
   Reproduces and comments on the introduction to a 1780 translation.

274 MARILLA, ESMOND L. The Central Problem of Paradise Lost: The Fall of Man. Essays and Stud. in Eng. Lang. and Lit., 15. Upsala: A. -B. Lundequistska Bokhandeln; Copenhagen: Ejnar Munksgaard; Cambridge: Harvard University Press, 1953. 36pp.
   "My purpose here is to bring the details of the scene [the fall of Adam and Eve] under careful focus and to argue for my view that the episode is a painstaking and carefully unified dramatization of issues which, in Milton's opinion, are always active in shaping the course of human history."
   Rev: Arnold Davenport, YWES, 206; Pierre Legouis, EA, 7, 1954, 119; J. Milton French, SN, 26, 1954, 201-2.

275 ------. Milton on Conjugal Love among the Heavenly Angels. MLN, 68, 1953, 485-6.
   On Raphael's comment in Paradise Lost, 8.

276 ------. Milton on Vain Wisdom and False Philosophie. SN, 25, 1953, 1-5.
   On Paradise Lost, 2, 557-68.
   Rev: Arnold Davenport, YWES, 209.

277 MAXWELL, I. R. Waldock and Milton. Southerly (Sidney, Australia), 12, 1951, 14-16.
   Criticizes Waldock's Paradise Lost and Its Critics.

278 MAXWELL, J. C. "Gods" in Paradise Lost. NQ, 193, 1948, 234-6, 242.
   Rev: L. C. Martin, YWES, 196.

279 ------. The Sensible of Pain: Paradise Lost, 2, 278. RES, 5, 1954, 268.
   Interprets the phrase as "that element in our pain which is apprehended by the senses."

280 McCARTHY, THOMAS J. Some Theological Aspects of Paradise Lost. Master's thesis, University of Western Ontario, 1933. 130pp.
   "Milton's works mirror the eclecticism of the age and indicate the prevailing trend of religious thought."

281 McCOLLEY, GRANT. The Astronomy of Paradise Lost. SP, 34, 1937, 209-47.
Rev: L. C. Martin, YWES, 184-5.

282 - - - - - -. The Book of Enoch and Paradise Lost. HTR, 31, 1938, 21-39.
Milton knew more of I Enoch than is commonly acknowledged.
Rev: L. C. Martin, YWES, 177.

283 - - - - - -. The Epic Catologue of Paradise Lost. ELH, 4, 1937, 180-91.
Rev: L. C. Martin, YWES, 183.

284 - - - - - -. Macbeth and Paradise Lost. SAB, 13, 1938, 146-50.
Milton's indebtedness.

285 - - - - - -. Milton and Moses Bar-Cepha. SP, 38, 1941, 246-51.
Parallels.

286 - - - - - -. Milton's Ariel. NQ, 177, 1939, 45.
Basil and Procopius were Milton's authorities for his making Ariel a follower of Satan.

287 - - - - - -. Milton's Battle in Heaven and Rupert of Saint Heribert. Spec., 16, 1941, 230-5.
Parallels suggest that Milton had read the twelfth century theologian.

288 - - - - - -. Milton's Dialogue on Astronomy: The Principal Immediate Sources. PMLA, 52, 1937, 728-62.
On Paradise Lost, 8. Suggests Bishop John Wilkins and Alexander Ross.
Rev: L. C. Martin, YWES, 183-4.

289 - - - - - -. Milton's Golden Compasses. NQ, 176, 1939, 97-8.
Milton following convention in using the metaphor in Paradise Lost, 7, 224-33.

290 - - - - - -. Paradise Lost. HTR, 32, 1939, 181-235.
"...I suggest that Paradise Lost was designed as a non-sectarian epic and more or less deliberately modelled as well as based upon conservative religious literature...."
Rev: L. C. Martin, YWES, 114-15.

291 - - - - - -. Paradise Lost: An Account of Its Growth and Major Origins, with a Discussion of Milton's Use of Sources and Literary Patterns. Chicago: Packard and Co., 1940. 362pp.
Rev: L. C. Martin, YWES, 169-70; Garland Greever, Pers., 22, 1941, 308; M. Kelley and T. S. K. Scott-Craig, MLN, 27, 1942, 295-6; S. A. Nock, SR, 49, 1942, 561-5.

292 - - - - - -. The Theory of the Diurnal Rotation of the Earth. Isis, 26, 1937, 392-402.
Rev: L. C. Martin, YWES, 183-4.

293 McKERAHAN, ANNABELLE L. Paradise Lost: A Sublimation of the Philosophical Concepts Found in Milton's Prose. Doctoral diss., University of Pittsburgh, 1936. Abs., University of Pittsburgh, Abstracts of Theses, 20, 1936, 168-74.

294 MEYERSTEIN, E. H. W. Ramiel (Paradise Lost, VI, 372), NQ, 189, 1945, 255.
Asks, "Where did Milton get the name?"

295 MILLER, MILTON. Paradise Lost: the Double Standard. UTQ, 20, 1951, 183-99.
The fallen angels exemplify the heroic standard of virtue, while Christ exemplifies the super-heroic standard of self-sacrifice.
Rev: Arnold Davenport, YWES, 189-90.

296 MODY, JEHANGIR R. P. Vondel and Milton. Bombay: Cooper, 1942. xiv, 326pp.
Rev: Helen Darbishire, RES, 19, 1943, 330.

297 MOHL, RUTH. Studies in Spenser, Milton and the Theory of Monarchy. New York: Columbia University Press, 1949.
Two essays of interest: The Theme of Paradise Lost, pp. 66-93; and. Milton and the Idea of Perfection, pp. 94-132. In the first essay, Mohl argues that Milton's purpose was to present the theme of the making of the greater man—not simply the greater man Christ but the human being everywhere. In the second, the author places Milton on the side of the Christian humanists, "whose conception of perfection implies life and growth."
Rev: L. C. Martin, YWES, 169; E. Sirluck, MP, 48, 1950, 60-4; Mindele Black, QQ, 57, 1950, 580-2; E. S. Gohn, MLN, 65, 1950, 562-4.

298 MORSE, J. MITCHELL. La Pucelle and Paradise Lost. CL, 9, 1957, 238-42.
Chapelain's poem as a possible source.

299 MÜLLER, URSULA. Miltons Satan. Die Gestalt Lucifers in der Dichtung vom Barock bis zur Romantik (Berlin: Emil Ebering, 1940), pp. 40-50.

300 MUIR, LYNETTE R. A Detail in Milton's Description of Sin. NQ, N. S., 3, 1956, 100-1.
The hounds in Sin's womb may derive from Malory's Questing Beast.

301 M(UNSTERBERG), M. Precursor of Paradise Lost. MB, 19, 1944, 24.
Andreini's L'Adamo and Vodel's Lucifer.

302 MUSGROVE, S. Is the Devil an Ass? **RES**, 21, 1945, 302-15.
"The Satan of the first two books, even if magnificent... is still intellectually rotten and is stil evil incarnate."
Rev: L. C. Martin, YWES, 146.

303 MUTSCHMANN, H. Further Studies Concerning the Origin of Paradise Lost (The Matter of the Armada). Dorpat, Estonia: Mattiessen, 1934. 55pp.
Milton's first epic plans were to glorify Britain in an epic and to celebrate the defect of the Armada. Echoes of such planning remain in Paradise Lost, especially in Book VI, which contains numerous parallels to contemporary accounts.
Rev: L. C. Martin, YWES, 235-6; TLS, Sept. 13, 1934, p. 616; H. O. Wilde, Ang. Bbl., 46, 1935, 238-9; Denis Saurat, MLN, 51, 1936, 263-4; E. H. Visiak, NC, 119, 1936, 506-12.

304 - - - - - -. Milton's Projected Epic on the Rise and Future Greatness of the Britannic Nation together with a Reprint of the Anonymous Pamphlet, Great Britain's Ruin Plotted by the Seven Sorts of Men, 1641. Dorpat, Estonia: J. G. Krüger, 1936.
Rev: TLS, Aug. 1, 1936, p. 633; S. Addleshaw, CQR, 124, 1937, 330-3; E. M. W. Tillyard, MLN, 53, 1938, 381-3; reply to Tillyard by Mutschmann, ibid., 54, 1939, 398.

305 NAZÀRI, EMILIO. Elementi Classici ed Italiani nel Paradiso Perduto. Problemi Miltoniani (Palermo: A. Priulla, 1951), pp. 44-217.

306 NELSON, LAWRENCE E. Streamlining Satan. Our Roving Bible (New York: Abington-Cokesbury, 1945), pp. 93-9.

307 NICOLSON, MARJORIE H. Milton's Hell and the Phlegraean Fields. UTQ, 7, 1938, 500-13.
Suggests that Milton may have remembered his visit to the Phlegraean Fields in southern Italy.
Rev: L. C. Martin, YWES, 178.

308 OGDEN, H. S. V. The Crisis of Paradise Lost Reconsidered. PQ, 36, 1957, 1-19.
Argues against Tillyard and Bell that Adam and Eve, though not perfect before the Fall, are by no means already fallen, "that the Fall is the central theological event in the poem, and that it is likewise the climax of the narrative."

309 ORAS, ANTS. Echoing Verse Endings in Paradise Lost. South Atlantic Studies for Sturgis E. Leavitt (Washington: Scarecrow Press, 1953), pp. 175-90.

310 - - - - - -. Goddess Humane (Paradise Lost IX, 732). MLR, 49, 1954, 51-3.
Prefers the reading "human" to "humane."
Rev: Arnold Davenport, YWES, 143.

311 - - - - - -. Milton's Blank Verse and the Chronology of His Major Poems. SAMLA Studies in Milton (Gainesville: University of Florida Press, 1953), pp. 128-97.
Accepts the traditional chronology.

312 PAKENHAM, THOMAS. On the Site of the Earthly Paradise. TLS, Feb. 15, 1957, p. 104. Replies by E. Ullendorff and W. G. L. Randles, ibid., Mar. 8, 1957, p. 151.
On Milton's indebtedness to Purchas and to Urreta, a Spanish Dominican, for his account of the true and of the false Paradise.

313 PARISH, JOHN E. Pre-Miltonic Representations of Adam as a Christian. RIP, 40, 1953, 332-3.
Rev: Arnold Davenport, YWES, 208-9.

314 PARTRIDES, C. A. Paradise Lost and the Mortalist Heresy. NQ, N. S., 4, 1957, 250-1.
Suggests a reconsideration of the belief that the mortalism of De Doctrina Christiana is reflected in the epic, since Adam (10, 808-13) is hardly in a position to argue about death.

315 PATRICK, JOHN M. Milton, Phineas Fletcher, Spenser, and Ovid—Sin at Hell's Gates. NQ, N S., 3, 1956, 384-6.

316 - - - - - -. More on the Dorian Mood in Paradise Lost. NQ, N. S., 4, 1957, 196-7.
Suggests that in 1, 549-61, Milton may have in mind a passage from Ammianus Marcellinus' Res Gestae.

317 PILATO, S. DE. Un inspirators del Paradiso Perduto: P. Serafino della Salandra. Potenza: Marchesiello, 1934. 26pp.
Rev: G. N. Giordano-Orsini, Leonardo, 6, 1935, 19-20.

318 POWELL, F. TOWNSHEND. Francis Atterbury. TLS, Mar. 3, 1932, p. 155.
On Atterbury's copy of Paradise Lost.

319 PRAZ, MARIO. Le Metamorfosi di Satan. La Carne, La Morte e il Diavolo nella Letterature Romantica (Milan and Rome: Soc. Editrice, 1930), pp. 49-90. Reprinted in The Romantic Agony, trans. by Angus Davidson (London: Oxford University Press, 1933), pp. 51-92.

320 PRITCHARD, HUGH C. A Study of Repetition as an Architectonic Device in Paradise Lost. Master's thesis, University of North Carolina, 1942.

321 PURCELL, J. M. Rime in Paradise Lost. MLN, 59, 1944, 171-2.

322 PUTZEL, ROSAMUND. A Re-examination of the Place of the Holy Spirit in Paradise Lost. Master's thesis, University of North Carolina, 1951.

323 QUARE. Paradise Lost in Latin. NQ, 174, 1938, 442-3.
Notes the existence of a complete Latin hexameter translation by William Dobson.

324 R., V. Milton: A Familiar Quotation. NQ, 165, 1933, 65.
Paradise Lost, 2, 146.

325 RAILO, EINO. Kadotetun Paratiisin maailmankuva (The Weltbild of Paradise Lost). Valvoja-Aika (Helsingfors), 1932.

326 RAJAN, B. Paradise Lost and the Seventeenth Century Reader. London: Chatto and Windus, 1947. 171pp.
Relates the epic to seventeenth-century thought and gives a critical analysis of its structure.
Rev: L. C. Martin, YWES, 189-90; TLS, Oct. 18, 1947, 539; Joan Bennett, NSN, Nov. 8, 1947, pp. 375-6; F. E. Hutchinson, Spect., Oct. 31, 1947, pp. 567-8; B. A. Wright, RES, 25, 1949, 75-83; A. S. P. Woodhouse, UTQ, 18, 1949, 202-5; A. N. Jeffares, ES, 30, 1949, 92-3.

327 RANSOM, JOHN CROWE. God Without Thunder. New York: Harcourt Brace, 1930. x, 334pp.
Discusses the Promethean elements of Satan, pp. 127-33.

328 READ, HERBERT. Milton. A Coat of Many Colors (London: Routledge, 1945), pp. 132-3.
On the virtues of Paradise Lost.

329 REGAN, DORIS B. Paradise Lost: An Enduring Monument. Reading and Collecting, 1, Oct., 1937, 11-12.

330 REYNOLDS, JOHN S. The Similes in Book I of Paradise Lost Compared with Those in Book I of The Faerie Queene. Master's thesis, University of North Carolina, 1940.

331 RICE, WARNER G. Fate in Paradise Lost. Papers of the Mich. Acad., 31, 1947 for 1945, 299-306.

332 ROBERTSON, D. S. The Odyssey and Paradise Lost. TLS, May 4, 1940, pp. 219, 221.

333 ROBINS, HARRY F. The Cosmology of Paradise Lost: A Reconsideration. Doctoral diss., Indiana University, 1951.

334 - - - - - -. The Crystalline Sphere and the Waters Above in Paradise Lost. PMLA, 69, 1954, 903-14.

335 - - - - - -. Milton's Golden Chain. MLN, 69, 1954, 76.

336 ROSE, PATRICIA A. Essentials of Epic Poetry: A Comparative Study of the Iliad, the Chanson de Roland, and Paradise Lost. Master's thesis, Florida State University, 1955.

337 ROSS, MALCOLM M. Poetry, Belief, and Paradise Lost. DR, 28, 1948, 177-88. Reprinted in Poetry and Dogma (New Brunswick: Rutgers University Press, 1954), pp. 205-27.
Rev: L. C. Martin, YWES, 194.
Holds that a correct understanding of the poem is possible not by a suspension of disbelief but in spite of disbelief. "Beyond this, the range of appreciation must depend upon the kind and degree of belief."

338 RUDWIN, MAXIMILIAN. The Devil in Legand and Literature. Chicago: Open Court, 1931. 354pp.

339 - - - - - -. Open Court, 43, 1929.
The volume contains several articles relevant to Paradise Lost: The Legend of Lucifer, pp. 193-208; The Number and Names of the Devils, pp. 282-93; The Form of the Fiend, pp. 321-40; The Organization of Pandemonium, pp. 463-73; Journeys to Hell, pp. 566-70; Diabolus Simia Dei, pp. 602-11; The Synagogue of Satan, pp. 728-48.

340 S., W. W. The Forbidden Fruit. NQ, 183, 1942, 226-7.
A query concerning the idea that the fruit was an apple. Replies by Hibernicus and George Percival-Kaye, ibid., p. 323; by Sayar, ibid., p. 383.

341 SAMUEL, IRENE. The Dialogue in Heaven: A Reconsideration of Paradise Lost, III, 1-417. PMLA, 72, 1957, 601-11.
On the centrality of the episode to the entire action of the poem.

342 SASEK, LAWRENCE A. Satan and the Epic Hero: Classical and Christian Tradition. Doctoral diss., Harvard University, 1953.

343 SAURAT, DENIS. Gods of the People. London: John Westhouse, 1947. 190pp.
Concerned with the evolution of ideas by "unknown people." Draws examples from the thought of Spenser and Milton and others. Of doubtful significance.

344 - - - - - -. Two Notes on Milton: 1. Did Milton Change His Views after Paradise Lost? 2. Light and the Son. RES, 12, 1936, 323-5.
Rev: L. C. Martin, YWES, 191.

345 SCHANZER, ERNEST. Milton's Fall of Mulciber and Troia Britannica. NQ, N. S., 4, 1957, 379-80.
Suggests Heywood's work (1609) as a source for Paradise Lost, 1, 740-6.

346 - - - - - -. Milton's Hell Revisited. UTQ, 24, 1955, 136-45.

347 SCHIRMER, W. F. Das Problem des religiösen Epos im 17. Jahrhundert in England. Deutsche Vierteljahrschrift, 14, 1936, 60-74.
Sees Paradise Lost as a fusion of the warring elements, the new religious feeling and the emergent scientific philosophy.

348 SCHULTZ, HOWARD. Satan's Serenade. PQ, 27, 1948, 17-26.
On the dream episode in the Garden.
Rev: L. C. Martin, YWES, 195.

349 - - - - - -. Warlike Flutes: Gellius, Castiglione, Montaigne, and Milton. MLN, 64; 1949, 96-8.
On the flutes of Paradise Lost, 1, 550-4.

350 SCOTT-CRAIG, T. S. K. Milton's Paradise Lost, V, 108-111. Expl., 3, 1945, item 37.

351 SCUDDER, HAROLD H. Satan's Artillery. NQ, 195, 1950, 334-47.
On Paradise Lost, 6, 568-78.
Rev: Arnold Davenport, YWES, 181.

352 SEIBERT, THEODOR. Egozentrisches in Mitons Schreibweise, mit besonderer Berucksichtigung des Satan in Paradise Lost. Ang., 43, 1931, 57-83.
Rev: F. S. Boas, YWES, 207.

353 SENSABAUGH, GEORGE F. Milton on Learning. SP, 43, 1946, 258-72.
On Raphael's discourse to Adam.
Rev: L. C. Martin, YWES, 173-4.

354 SERONSY, CECIL C. Samuel Daniel and Milton. NQ, 197, 1952, 135-6.
Possible borrowings in Paradise Lost and Paradise Regained.
Rev: Arnold Davenport, YWES, 178.

355 SEWELL, W. A., and DENIS SAURAT. Two Notes on Milton. I. Did Milton Change His Views after Paradise Post? II. The Interpretation of Paradise Lost, Book VII, 11. 168ff. RES, 15, 1939, 73-80.
The authors have opposing views on both issues. Sewell reiterates his view in RES, 15, 1939, 335.

356 SHUMAKER, WAYNE. The Fallacy of the Fall in Paradise Lost. PMLA, 70, 1955, 1185-7.
Disagrees with Bell, PMLA, 68, 1953, 863-83. Reply by Bell, pp. 1187-97, a rejoinder by Shumaker, pp. 1197-1202, and a surrejoinder by Bell, p. 1203.

357 SIEGEL, PAUL. "A Paradise within Thee" in Milton, Byron, and Shelley. MLN, 56, 1941, 615-17.
Considers Paradise Lost, Cain, and The Revolt of Islam.

358 SISTER MIRIAM JOSEPH, C. S. C. Orthodoxy in Paradise Lost. Laval Theologique et Philosophique, 8, 1952, 243-84.
"...it seems fair to conclude that an intelligent Catholic reader can enjoy in Paradise Lost the expression of dogmatic, moral, and philosophical truths impregnated with a power to poetry, the power not merely to teach but to delight and move."
Rev: Arnold Davenport, YWES, 141.

359 SLAUGHTER, E. E. Milton's Demogorgon. PQ, 10, 1931, 310-12.
On Paradise Lost, 2, 963-5. Locrine a possible source.
Rev: F. S. Boas, YWES, 207.

360 SMITH, HALLETT. No Middle Flight. HLQ, 15, 1952, 159-72.
"...Milton was able to speak out... not only because he believed the argument, but also because he had found an area of belief which encompassed at once serious doctrine and poetic fiction."
Rev: Arnold Davenport, YWES, 184.

361 SMITH, PAUL R. A Comparison of Paradise Lost and Mundorum Explicatio. Master's thesis, University of Georgia, 1951.

362 SMITH, REBECCA W. The Source of Milton's Pandemonium. MP, 29, 1931, 187-98.
His recollection of St. Peter's Cathedral.
Rev: F. S. Boas, YWES, 207.

363 SPADALA, ENRICO. Tre i principi dei diavoli: Lucifer di Dante. Plutone di Tasso, Satana di J. Milton. Ragusa: Puglisi, 1937. 116pp.

364 SPAETH, J. DUNCAN. Epic Conventions in Paradise Lost. Elizabethan Studies... in Honor of George F. Reynolds. University of Colorado Stud., Ser. B., Stud. in the Humanities, 2 (Boulder: University of Colorado Press, 1945), pp. 201-10.

365 STARNES, D. T. Gehenna and Tophet. NQ, 192, 1947, 369-70.
Addenda to Whiting, ibid., 225-30.

366 - - - - - -. Tityos and Satan. NQ, 197, 1952, 379-80.
Suggests Tityos as Milton's model for the size of Satan in
Paradise Lost, 1, 194-8, 209-10.

367 STEADMAN, JOHN M. The Bee-Simile in Homer and
Milton. NQ, N. S., 3, 1956, 101-2.
On Paradise Lost, 1, 768-76.

368 - - - - - -. Dante's Commedia and Milton's Paradise Lost:
A Consideration of the Significance of Genre for Source
Studies and Compartive Literature. Doctoral diss.,
Princeton University, 1954. Abs., DA, 15, 1955, 593-4.

369 - - - - - -. A Milton-Claudian Parallel. NQ, N. S., 3, 1956,
202.
Compares the opening of the infernal portals, Paradise
Lost, 2, 881ff., and a passage in Claudian's De Consulatu
Stilichonis.

370 - - - - - -. John Collop and the Flames without Light
(Paradise Lost, I, 62-3). NQ, N. S., 2, 1955, 382-3.

371 - - - - - -. Satan's Metamorphoses and the Heroic Convention of the Ignoble Disguise. MLR, 52, 1957, 81-5.
Believes that Satan's voluntary disguises possess a recognizable
affinity with the heroic tradition.

372 - - - - - -. Sin and the Serpent of Genesis 3: Paradise Lost,
II, 650-53. MP, 54, 1956, 217-20.

373 STEIN, ARNOLD. Answerable Style: Essays on Paradise
Lost. Minneapolis: University of Minnesota Press, 1953.
ix, 166pp.
Chapters: Satan, The War in Heaven, A Note on Hell, The
Garden, The Fall, Answerable Style.
Rev: Arnold Davenport, YWES, 207; Cleanth Brooks, KR,
15, 1953, 638-47; J. H. Hanford, SCN, 11, 1953, 29; TLS,
May 7, 1954, p. 298; C. S. Holmes, SR, 62, 1954, 509-19;
Kester Svendsen, BA, 28, 1954, 223; MGW, Feb. 4, 1954,
p. 10; E. Duncan-Jones, MLR, 50, 1955, 106-7.

374 - - - - - -. Milton's War in Heaven—An Extended Metaphor. ELH, 18, 1951, 201-20. Reprinted in Answerable
Style. (Minneapolis: University of Minnesota Press,
1953), pp. 17-37.
Rev: Arnold Davenport, YWES, 190.

375 - - - - - -. Satan: The Dramatic Role of Evil. PMLA, 65,
1950, 221-31. Reprinted in Answerable Style (Minneapolis: University of Minnesota Press, 1953), pp. 3-16.
Rev: Arnold Davenport, YWES, 180.

376 STEWART, FLORENCE M. Paradise Lost, Bk. I, 636:
Different. NQ, 166, 1934, 79.
Milton uses "different" in its old sense of "deferent."

377 STOCKLEY, W. F. P. Paradise Lost, 1, 301. TLS, Feb. 18, 1932, p. 112.

378 STOLL, ELMER E. Belial as an Example. MLN, 48, 1933, 419-27.
Of literature as imagination rather than life.

379 - - - - - -. From the Superhuman to the Human in Paradise Lost. UTQ, 3, 1933, 3-16. Reprinted in From Shakespeare to Joyce (New York: Doubleday, 1944), pp. 422-35.
Rev: L. C. Martin, YWES, 253.

380 - - - - - -. Give the Devil His Due: a Reply to Mr. Lewis. RES, 20, 1944, 108-24.
Attacks Lewis' interpretation of Satan in his Preface to Paradise Lost.

381 - - - - - -. A Postscript to Give the Devil His Due. PQ, 28, 1949, 167-84.
Rev: L. C. Martin, YWES, 165.

382 STRICKLAND, LAURA L. Christ of the Bible in Paradise Lost. Master's thesis, University of Alabama, 1948.

383 SUMMERS, JOSEPH H. Grateful Vicissitude in Paradise Lost. PMLA, 69, 1954, 251-64.

383a - - - - - -. The Voice of the Redeemer in Paradise Lost. PMLA, 70, 1955, 1082-9.

384 SVENDSEN, KESTER. Adam's Soliloquy in Book X of Paradise Lost. CE, 10, 1949, 366-70.
Rev: L. C. Martin, YWES, 167.

384a - - - - - -. Epic Address and Reference and the Principle of Decorum in Paradise Lost. PQ, 28, 1949, 185-206.
Rev: L. C. Martin, YWES, 167.

385 - - - - - -. "Found out the Massie Ore." NQ, 177, 1939, 331.
On an emendation of Paradise Lost, 1, 703.

386 - - - - - -. Milton and Malleus Maleficarum. MLN, 60, 1945, 118-19.
Adam's remark to Eve concerning the rib (10, 884-8) is clarified by a passage in the Malleus Maleficarum (c. 1484).

387 - - - - - -. Milton's Chariot of Paternal Deity (P. L., VI, 749-759). NQ, 193, 1948, 339.
Comments of Bartholomew Anglicus in De Proprietatibus Rerum closely parallel Milton's description.
Rev: L. C. Martin, YWES, 195.

388 - - - - - -. Milton's Paradise Lost, V, 108-111. Expl., 4, 1945, item 2.

389 ------. Milton's Paradise Lost, IV, 347-350. Expl., 8, 1949, item 11.

390 ------. The Power to Reason: A Milton Paradox. NQ, 184, 1943, 368-70.
   On Milton and the reasoning ability of animals. See also H. W. Crundell, ibid., 185, 1943, 113.
   Rev: L. C. Martin, YWES, 155.

391 ------. The Prudent Crane: Paradise Lost, VII, 425-431. NQ, 183, 1942, 66-7.
   Testimony of the crane's qualities from popular encyclopedias of science.

392 TAYLOR, DICK, JR. The Battle in Heaven in Paradise Lost. Tulane Stud. Eng., 3, 1952, 69-92.

393 TAYLOR, GEORGE C. Did Milton Read Robert Crofts' A Paradice within Us or The Happie Mind? PQ, 28, 1949, 207-10.
   Expresses the affirmative view.
   Rev: L. C. Martin, YWES, 166-7.

394 ------. Milton's Use of Du Bartas. Cambridge: Harvard University Press; London: Milford, 1934. 129pp.
   Rev: L. C. Martin, YWES, 235; TLS, Aug. 23, 1934, pp. 578-9; H. F. Fletcher, JEGP, 34, 1935, 119-20; H. O. Wilde, Ang. Bbl., 46, 1935, 237-8; D. Saurat, RES, 12, 1936, 216-18, and MLN, 51, 1936, 263-4; B. A. Wright, MLR, 31, 1936, 84-5; J. H. Hanford, MP, 35, 1937, 200-1.

395 THOMPSON, ELBERT N. S. For Paradise Lost, XI-XII. PQ, 22, 1943, 376-82.
   In refutation of C. S. Lewis, the author expresses a liking for the books and argues that they are artistically justified.
   Rev: L. C. Martin, YWES, 155.

396 THOMPSON, J. A. K. The Epic Tradition in Modern Times: Milton. Classical Influences on English Poetry (London: Allen and Unwin, 1951), pp. 53-74.
   Indicates lines along which the relation of Milton to Homer and Virgil may be pursued.
   Rev: TLS, Sept. 28, 1951, p. 614; Peter Russell, TT, Oct. 13, 1951, pp. 986-7.

397 TILLYARD, E. M. W. The Causeway from Hell to the World in the Tenth Book of Paradise Lost. SP, 38, 1941, 266-70.

398 ------. Milton. The English Epic and Its Background (New York: Oxford University Press, 1954), pp. 430-47.
   Discusses Milton as the nodal figure in the English epic, corresponding to Virgil in Latin.
   Rev: TLS, Apr. 30, 1954, p. 280; L. Cazamian, EA, 7,

1954, 343-4; J. C. Ghosh, CR, 186, 1954, 125-6; Andrew Wordsworth, NER, 143, 1954, 49-50; David Daiches, MGW, May 20, 1954, p. 804; Bonamy Dobrée, Spect., Apr. 16, 1954, p. 470; B. E. Owen, FR, N. S., 1050, 1954, 427; J. C. Maxwell, DUJ, 47, 1954-5, 38-9.

399 — — — — — —. The English Epic Tradition. Warton Lecture on English Poetry. Proc. Brit. Acad., 22. London: Humphrey Milford, 1936. 23pp. Reprinted in The Miltonic Setting (Cambridge: Cambridge University Press, 1938), pp. 141-67.

> i. a., considers Paradise Lost as an epic which "resumes the essential medieval theme and combines with it Renaissance culture and exuberance and with neo-classic compression of form."
> Rev: E. C. Batho, MLR, 33, 1938, 87-8.

400 — — — — — —. Milton and Sidney's Arcadia. TLS, Mar. 6, 1953, p. 153.

> On the resemblance between Paradise Lost, 11, 836-9, and the passage describing the shipwreck early in the Arcadia.

401 — — — — — —. Milton and Statius. TLS, July 1, 1949, p. 429.

> Notices a parallel between Paradise Lost, 9, 886-93, and the Thebiad, 7, 148-50.

402 — — — — — —. Milton and the English Epic Tradition. Seventeenth Century Studies Presented to Sir Herbert Grierson (Oxford: Clarendon Press, 1938), pp. 211-34. Reprinted as The Growth of Milton's Epic Plans in The Miltonic Setting (Cambridge: Cambridge University Press, 1938), pp. 168-204.

403 — — — — — —. Studies in Milton. London: Chatto and Windus, 1951. 176pp.

> Contains, i. a., chapters on the crisis of Paradise Lost, on Satan, and on Adam and Eve.

404 TOLA MENDOZA, FERNANDO. Una nota sobre el Paradiso Perdito de Milton. Sphinx (Lima, Peru), 2, No. 3, 1937, 91-4.

405 TURNER, PAUL. The Dorian Mood (A Note on Paradise Lost, I, 549-61). NQ, N. S., 4, 1957, 10-11.

> Suggests that Milton is alluding to a passage from Plutarch's Lycurgus.

406 — — — — — —. Miltonic Negligence. NQ, 192, 1947, 358.

> On Paradise Lost, 10, 775-9.

407 — — — — — —. Woman and the Fall of Man. ES, 29, 1948, 1-18. On Adam's attitude toward Eve and the metaphysical love poetry of Milton's age.

> Rev: L. C. Martin, YWES, 194.

408 URGAN, MINA. Satan and His Critics. English Department Stud., Istanbul University, 2, 1951, 61-81.
Surveys the Satanist controversy.

409 VAN DOREN, MARK. Paradise Lost. The Noble Voice: A Study of Ten Great Poems (New York: Holt, 1946), pp. 122-47.
"Paradise Lost is as near to greatness as a poem without simple vision can go. Since its vision is not simple, however, or its author's mind made up, as an epic it suffers a serious handicap. It comes last in the great list, walking lame."
Rev: Irwin Edman, NYHTBR, Nov. 24, 1946, p. 3; Carlos Baker, NYTBR, Nov. 24, 1946, p. 3; Delmore Schwartz, SR, 55, 1947, 707-9; M. F. Lindsley, CW, 164, 1947, 476-7.

410 VISIAK, E. H. Milton's Magic Shadow. NC, 134, 1943, 135-40.
"Satan is the projection, the shadow-shape, of a mind disillusioned by the ideal that had possessed it."

411 WALDOCK, A. J. A. Masson's Diagram of Milton's Spaces. RES, 22, 1946, 56-8.
On Paradise Lost, 1, 73-4.

412 - - - - - -. Mr. C. S. Lewis and Paradise Lost. Australian English Assn., Sept., 1943.
A disparagement of the epic.

413 - - - - - -. Paradise Lost and Its Critics. Cambridge: Cambridge University Press, 1947. 147pp.
Concerned with Milton's success or failure in accomplishing his purpose.
Rev: L. C. Martin, YWES, 188-9; TLS, Aug. 2, 1947, p. 395, and Nov. 1, 1947, p. 560; F. R. Leavis and TLS reviewer, TLS, Nov. 22, 1947, p. 603; C. S. Lewis, TLS, Nov. 29, 1947, p. 615; NQ, 192, 1947, 395; Herman Peschmann, Eng., 6, 1947, 311-12; W. G., QQ, 54, 1947, 528-30; Joan Bennett, NSN, Aug. 23, 1947, pp. 154-5; Camb. Jour., 1, 1947, 70; H. F. Fletcher, JEGP, 47, 1948, 203; A. N. J., ES, 29, 1948, 94; B. A. Wright, RES, 25, 1949, 75-83; Elizabeth M. Pope, MLN, 64, 1949, 208-9; D. C. Allen, MLQ, 10, 1949, 115-17.

414 WEATHERS, WINSTON. Paradise Lost as Archetypal Myth. CE, 14, 1952-3, 261-4.

415 WEISINGER, HERBERT. Tragedy and the Paradox of the Fortunate Fall. London: Routledge and Kegan Paul, 1953. 300pp.
A background study.
Rev: J. A. Bryant, SR, 62, 1954, 319-28.

416 WEISMILLER, E. R. The Versification of Paradise Lost and Paradise Regained: a Study of Movement and Structure in Milton's Non-Dramatic Blank Verse. Doctoral diss., Merton College, Oxford, 1951.

417 WERBLOWSKY, R. J. ZWI. Lucifer and Prometheus: a
Study of Milton's Satan. Introd. by C. G. Jung. London:
Routledge, 1952. xix, 120pp.
"The claim made in this study is that Milton's Satan in
fact contains Promethean elements, and that these are the
reasons for his powerful appeal—an appeal which has proved
detrimental to the unity and purpose of the poem."
Rev: Arnold Davenport, YWES, 183; NSN, Aug. 9, 1952,
p. 168.

418 - - - - - -. Milton and the Conjectura Cabbalistica. Jour. of
the Warburg and Courtauld Institute, 18, 1955, 90-113.
Shows that no direct relation exists between Paradise Lost
and the Zohar and argues that kabbalistic influences come
from post-Renaissance Kabbalah in its pre-Lurianic phase.

419 WEST, ROBERT H. Milton and the Angels. Athens:
University of Georgia Press, 1955. ix, 237pp.
Rev: Arnold Davenport, YWES, 160; R. H. Bowers, SAB,
22, No. 2, 1956, pp. 17-18; Marvin Murdrick, Hudson Rev.,
9, 1956, 126-33; NQ, N. S., 3, 1956, 90-1; Charles M.
Coffin, QQ, 63, 1956, 138-44; TLS, Jan. 20, 1956, p. 38;
Thomas H. English, Georgia Rev., 10, 1956, 19-21; T. S.
K. Scott-Craig, Religion in Life, 25, 1956, 477-8; H. F.
Fletcher, JEGP, 55, 1956, 323; R. A. Fraser, SAQ, 55,
1956, 388-9; M. Y. Hughes, MLN, 71, 1956, 526-9; Kester
Svendsen, BA, 30, 1956, 331; Arnold Williams, MP, 54,
1957, 202-3; F. T. Prince, RES, 8, 1957, 348-9; B. A.
Wright, MLR, 52, 1957, 101-2.

419a - - - - - -. Milton and Michael Psellus. PQ, 28, 1949, 477-89.
A study of likenesses and differences in demonology and
angelology.
Rev: L. C. Martin, YWES, 166.

420 - - - - - -. Milton's Angelological Heresies. JHI, 14, 1953,
116-23.
Provides the basis for another heresy concerning the good-
ness of matter.

421 - - - - - -. Milton's Giant Angels. MLN, 67, 1952, 21-3.
On Paradise Lost, 7, 605.

422 - - - - - -. The Names of Milton's Angels. SP, 47, 1950,
211-23.
Rev: Arnold Davenport, YWES, 181.

423 - - - - - -. The Substance of Milton's Angels. SAMLA
Studies in Milton (Gainesville: University of Florida
Press, 1953), pp. 20-53.

424 - - - - - -. The Terms of Angelic Rank in Paradise Lost.
Essays in Honor of W. C. Curry (Nashville: Vanderbilt
University Press, 1954), pp. 261-8.

425 WHALER, JAMES. Animal Simile in Paradise Lost. PMLA, 47, 1932, 534-53.
Rev: L. C. Martin, YWES, 210-11.

426 ------. The Compounding and Distribution of Similes in Paradise Lost. MP, 28, 1931, 313-27.

427 WHITING, GEORGE W. Before the Flood: Paradise Lost and the Geneva Bible. NQ, 194, 1949, 74-5.
Rev: L. C. Martin, YWES, 166.

428 ------. Cherubim and Sword. NQ, 192, 1947, 469-70.
On Paradise Lost, 12, 632-4.

429 ------. The Golden Compasses in Paradise Lost (Bk. VII, 11. 224-31). NQ, 172, 1937, 294-5.

430 ------. Milton's Crystalline Sphere and Ben Gerson's Heavens. RES, 8, 1932, 450-3.
Questions Fletcher's (Milton's Rabbinical Readings) interpretation of Paradise Lost, 7, 263-74.
Rev: L. C. Martin, YWES, 210.

431 ------. The Politics of Milton's Apostate Angels. NQ, 163, 1932, 384-6.
Rev: L. C. Martin, YWES, 211.

432 ------. Tormenting Tophet. NQ, 192, 1947, 225-30.
Henry Greenwood's Tormenting Tophet (1624) illustrates the comonplaceness of many elements in Milton's picture of hell.
Rev: L. C. Martin, YWES, 191.

433 WICKERT, MARIA. Miltons Entwürfe zu einem Drama vom Sudenfall. Ang., 73, 1955, 171-206.

434 WILLIAMS, ARNOLD. Commentaries on Genesis as a Basis for Hexaemeral Material in the Literature of the Late Renaissance. SP, 34, 1937, 191-208.
Suggests that Milton may have followed Ralegh and Sir Thomas Browne in leaning heavily upon Pererius and others.

435 ------. The Common Expositor: An Account of the Commentaries on Genesis, 1527-1633. Chapel Hill: University of North Carolina Press, 1948. ix, 297pp.
Renaissance commentaries on Genesis and their influence on Milton and others.
Rev: L. C. Martin, YWES, 194-5.

436 ------. Milton and the Book of Enoch—An Alternative Hypothesis. HTR, 33, 1940, 291-9.
Suggests that the fragments themselves are sufficient as a source for Paradise Lost.

437 - - - - - -. The Motivation of Satan's Rebellion in Paradise Lost. SP, 42, 1945, 253-68.
   On the fusion of several motives and the traditions that lie behind them.
   Rev: L. C. Martin, YWES, 146.

438 - - - - - -. Renaissance Commentaries on Genesis and Some Elements of the Theology of Paradise Lost. PMLA, 56, 1941, 151-64.

439 WINKLER, HERTHA. Das biblisch-religiöse Epos des 17. Jahrhunderts bis zu Miltons Paradise Lost. Doctoral diss., Wien, 1949. 249pp.

440 WINTERICH, JOHN T. Paradise Lost. Twenty-Three Books and the Stories Behind Them (Philadelphia: Lippincott, 1939), pp. 1-12.
   General information.

441 WOODHOUSE, A. S. P. Pattern in Paradise Lost. UTQ, 22, 1953, 109-27.
   Rev: Arnold Davenport, YWES, 207-8.

442 WORDEN, W. S. Milton's Approach to the Story of the Fall. ELH, 15, 1948, 295-305.
   Rev: L. C. Martin, YWES, 194.

443 WRIGHT, B. A. Found out the Massie Ore (Paradise Lost, I, 703). TLS, Aug. 9, 1934, p. 553.
   Rev: L. C. Martin, YWES, 237.

444 - - - - - -. Mainly: Paradise Lost, XI, 519. RES, 4, 1953, 143.
   Interprets "mainly" as "considerably, a great deal," not "chiefly."

445 - - - - - -. Masson's Diagram of Milton's Spaces. A Note on Paradise Lost, I, 73-4. RES, 21, 1945, 42-3.
   The "as...as" construction indicates a simile, not a comparison of exact measurement.
   Rev: L. C. Martin, YWES, 27, 1946, 172.

446 - - - - - -. Milton's Treason. TLS, June 20, 1929, p. 494.
   On Paradise Lost, 1, 594-9, which, according to Toland, was objected to by the censor.

447 - - - - - -. A Note on Milton's Punctuation. RES, 5, 1954, 170.
   On Paradise Lost, 9, 922.

448 - - - - - -. Note on Milton's Use of the Word "danger." RES, 22, 1946, 225-6.
   On Paradise Lost, 2, 1004-9. Used in the sense of "power to hurt or harm" or "mischief, harm, and damage."
   Rev: L. C. Martin, YWES, 172.

449 ------. Note on Paradise Lost, II, 879-83. RES, 22, 1946, 130-1.
   "Erebus" used here to designate the dark surrounding void of Chaos out of which hell and the new world of man were created.
   Rev: L. C. Martin, YWES, 172.

450 ------. Note on Paradise Lost, I, 230. RES, 23, 1947, 146-7.
   Rev: L. C. Martin, YWES, 191.

451 ------. Paradise Lost, I, 341. RES, 21, 1945, 238-9.
   Suggests the meaning "veering" for "warping."

452 WRIGHT, CELESTE T. Something More About Eve. SP, 41, 1944, 156-68.
   Collects Renaissance opinions on the nature of women.

453 YOFFIE, LEAH R. C. Chaucer's White Paternoster, Milton's Angels, and.a Hebrew Night Prayer. SFQ, 15, 1951, 203-10.
   Suggests that Chaucer and Milton used the prayer.

453a ------. Creation, the Angels, and the Fall of Man in Milton's Paradise Lost and Paradise Regained, and in the Works of Sir Richard Blackmore. Doctoral diss., University of North Carolina, 1942. Abs., University of North Carolina Record, No. 383, 1942, pp. 77-8.

454 John Milton. Paradise Regained. London: Cresset Press, 1931. 88pp.
Rev: TLS, Dec. 24, 1931, pp. 1033-4.

455 John Milton. Paradise Regained. London: Partridge, 1932. x, 187pp.

456 John Milton. Paradise Regained. Newly Edited with an Introd. and Commentary by E. H. Blakeney. London: Scholartis Press, 1932. ix, 187pp.
Rev: L. C. Martin, YWES, 211; S. B. Liljegren, Ang. Bbl., 43, 1932, 365-80; TLS, May, 26, 1932, p. 384; QR, 259, 1932, 380; J. E. G. de M., CR, 141, 1932, 797-800; G. Bullett, Obs., Sept. 18, 1932; B. A. Wright, MLR, 28, 1933, 105-10.

457 John Milton. Paradise Regained, the Minor Poems and Samson Agonistes. Complete and Arranged Chronologically. Ed. by Merritt Y. Hughes. New York: Odyssey Press; Garden City; Doubleday, 1937. lxiii, 633pp.
A selected bibliography, pp. lvi-lxiii. Good introductions.

458 ALLEN, DON C. The Harmonious Vision: Studies in Milton's Poetry. Baltimore: Johns Hopkins University Press, 1954.
Contains a chapter on Paradise Regained.

459 BALDWIN, EDWARD C. Shook the Arsenal: A Note on Paradise Regained. PQ, 18, 1939, 218-22.
On Paradise Regained, 4, 270.
Rev: L. C. Martin, YWES, 117.

460 BANKS, THEODORE H. The Banquet Scene in Paradise Regained. PMLA, 55, 1940, 773-6.
Interprets the scene as a connecting device between the first and second temptations.

461 BARNES, C. L. Error in Paradise Regained. NQ, 156, 1929, 440.
On Paradise Regained, 1, 383. Cf. ibid., 157, 1929, 177-8, 251.

462 BECK, R. J. A Commentary on Paradise Regained. Doctoral diss., St. Andrews College, 1954.

462a ------. Urim and Thummim. NQ, N. S., 4, 1957, 27-9.
On the nature of the gems mentioned by Satan in Paradise Regained, 3, 13-16.

463 BRODRIBB, C. W. A Neglected Correction in Milton (Paradise Regained, IV, 157-158). TLS, May 17, 1941, pp. 239, 241.
Would replace "the" with "thee" as the fourth word in the line.

464 CARLISLE, A. I. Milton and Ludwig Lavater. RES, 5, 1954, 249-55.
Believes that Paradise Regained, 1, 365-77, 387-96, 407-53 (Christ's argument with Satan) is taken from Lavater on 2 Chronicles 18.

465 CLEVELAND, EDWARD. On the Identity Motive in Paradise Regained. MLQ, 16, 1955, 232-6.
Examines the motive of Satan's attempt to discover Christ's identity against the Old Testament background.

466 DAUBE, DAVID. Three Notes on Paradise Regained. RES, 19, 1943, 205-13.
On the second temptation, the order of the temptations, and Schiller's indebtedness in his Fiesko.
Rev: L. C. Martin, YWES, 155-6.

467 FARNELL, LEWIS R. Milton and Pindar. TLS, Oct. 1, 1931, p. 754.
   On Paradise Regained and the Ninth Pythian Ode.
   Rev: F. S. Boas, YWES, 206.

468 FINK, ZERA S. The Political Implications of Paradise Regained. JEGP, 40, 1941, 482-8.
   Summarized in The Classical Republicans (Evanston: Northwestern University Press, 1945), pp. 195-6. On Milton's distrust of seventeenth-century forms of dictatorship.

469 FIXLER, MICHAEL. The Unclean Meats of the Mosaic Law and the Banquet Scene in Paradise Regained. MLN, 70, 1955, 573-7.

470 FRYE, NORTHROP. The Typology of Paradise Regained. MP, 53, 1956, 227-38.

471 GALVIN, ANSELM. Paradise Regained: Milton and the Tradition of the Fathers. Master's thesis, University of Toronto, 1946.

472 HALL, ALFREDA C. N. The Biblical Elements in Milton's Paradise Regained. Part 1 of Master's thesis, McMaster University, 1933.

473 HOOPER, CHARLOTTE L. The Bible and Paradise Regained. Master's thesis, Duke University, 1942.

474 HUGHES, MERRITT Y. The Christ of Paradise Regained and the Renaissance Heroic Tradition. SP, 35, 1938, 254-77.
   Rev: L. C. Martin, YWES, 178-9.

475 JONES, CHARLES W. Milton's Brief Epic. SP, 44, 1947, 209-27.
   On the genre of Paradise Regained.
   Rev: L. C. Martin, YWES, 192.

476 KENDALL, LYLE H., JR. Two Notes on the Text of Paradise Regained. NQ, N. S., 4, 1957, 523.
   On 4, 387, and 2, 485.

477 KERMODE, FRANK. Milton's Hero. RES, 4, 1953, 317-30.
   "My purpose here is... to show that Paradise Regained contains within itself the reasons why its hero is as he is and not otherwise, and that Milton's thought was... always and heroically consistent."
   Rev: Arnold Davenport, YWES, 210.

478 KLIGER, SAMUEL. The Urbs Aeterna in Paradise Regained. PMLA, 61, 1946, 474-91.
   On the tradition behind the passage on Rome.
   Rev: L. C. Martin, YWES, 173.

479 L(OANE), G(EORGE) G. The Crisis of Paradise Regained. NQ, 175, 1938, 185 and 187, 1944, 39.

480 MARILLA, E. L. Paradise Regained: Observations on Its Meaning. SN, 27, 1955, 179-91.
Argues that Paradise Regained "is inspired primarily by dynamic interest in the 'practical' problems of the temporal world and that it strives, principally, to set forth the issues which condition the course of human history."
Rev: Arnold Davenport, YWES, 164.

481 NEWELL, SAMUEL WILLIAM, JR. Milton's Paradise Regained: A Historical and Critical Study. Master's thesis, Emory University, 1942.

482 PITTS, DESSIE D. A Study of Milton's Paradise Regained. Master's thesis, University of South Carolina, 1941.

483 POPE, ELIZABETH M. Paradise Regained: the Tradition and the Poem. Doctoral diss., Johns Hopkins University, 1944. Baltimore: Johns Hopkins University Press, 1947. xvi, 135pp.
Rev: L. C. Martin, YWES, 191-2; H. F. Fletcher, JEGP, 47, 1948, 203-4; E. N. S. Thompson, PQ, 27, 1948, 288; B. A. Wright, RES, 25, 1949, 75-83; E. Sirluck, MP, 46, 1949, 277-9.

484 RANSOM, JOHN CROWE. God Without Thunder. New York: Harcourt Brace, 1930. x, 334pp.
Discusses Paradise Regained, pp. 141-5.

485 RICE, WARNER G. Paradise Regained. Papers Mich. Acad., 22, 1938, 493-503.
A critical analysis.

486 SACKTON, ALEXANDER H. Architectonic Structure in Paradise Regained. UTSE, 33, 1954, 33-45.

487 SCHULTZ, HOWARD. Christ and Antichrist in Paradise Regained. PMLA, 67, 1952, 790-808.
Rev: Arnold Davenport, YWES, 186.

488 SENSABAUGH, GEORGE F. Milton on Learning. SP, 43, 1946, 258-72.

489 STEIN, ARNOLD. Heroic Knowledge: An Interpretation of Paradise Regained and Samson Agonistes. Minneapolis: University of Minnesota Press, 1957. xi, 237pp.
Paradise Regained, pp. 3-134.

489a - - - - - -. The Kingdoms of the World: Paradise Regained. ELH, 23, 1956, 112-26.

490   SVENDSEN, KESTER. Milton's Aerie Microscope. MLN, 64, 1949, 525-7.
      On Paradise Regained, 4, 55-60.
      Rev: L. C. Martin, YWES, 167.

491   TAYLOR, DICK, JR. The Storm Scene in Paradise Regained: a Reinterpretation. UTQ, 24, 1955, 359-76.

492   TILLYARD, E. M. W. The Christ of Paradise Regained and the Renaissance Heroic Tradition. SP, 36, 1939, 247-52. Reprinted in Studies in Milton (London: Chatto and Windus, 1951), pp. 100-6.
      Agrees with Hughes with some qualifications.

493   WEISMILLER, E. R. The Versification of Paradise Lost and Paradise Regained. Doctoral diss., Merton College, Oxford, 1951.

494   WENZL, JOSEF. Paradise Regained und seine Stellung innerhalb der geistigen Entwicklung Miltons. Doctoral diss., Wien, 1940. 148pp.

495   WEST, ROBERT H. Milton's Sons of God. MLN, 65, 1950, 187-91.
      On Paradise Regained, 2, 178-81.

496   WHITING, GEORGE W. Christ's Miraculous Fast. MLN, 66, 1951, 12-16.
      Emphasizes the divine nature of the Christ of Paradise Regained.
      Rev: Arnold Davenport, YWES, 191.

497   - - - - - -. Milton's Taprobane (Paradise Regained IV, 75). RES, 13, 1937, 209-12.
      Identifies Taprobane as Sumatra.

498   WOLFE, DON M. The Role of Milton's Christ. SR, 51, 1943, 467-75.
      Argues that Milton's own principles and prejudices are reflected in the Christ of Paradise Regained.
      Rev: L. C. Martin, YWES, 156.

499   WOODHOUSE, A. S. P. Theme and Pattern in Paradise Regained. UTQ, 25, 1956, 167-82.

500 samson agonistes a dramatic poem the author john milton.
florence: stamperia del santuccio, 1930/31. 76pp.
Printed in semi-uncial characters without capitals.

501 John Milton. Samson Agonistes. Printed under the direction
of Victor Hammer. Florence: Stamperia del Santuccio,
1931.
Rev: TLS, Mar. 17, 1932, p. 186; SRL, 7, 1932, 451.

502 John Milton. Samson Agonistes: A Dramatic Poem. With
wood engravings by Robert A. Maynard. Harrow Weald:
Raven Press, 1931. xi, 63pp.
Rev: B. H. Newdigate, Merc., 25, 1931, 200-1; Frank
Kendon, FR, N. S., 131, 1932, 113-16.

503 John Milton. Samson Agonistes and English Sonnets.
Introd. and Notes by A. M. Percival. Sonnets, ed. by
W. Bell. New York: Macmillan, 1931. xlviii, 219pp.
A reprint of Stevens' No. 1141.

504 Milton's Samson Agonistes, with Introd., Notes, Glossary
and Indexes by A. W. Verity. Cambridge: Cambridge
University Press, 1932.
A reprint of Stevens' No. 1142.

505 John Milton. Samson Agonistes. Ed. by A. J. Wyatt and
A. J. F. Collins. The Sonnets. Ed. by A. R. Weeks.
London: University Tutorial Press, 1932. viii, 160pp.

506 John Milton: Samson Agonistes. A Dramatic Poem. The
Author John Milton. Florence. Stamperia del Santuccio,
1933.
Rev: Bibliofilia, 35, 1933, 105-6.

507 John Milton. Samson Agonistes. Ed. with Introd. and
Notes by John Churton Collins. Oxford: Clarendon
Press, 1938. 94pp.
A reprint of Stevens' No. 1139.

508 John Milton. Samson Agonistes. Ed. by F. T. Prince, with
an Introd., Notes, and Appendices. London and New
York: Oxford University Press, 1957.

SAMSON AGONISTES: CRITICISM

509 ALLEN, DON C. The Harmonious Vision: Studies in Milton's Poetry. Baltimore: Johns Hopkins University Press, 1954.
Contains a chapter on Samson Agonistes.

510 BEERBOHM, SIR MAX. Agonising Samson. Around Theatres (London: British Book Centre, 1953), pp. 527-31.

511 BOUGHNER, DANIEL C. Milton's Harapha and Renaissance Comedy. ELH, 11, 1944, 297-306.
Harapha and his forebears in Italian Renaissance comedy.

512 BOWRA, SIR CECIL MAURICE. Samson Agonistes. Inspiration and Poetry (London: Macmillan, 1955), pp. 112-29.
"In Samson Milton has rediscovered his taste for action and abandoned the quietism of Paradise Regained."

513 BUCHANAN, EDITH. The Italian Neo-Senecan Background of Samson Agonistes. Doctoral diss., Duke University, 1952.

514 BURKE, KENNETH. The Imagery of Killing. Hudson Rev., 1, 1948, 151-67.
In Samson Agonistes Milton unites the images of the suicide and of the warlike death.

515 CONDELL, KATHLEEN. Samson Agonistes and Prometheus Bound: a Comparison. Master's thesis, McMaster University, 1931. 65pp.

516 DURLING, DWIGHT. Coghill's Samson Agonistes at Oxford. SCN, 11, 1951, 63.
On a presentation at Oxford in July, 1951.

517 ELLIS-FERMOR, UNA. Samson Agonistes and Religious Drama. The Frontiers of Drama (London: Methuen, 1945), pp. 17-33.
Rev: Harley Granville-Barker, RES, 22, 1946, 144-7; Paul Dombey, NSN, Jan. 5, 1946, pp. 13-14; Elizabeth Sweeting, MLR, 41, 1946, 324-6; Alwyn Andrew, LL, 48, 1946, 130-40.

518 FELL, KENNETH. From Myth to Martyrdom: Towards a View of Milton's Samson Agonistes. ES, 34, 1953, 145-55.
On the martyrdom in Samson Agonistes and in Eliot's Murder in the Cathedral.
Rev: Arnold Davenport, YWES, 210.

519 FINNEY, GRETCHEN L. Chorus in Samson Agonistes. PMLA, 58, 1943, 649-64.
On Samson Agonistes and the Italian dramatic background.
Rev: L. C. Martin, YWES, 156-7.

520 FLATTER, RICHARD. Samson Agonistes and Milton. TLS, Aug. 7, 1948, p. 443.
Replies by F. F. Farnham-Flower and Maurice Kelley, ibid., Aug. 21, 1948, p. 471; rejoinder by Flatter, ibid., Sept 4, 1948, p. 499. Flatter believes that the last lines of Samson Agonistes refer to the projected publication of De Doctrina Christiana; Farnham-Flower and Kelley present contradictory evidence.
Rev: L. C. Martin, YWES, 196.

521 FOWLER, LOUIS HEATH. Samson Agonistes. Master's thesis, McMaster University, 1932. 27pp.
A study of Samson Agonistes in terms of dramatic form, style, verse technique, autobiographical references, theme, and religious teaching.

522 FREEDMAN, MORRIS. All for Love and Samson Agonistes. NQ, N. S., 3, 1956, 514-17.

523 GALLAND, RENÉ. Milton et Buchanan. RA-A, 13, 1936, 326-33.
Cites parallels between Samson Agonistes and Buchanan's Baptistes, sive Calumnia.
Rev: L. C. Martin, YWES, 189.

524 GILBERT, ALLAN H. Is Samson Agonistes Unfinished? PQ, 28, 1949, 98-106.
Argues that Samson Agonistes is an early work which Milton never found time to revise.
Rev: L. C. Martin, YWES, 168.

525 GOSSMAN, ANN MARY. The Synthesis of Hebraism and Hellenism in Milton's Samson Agonistes. Doctoral diss., Rice Institute, 1957.

526 GRENANDER, M. E. Samson's Middle: Aristotle and Dr. Johnson. UTQ, 24, 1955, 377-89.

527 GRIERSON, H. J. C. A Note upon the Samson Agonistes of John Milton and Sampson of Heilige Wraeck by Joost van den Vondel. Mélanges d'histoire littéraire générale... offerts à Fernand Baldensperger (Paris: Champion, 1930), 1, 332-9. Reprinted in Essays and Addresses (London: Chatto and Windus, 1940), pp. 55-64.

528 HALL, ALFREDA C. N. The Classical Features of Milton's Samson Agonistes. Part 2 of Master's thesis, McMaster University, 1933.

529 KELLEY, MAURICE. Samson Agonistes and Milton. TLS, Aug. 21, 1948, p. 471.
>On Samson Agonistes, 1423-6.

530 KERMODE, FRANK. Samson Agonistes and Hebrew Prosody. DUJ, 14, 1953, 59-63.
>On Milton's imitation of Hebrew lyric measures and rhymes.
>Rev: Arnold Davenport, YWES, 210.

531 KIRKCONNELL, WATSON. Six Sixteenth-Century Forerunners of Milton's Samson Agonistes. TRSC, 3rd Ser., 43, 1949, 73-85.
>Analogues.
>Rev: Arnold Davenport, YWES, 31, 1950, 182.

532 KREIPE, C. E. Milton's Samson Agonistes. Halle: Niemeyer, 1926. 70pp.
>Rev: K. Brunner, ESt., 64, 1929, 130-1; H. Jantzen, Zs. f. franz. u. engl. Unterr, 28, 1929, 388.

533 KROUSE, F. MICHAEL. Milton's Samson and the Christian Tradition. Doctoral diss., Johns Hopkins University, 1946. Princeton: Princeton University Press for the University of Cincinnati, 1949. viii, 159pp.
>Rev: L. C. Martin, YWES, 167-8; Moses Hadas, Class. Week., 43, 1949, 28; H. F. Fletcher, JEGP, 49, 1950, 115-17; E. Sirluck, MP, 48, 1950, 70-2; Arthur Barker, PQ, 29, 1950, 93-4; A. H. Gilbert, SAQ, 49, 1950, 254-5; A. Williams, Spec., 25, 1950, 139-41; A. S. P. Woodhouse, MLN, 66, 1951, 116-18; C. T. Harrison, SR, 59, 1951, 699; E. L. Allen, RES, 2, 1951, 281-2; William R. Parker, MLQ, 13, 1952, 103-5.

534 LEGETT, ELVA. The Dramatic Poems of John Milton. Master's thesis, Louisiana State University, 1933.

535 LITTLE, MARGUERITE. Some Italian Elements in the Choral Practice of Samson Agonistes. Doctoral diss., University of Illinois, 1946. Abs., Urbana: University of Illinois Press, 1946.

536 LYNCH, JAMES J. Evil Communications. NQ, N. S., 3, 1956, 477.
>Points out that neither Fielding nor Milton (in his Preface to Samson Agonistes) attributes the phrase to Menander, its original author.

537 MARILLA, E. L. Samson Agonistes: An Interpretation. SN, 29, 1957, 67-76.
>Shows that the poem embodies a unification of the basic arguments in Paradise Lost and Paradise Regained.

538 MATHIES GEB. DORNER, MARIA ELIZABETH. Untersuchungen zu Miltons Samson Agonistes. Doctoral diss., Hamburg, 1949. 271pp.

539 MAXWELL, J. C. Milton's Knowledge of Aeschylus: the Argument from Parallel Passages. RES, N. S., 3, 1952, 366-71.
Conclusions are negative.
Rev: Arnold Davenport, YWES, 177-8.

540 ------. Milton's Samson and Sophocles' Heracles. PQ, 33, 1954, 90-1.

541 McCALL, LOIS G. Imagery and Symbolism in Samson Agonistes. Master's thesis, Mt. Holyoke College, 1949.

542 McDAVID, RAVEN I., JR. Samson Agonistes 1096: a Re-examination. PQ, 33, 1954, 86-9.
Favors "wish" instead of "with."

543 McMANAWAY, JAMES G. Milton and Harrington. TLS, Feb. 20, 1937, p. 131.
Cf. G. M. Young, ibid., Jan. 9, 1937, p. 28.

544 PARKER, WILLIAM R. The Date of Samson Agonistes. PQ, 28, 1949, 145-66.
c. 1646-8.
Rev: L. C. Martin, YWES, 168.

545 ------. The Greek Spirit in Milton's Samson Agonistes. E&S, 20, 1934, 21-44.

546 ------. The "Kommos" of Milton's Samson Agonistes. SP, 32, 1935, 240-4.
Rev: L. C. Martin, YWES, 256.

547 ------. Milton's Debt to Greek Tragedy in Samson Agonistes. Baltimore: Johns Hopkins University Press; London: Milford, 1937. xvi, 260pp.
Rev: L. C. Martin, YWES, 185-6; E. M. W. Tillyard, MLN, 53, 1938, 381-3; D. Grene, MP, 35, 1938, 454-7; E. N. S. Thompson, PQ, 17, 1938, 416; F. Delattre, EA, Oct., 1938, pp. 401-2; A. v. Blumenthal, Ang. Bbl., 49, 1938, 154-5; J. H. Hanford, JEGP, 38, 1939, 456-7; L. R. Lind, CJ, 34, 1939, 178-9.

548 ------. Misogyny in Milton's Samson Agonistes. PQ, 16, 1937, 139-44.

549 ------. Symmetry in Milton's Samson Agonistes. MLN, 50, 1935, 355-60.

550 ------. Tragic Irony in Milton's Samson Agonistes. EA, 1, 1937, 314-20.

551 SAMS, ALMA F. Samson Agonistes: Its Date and Fallacies in the Autobiographical Interpretation. Master's thesis, Duke University, 1942.

552 SCOTT-CRAIG, T. S. K. Concerning Milton's Samson. RN, 5, 1952, 45-53.
   Interprets Samson Agonistes as a lustration, a Protestant equivalent of the Mass.
   Rev: Arnold Davenport, YWES, 186.

553 SPENCER, TERENCE. Samson Agonistes in London. SCN, 9, 1951, 35.
   On a performance in the Church of St. Martin's-in-the Fields in May, 1951.

554 - - - - - -, and JAMES WILLIS. Milton and Arnobius. NQ, 196, 1951, 387.
   Cites parallels between Samson Agonistes and Arnobius' Libri Septem Adversus Gentes.

555 STEIN, ARNOLD. Heroic Knowledge: An Interpretation of Paradise Regained and Samson Agonistes. Minneapolis: University of Minnesota Press, 1957. xi, 237pp.
   Samson Agonistes, pp. 137-202.

556 STEPHENSON, ANDREW. Samson Agonistes. Theatre Arts Monthly, 22, 1938, 914-16.

557 TIMBERLAKE, P. W. Milton and Euripides. Parrott Presentation Volume (Princeton: Princeton University Press, 1935), pp. 315-40.
   Rev: L. C. Martin, YWES, 256.

558 TINKER, CHAUNCEY B. Samson Agonistes. Tragic Themes in Western Literature. Ed. by Cleanth Brooks (New Haven: Yale University Press, 1955), pp. 59-76.
   Considers the transformation of the Biblical story to drama.

559 URE, PETER. A Simile in Samson Agonistes. NQ, 195, 1950, 298.
   Cites parallels to the woman-ship figure (710-18) from Jonson's The Devill is an Asse and The Staple of News.

560 WHITING, GEORGE W. Samson Agonistes and the Geneva Bible. RIP, 38, 1951, 18-35.
   On the Hebraic elements in Milton's drama.
   Rev: Arnold Davenport, YWES, 192.

561 WILLIAMS, ARNOLD. A Note on Samson Agonistes 11. 90-94. MLN, 63, 1948, 537.
   Concerning the indivisibility of the soul.
   Rev: L. C. Martin, YWES, 196.

562 WILSON, J. DOVER. Shakespeare, Milton, and Congreve. TLS, Jan. 16, 1937, p. 44.
   "Cleopatra—Dalila—Millamant make a pretty daisy-chain." Reply by G. G. Loane, ibid., Jan. 23, 1937, p. 60.

563   WOMACK, LUCILLE. A General Commentary on Samson Agonistes. Master's thesis, Emory University, 1945.

564   WOODHOUSE, A. S. P. Samson Agonistes and Milton's Experience. TRSC, 3rd Ser., 43, Sec. 2, 1949, 157-75.
      Argues for the validity of relating Milton's art and his experience; suggests a late date of composition.
      Rev: Arnold Davenport, YWES, 182.

565   YOUNG, G. M. Milton and Harrington. TLS, Jan. 9, 1937, p. 28.
      On the ship-woman image in Milton and Harrington.
      Rev: L. C. Martin, YWES, 186.

566 Early Poems of John Milton. Selected and ed. by Mercy A. Brann. Illus. by Isabel Bacheler. New York: Holt, 1929. xi, 235pp.

567 John Milton. The Nativity Ode, Lycidas, Sonnets, etc. Ed. by William Bell. London: Macmillan, 1929. xx, 230pp.
A reprint of Stevens' No. 283.

568 The Sonnets of Mr. John Milton, both English and Italian. Maastricht: Halycon Press, 1929. 28pp.
Printed with the italic type cut by Christoffel Van Dyck (1601-70).
Rev: TLS, July 18, 1929, p. 579.

569 The Latin Poems of John Milton. Ed. by Walter Mackellar. Cornell Stud. in Eng., 15. New Haven: Yale University Press for Cornell University; London: Milford, 1930. xli, 382pp.
Introd. pp. 1-67. Includes English prose translations.
Rev: H. J. C. Grierson and A. Melville Clark, YWES, 228; E. N. S. Thompson, PQ, 9, 1930, 320; L. Bradner, MP, 28, 1930, 116-17; C. S. Northup, Cornell Alumni News, 32, 1930, 392; D. Saurat, RES, 6, 1930, 473; TLS, Apr. 24, 1930, p. 533; E. C. Batho and E. J. Vaughan, MLR, 26, 1931, 203; J. H. Hanford, MLN, 46, 1931, 534-6; S. Gaselee, Class. Rev., 45, 1931, 155-6, and NQ, 163, 1932, 249; H. F. Fletcher, JEGP, 31, 1932, 158-9; C. W. Brodribb, NQ, 162, 1932, 188; T. O. Mabbott, NQ, 162, 1932, 263-4, and 163, 1932, 170; V. R., NQ, 163, 1933, 209, 371; F. Delatte, Rev. belge de philol. et d'hist., 12, 1933, 315.

570 Minor Poems by John Milton. Ed. by S. E. Allen. Rev. by H. Y. Moffett. Illus. by W. M. Berger. New York: Macmillan, 1930. xliii, 140pp.
A revision of Stevens' No. 339. Also contains Macaulay's Essay on Milton and Arnold's Address on Milton.

571 John Milton. Comus. Illus. by Blair Hughes-Stanton. London: Gregynog Press, 1932.
Rev: R. E. R., NSN, N. S., 3, 1932, xii, xiv; B. H. Newdigate, Merc., 25, 1932, 294.

572 Milton's Minor Poems, with Descriptive Poetry of the Eighteenth, Nineteenth, and Twentieth Centuries. Ed. by Kenneth W. Wright. New York: Noble, 1932. x, 146pp. Reprinted, 1934.
Descriptive poems by George Crabbe, William Wordsworth, Rupert Brooke, and Edna St. Vincent Millay.

573 The Cambridge Manuscript of John Milton. Lycidas and Some of the Other Poems Reproduced from the Collotype Facsimile. With a Bibliographical Note by Frank A. Patterson. New York: Columbia University Press for the Facsimile Text Society; London: Milford, 1933.
"An offset reproduction of the collotype of W. Aldis Wright, who in 1899 printed the manuscript."
Rev: A. H. Gilbert, SAQ, 33, 1934, 111-12; H. F. Fletcher, JEGP, 13, 1934, 338.

574 John Milton. Epitaphium Damonis. Printed from the First Edition. With a new translation by W. W. Skeat. In memory of Israel Gollancz. New York: Macmillan; Cambridge: Cambridge University Press, 1933. 21pp.
Rev: A. Brandl, Archiv, 164, 1933, 134; TLS, July 13, 1933, p. 482; NQ, 165, 1933, 143-4; J. H. Hanford, MLN, 51, 1936, 53-4; E. Bensly, RES, 12, 1936, 92-3.

575 Four Poems by John Milton: L'Allegro, Il Penseroso, Arcades, Lycidas. With wood-engravings by Blair Hughes Stanton. London: Gregynog Press, 1934. 33pp.
Rev: B. H. Newdigate, Merc., 29, 1934, 257.

576 John Milton. Minor Poems. New York: Columbia University Press for the Facsimile Text Society, 1934. 120pp.
A facsimile of the 1645 volume.

577 John Milton. Lament for Damon and Other Latin Poems. Rendered into English by Walter Skeat, with an Introd. by E. H. Visiak. Oxford: Oxford University Press, 1935.
Rev: L. C. Martin, YWES, 253; H. I. Bell, Class. Rev., 50, 1936, 204-5; Arnold Wilson, NC, 119, 1936, 495-506; E. L., RA-A, 13, 1936, 516; TLS, Jan. 11, 1936, p. 26; NQ, 170, 1936, 17; W. R. Parker, MLN, 52, 1937, 388.

578 John Milton. Minor Poems. Reproduced from the Edition of 1645. New York: Columbia University Press, 1935.

579 Milton's Minor Poems. Ed. by Tom Peete Cross. Illus. by Marguerite Benjamin. Boston: Ginn, 1936. viii, 129pp.

580 The Mask of Comus. The Poem Originally Called A Mask Presented at Ludlow Castle, 1634, &c., ed. by E. H. Visiak. The Airs of Five Songs Reprinted from the Composer's Autograph Manuscript, ed. by Hubert J. Foss, with a Foreword by the Earl of Ellesmere. Ornamented by M. R. H. Farrar. London: Nonesuch Press, 1937. xxiv, 44pp.
Rev: TLS, Jan. 15, 1938, p. 40; B. H. Newdigate, Merc., 37, 1938, 455; E. M. W. Tillyard, NC, 124, 1938, 479-81; MGW, Jan. 28, 1938, p. 75.

581 The Shorter Poems of John Milton. Ed. by B. A. Wright. London: Macmillan, 1938. xliv, 209pp.

582 Justa Edovardo King. Reproduced from the Original Edition, 1638, with an Introd. by Ernest C. Mossner. New York: Columbia University Press for the Facsimile Text Society, 1939. 61pp.

583 Lament for Damon. The Epitaphium Damonis of Milton. Trans. by Helen Waddell. UTQ, 16, 1947, 341-8.

584 VAN SINDEREN, ADRIAN. Blake, the Mystic Genius. Syracuse: Syracuse University Press, 1949. 119pp.
   Blake's text of L'Allegro and Il Penseroso and illustrations in color, pp. 45-112. Notes on the Poems, pp. 113-15.

585 Poems of Mr. John Milton: the 1645 Edition with Essays in Analysis. Ed. by Cleanth Brooks and John E. Hardy. New York: Harcourt, Brace and Co., 1951. xxi, 353pp.
   Part 1: The Poems, pp. 3-94; Part 2: Essays in Analysis, pp. 95-270; several appendices.
   Rev: J. H. Hanford, YR, 41, 1951-2, 634-6; Arnold Davenport, YWES, 33, 1952, 179-80; Ben R. Redman, SRL, June 21, 1952, p. 41; Kester Svendsen, SR, 60, 1952, 548-54; T. B. Stroup, SCN, 10, 1952, 48; Max Selinger, BA, 27, 1953, 193; QR, 295, 1957, 483; TLS, July 12, 1957, p. 428.

586 Comus and Some Shorter Poems of Milton. Ed. by E. M. W. and Phyllis B. Tillyard. London: Harrap, 1952. 223pp.

587 English Pastoral Poetry from the Beginnings to Marvell. Ed. by Frank Kermode. London: Harrap, 1952.
   Includes L'Allegro, two songs from Arcades, passages from Comus, and Lycidas.

588 A Selection of Poems by John Milton. With an Introd. by Howard Sergeant. Crown Classics. London: Gray Wall Press, 1954. 64pp.

589 The Masque of Comus. The Poem by John Milton, with a Preface by Mark Van Doren. The Airs by Henry Lawes, with a Preface by Hubert Foss. New York: Heritage Press, 1954.

590 John Milton. L'Allegro (and) Il Penseroso, with the Paintings by William Blake together with a Note upon the Poems by W. P. Trent (and) a Note upon the Paintings by Chauncey Brewster Tinker. New York: Heritage Press, 1954.

591 The Shorter Poems of John Milton. Ed. by B. A. Wright. London: St. Martin's Press, 1954.

592 ABERCROMBIE, LASCELLES. Milton Sonnet XVII. TLS, Apr. 11, 1936, p. 316.

593 ADAMS, HENRY H. The Development of the Flower Passage in Lycidas. MLN, 65, 1950, 468-72.
Rev: Arnold Davenport, YWES, 177-8.

594 ADAMS, RICHARD P. The Archetypal Pattern of Death and Rebirth in Milton's Lycidas. PMLA, 64, 1949, 183-8.
Rev: L. C. Martin, YWES, 163.

595 ADAMS, ROBERT M. Reading Comus. MP, 51, 1953, 18-32.
Believes that modern criticism has resulted in the "over-reading" of Lycidas, the Nativity Ode, and especially Comus.
Rev: Arnold Davenport, YWES, 203.

596 AIMAR, CAROLINE P. The Psalms as Milton Sings Them. Master's thesis, Duke University, 1942.

597 AINSWORTH, EDWARD G. Reminiscences of the Orlando Furioso in Comus. MLN, 46, 1931, 91-2.
Rev: F. S. Boas, YWES, 206.

598 ALLEN, DON C. The Harmonious Vision: Studies in Milton's Poetry. Baltimore: Johns Hopkins Press, 1954.
Contains chapters on the Nativity Ode, L'Allegro and Il Penseroso, Comus, and Lycidas.

599 - - - - - -. Milton's Alpheus. MLN, 71, 1956, 172-3.
In Lycidas.

600 - - - - - -. Milton's Comus as a Failure in Artistic Compromise. ELH, 16, 1949, 104-19.
Rev: Arnold Davenport, YWES, 162.

601 - - - - - -. A Note on Comus. MLN, 64, 1949, 179-80.
On the Renaissance theory of the generation of diamonds and Comus, 731-5.

602 ARNOLD, JAMES A. John Milton's Masque: an Historical and Critical Study of Comus. Doctoral diss., Princeton University, 1951. Abs., DA, 13, 1953, 385-6.

603 ARTHOS, JOHN. On A Mask Presented at Ludlow-Castle by John Milton. University of Michigan Contributions in Modern Philology, 20. Ann Arbor: University of Michigan Press, 1954. 50pp.
A critical analysis.
Rev: Arnold Davenport, YWES, 140-1; TLS, June 10, 1955, p. 311; J. C. Maxwell, RES, 6, 1955, 202-3; NQ, N. S., 2, 1955, 275-6; William B. Hunter, MLN, 70, 1955, 295-6.

604 AUSTIN, WARREN B. Milton's Lycidas and Two Latin Elegies by Giles Fletcher, the Elder. SP, 44, 1947, 41-55.
On the influence of Fletcher's elegies on the death of Walter Haddon and that of his son.
Rev: L. C. Martin, YWES, 187.

605 BABB, LAWRENCE. The Background of Il Penseroso. SP, 37, 1940, 257-73.
On the two conceptions of melancholy in the Renaissance, one banished in L'Allegro and the other accepted in Il Penseroso. Presents the same view in The Elizabethan Malady: a Study in English Literature from 1580 to 1642 (East Lansing: Michigan State College Press, 1951), pp. 178-80.

606 BAINES, A. H. J. The Topography of L'Allegro. NQ, 188, 1945, 68-71.

607 BANKS, THEODORE H. A Source for Lycidas, 154-158. MLN, 62, 1947, 39-40.
Pericles, 3, 1, 57-65.
Rev: L. C. Martin, YWES, 187.

608 BARKER, ARTHUR. The Pattern of Milton's Nativity Ode. UTQ, 10, 1941, 167-81.

609 BARRETT, JAMES A. S. A Line in Lycidas (11. 19-22). TLS, Jan. 11, 1934, p. 28.
Reply by G. M. Gathorne-Hardy, ibid., Jan. 18, 1934, p. 44.

610 BATESON, F. W. The Money-Lender's Son: L'Allegro and Il Penseroso. English Poetry, a Critical Introduction (London: Longmans, 1950), pp. 149-64.
Also pertinent comment on Lycidas.
Rev: Geoffrey Bullough, YWES, 10; M. Mack, YR, 40, 1950, 338-40; Rex Warner, NSN, Aug. 12, 1950, p. 181; reply by Bateson, ibid., Aug. 19, 1950, p. 181.

611 BATTESTIN, MARTIN C. John Crowe Ransom and Lycidas: A Reappraisal. CE, 17, 1955-6, 223-28.
Attacks Ransom's article on Lycidas in Amer. Rev., 1, 1933, 179-203.

612 BELLOC, HILAIRE. The Sonnets of Milton. Selected Essays (Philadelphia: Lippincott, 1936), pp. 133-64.

613 BERKELEY, DAVID S. Milton's On the Late Massacre in Piedmont. Expl., 15, 1957, item 58.
Suggests that line 4 is reminiscent of Jeremiah 2 : 27.

614 BLENNER-HASSETT, R. Geoffrey of Monmouth and Milton's Comus. MLN, 64, 1949, 315-18.
Concerning the Sabrina episode.

615 ------. Geoffrey of Monmouth and Milton's Comus: A
Problem in Composition. SN, 21, 1949, 216-21.
> Insists that the deftness of Milton's transmutation of Sabrina
> from Geoffrey of Monmouth into the figure in Comus
> furnishes us with an insight into the processes of artistic
> re-creation.

616 BLONDEL, JACQUES. Le Thème de la tentation dans
le Comus de Milton. Rev. d'hist. et de philosophie
religieuses, 28-9, 1948-9, 43-8.

617 BOLING, EDGAR, JR. The Masque Conventions in
Milton's Comus. Master's thesis, Emory University, 1955.

618 BONHAM, M. E. Milton's Comus Lives Again at Ludlow
Castle. Scholastic, Sept. 29, 1934, pp. 9-10.

619 BOWLING, WILLIAM G. The Travelogue Sections of
L'Allegro and Il Penseroso. EJ, 25, 1936, 220-3.

620 BREWER, WILMON. Sonnets and Sestinas. Boston:
Cornhill, 1937.
> Milton's sonnets discussed in their historical perspective in a
> chapter called The History of the Sonnet, pp. 91-178.

621 BRODRIBB, C. W. Milton and Persius. NQ, 159, 1930,
39.
> Cites several references to Persius in the Latin poems.

622 ------. Milton's L'Allegro and Il Penseroso. NQ, 163,
1932, 201.
> Believes that the Declaration of Sports, Oct. 10, 1633,
> prompted Milton to write the poems.
> Rev: L. C. Martin, YWES, 207.

623 ------. Stoic Fur (Comus, 1. 707). TLS, May 8, 1937,
p. 364.
> Rev: L. C. Martin, YWES, 182.

624 ------. That two-handed engine. TLS, June, 12, 1930,
p. 496.

625 ------. That Two-Handed Engine. TLS, June 5, 1943,
p. 271.
> Replies by Kathleen Tomlinson and by W. R. Dunstan,
> ibid., June 12, 1943, p. 283; by Katharine A. Esdaile, ibid.,
> June 19, 1943, p. 295; by H. Beckett, ibid., July 3, 1943,
> p. 319.

626 BROOKE, E. L. Lycidas and Bible Pastoral. NQ, N. S., 3,
1956, 67-8.
> On the resemblance between Peter's address in Lycidas and
> Ezekiel 34.

627 BROOKS, CLEANTH. The Light Symbolism in L'Allegro and Il Penseroso. The Well Wrought Urn; Studies in the Structure of Poetry (New York: Reynal and Hitchcock, 1947; London: Dobson, 1949), pp. 47-61.
> Rev: D. A. Stauffer, MLN, 62, 1947, 427-9; Dudley Fitts, KR, 9, 1947, 612-16; A. Mizener, SR, 55, 1947, 460-9; W. Empson, SR, 55, 1947, 690-7; Theodore Maynard, CW, 165, 1947, 570; R. P. Blackmur, NYTBR, June 8, 1947, p. 6; G. F. Whicher, NYHTBR, Apr. 20, 1947, p. 2; H. W. Wells, SRL, Apr. 12, 1947, p. 50; J. W. R. Purser, MLR, 42, 1947, 541-2; Josephine Miles, JAAC, 6, 1947, 185-6; R. S. Crane, MP, 45, 1948, 226-45; Norman Callan, RES, 24, 1948, 347-9.

628 BRUSER, FREDELLE. Comus and the Rose Song. SP, 44, 1947, 625-44.
> On the carpe diém theme and Comus.
> Rev: L. C. Martin, YWES, 186.

629 BUSH, DOUGLAS. An Allusion in Milton's Elegia tertia. Harvard Libr. Bull., 9, 1955, 392-6.
> Lines 9-10 may contain a reference to King James and Maurice, Prince of Orange.

630 C., T. C. Milton: Marble for Thinking. NQ, 184, 1943, 314.
> Explanation of the "marble of" of the Nativity Ode, On Shakespeare, and Il Penseroso. Comments by Richard Hussey and the editor, ibid., p. 381.
> Rev: L. C. Martin, YWES, 151.

631 CARPENTER, NAN C. The Place of Music in L'Allegro and Il Penseroso. UTQ, 22, 1953, 354-67.
> Rev: Arnold Davenport, YWES, 202.

632 ------. Spenser's Epithalamion as Inspiration for Milton's L'Allegro and Il Penseroso. NQ, N. S., 3, 1956, 289-92.

633 CHEEK, MACON. Milton's In Quintum Novembris: An Epic Foreshadowing. SP, 54, 1957, 172-84.
> Feels that the poem affords an insight into Milton's earliest conception of epic technique and style and into his earliest conception of Satan.

634 ------. Of Two Sonnets of Milton. Renaissance Papers, 1956 (Columbia: University of South Carolina Press, 1956), pp. 82-91.
> A comparison of On Having Arrived at the Age of Twenty-three and On His Blindness reveals a close sequence of thoughts and images, illustrating the unity in Milton's thinking.

635 CLARKE, A. H. T. That Two-Handed Engine at the Door. TLS, Apr. 11, 1929, pp. 295-6.
> Replies by G. M. Trevelyan, Harold Van Tromp, and George G. Loane, ibid., Apr. 25, 1929, p. 338.

636 COFFMAN, GEORGE R. The Parable of the Good Shepherd, De Contemptu Mundi, and Lycidas: Excerpts for a Chapter on Literary History and Culture. ELH, 3, 1936, 101-13.
Rev: L. C. Martin, YWES, 188-9.

637 COLLINS, DAN S. The Influence of Formal Rhetoric on the Treatment of Nature in the Early English Poems of John Milton. Master's thesis, University of North Carolina, 1951.

638 Comus Produced in 1953 at Ludlow Castle—Where It Was First Presented in 1634. Illus. London News, July 11, 1953, p. 75.
Photographs with text.

639 COOLIDGE, LOWELL W. That Two-handed Engine. PQ, 29, 1950, 444-5.
Rev: Arnold Davenport, YWES, 178.

640 CURGENVEN, J. P. Milton and the Lark (L'Allegro, 41-48). TLS, Oct. 18, 1934, p. 715.
Replies by H. J. C. Grierson, ibid., Nov. 1, 1934, p. 755; by T. Sturge Moore, ibid., Oct. 25, 1934, p. 735; by Moore and B. A. Wright, ibid., Nov. 8, 1934, p. 775; by Grierson, E. M. W. Tillyard, and M. Joan Sargeaunt, ibid., Nov. 15, 1934, p. 795; by Wright and B. R. Rowbottom, ibid., Nov. 22, 1934, p. 840; by Grierson and W. A. Jones, ibid., Nov. 29, 1934, p. 856.

641 CURIOUS. Archie Armstrong and Milton. NQ, 178, 1940, 353-4.
Milton's Hobson poems and Armstrong's A Banquet of Jests (1630?).
Reply by William Jaggard, ibid., p. 393.

642 DAICHES, DAVID. A Study of Literature for Readers and Critics. Ithaca: Cornell University Press, 1948.
Contains a detailed analysis of Lycidas, pp. 170-95.
Rev: G. F. Whicher, NYHTBR, Sept. 26, 1948, p. 9.

643 DAY, MABEL. Milton and Lydgate. RES, 13, 1947, 144-6.
Believes that three passages of the Troy Book are reflected in Il Penseroso and Comus.
Rev: L. C. Martin, YWES, 186.

644 DE BEER, E. S. Milton's Old Damaetas. NQ, 194, 1949, 336-7.
Rev: L. C. Martin, YWES, 163.

645 - - - - - -. St. Peter in Lycidas. RES, 13, 1947, 59-63.
On the two-handed engine.
Rev: L. C. Martin, YWES, 186-7.

646 DE FILIPPIS, MICHELE. Milton and Manso: Cups or Books? PMLA, 51, 1936, 745-56.
   On Epitaphium Damonis, 181-97.
   Rev: L. C. Martin, YWES, 189.

647 DIEKHOFF, JOHN S. Lycidas, Line 10. PQ, 16, 1937, 408-10.
   Rev: L. C. Martin, YWES, 182.

648 - - - - - -. The Milder Shades of Purgatory. MLN, 52, 1937 409-10.
   Interprets the sonnet to Lawes.
   Rev: L. C. Martin, YWES, 183.

649 - - - - - -. A Note on Comus, Lines 75-77. PQ, 20, 1941, 603-4.

650 - - - - - -. The Punctuation of Comus. PMLA, 51, 1936, 757-68.
   Rev: L. C. Martin, YWES, 188.

651 - - - - - -. The Text of Comus, 1634 to 1645. PMLA, 52, 1937, 705-28.
   Rev: L. C. Martin, YWES, 182.

652 DILLARD, KATHRYN. Milton's Use of the Psalms. Master's thesis, Duke University, 1939.

653 DORIAN, DONALD C. Milton's Epitaphium Damonis, Lines 181-197. PMLA, 54, 1939, 612-3.

654 - - - - - -. Milton's On His Blindness. Expl., 10, 1951, item 16.
   Rev: Arnold Davenport, YWES, 187.

655 - - - - - -. Milton's On His Having Arrived at the Age of Twenty-Three. Expl., 8, 1949, item 10.

656 - - - - - -. Milton's Two-Handed Engine. PMLA, 45, 1930, 204-15.

657 - - - - - -. On the new forces of Conscience, line 17. MLN, 56, 1941, 62-4.

658 - - - - - -. The Question of Autobiographical Significance in L'Allegro and Il Penseroso. MP, 31, 1933, 175-82.

659 DUNCAN-JONES, E. E. Lycidas and Lucan. NQ, N. S., 3, 1956, 249.

660 DYSON, A. E. The Interpretation of Comus. E&S, 8, 1955, 89-114.

661 ELLEDGE, SCOTT. Milton, Sappho?, and Demetrius. MLN, 58, 1943, 551-3.

On the source of Comus, 631-5, 637.
Rev: L. C. Martin, YWES, 152.

662 ELTON, WILLIAM. Two Milton Notes. NQ, 192, 1947, 428-9.

On the possibility that Thomas Robinson's Life and Death of Mary Magdalene (c. 1621) is a source for L'Allegro and and the Dantean character of "blind mouths."
Rev: L. C. Martin, YWES, 186.

663 EMERSON, FRANCIS W. Why Milton Uses Cambuscan and Camball. MLN, 47, 1932, 153-4.

Suggests that John Lane is the source of the words used in Il Penseroso.
Rev: L. C. Martin, YWES, 207.

664 EVANS, G. BLAKEMORE. Milton and the Hobson Poems. MLQ, 4, 1943, 281-90.

Prints seven poems by various writers on the death of Hobson.
Rev: L. C. Martin, YWES, 151.

665 - - - - - -. Some More Hobson Verses. MLQ, 9, 1948, 10, 184.

Prints four additional sets of verses.

666 - - - - - -. Two New Manuscript Versions of Milton's Hobson Poems. MLN, 57, 1943, 192-4.

667 EVANS, WILLA McCLUNG. Hobson Appears in Comic Song. PQ, 26, 1947, 321-7.

668 FINK, ZERA S. Il Penseroso, Line 16. PQ, 19, 1940, 309-13.

669 - - - - - -. Wine, Poetry, and Milton's Elegia Sexta. ES, 21, 1939, 164-5.

670 FINLEY, JOHN H., JR. Milton and Horace: A Study of Milton's Sonnets. Harvard Stud. in Class. Phil., 48, 1937, 29-73.

A detailed study.
Rev: L. C. Martin, YWES, 183.

671 FINNEY, GRETCHEN L. Comus, Dramma per Musica. SP, 37, 1940, 102-15.

Comus and the drama of Italy.

672 - - - - - -. A Musical Background for Lycidas. HLQ, 15, 1952, 325-50.

Lycidas and Italian music.
Rev: Arnold Davenport, YWES, 180-1.

673 FLETCHER, G. B. A. Milton's Latin Poems. MP, 37, 1940, 343-50.

674 FLETCHER, HARRIS F. Grierson's Suggested Date for Milton's Ad Patrem. Fred Newton Scott Anniversary Papers (Chicago: University of Chicago Press, 1929), pp. 199-205.
Supports Grierson and holds that the poem was written after Milton returned from Italy.

675 ------. Milton's Apologus and Its Mantuan Model. JEGP, 55, 1956, 230-3.
Argues for Mantuan's influence.

676 FOX, ROBERT C. Milton's Lycidas, 192-193. Expl., 9, 1951, item 54.
Rev: Arnold Davenport, YWES, 186.

677 FRENCH, J. MILTON. The Digressions in Milton's Lycidas. SP, 50, 1953, 485-90.
Rev: Arnold Davenport, YWES, 202.

678 ------. Milton's Two Handed Engine. MLN, 68, 1953, 229-31.
See also SP, 49, 1953, 548-50.

679 FRYE, ROLAND M. Milton's Sonnet 23 on His Late Espoused Saint. NQ, 194, 1949, 321.
Mary or Katherine? Addendum by Charles R. Dahlberg on the same page.

680 FUSSELL, E. S. Milton's Two-handed Engine yet once more. NQ, 193, 1948, 338-9.
Reply by Maurice Hussey, ibid., 503.

681 GATHORNE-HARDY, G. M. A Line in Lycidas. TLS, Jan. 18, 1934, p. 44.
Believes that lines 20-22 indicate that the poem itself will take the place of an ordinary funeral.

682 GHOSH, P. C. A Note on Comus (95). TLS, Feb. 19, 1931, p. 135.
Reply by A. W. Verity, ibid., Feb. 26, 1931, p. 154.
Rev: F. S. Boas, YWES, 206.

683 GODOLPHIN, F. R. B. Milton, Lycidas, and Propertius Elegies, III, 7. MLN, 49, 1934, 162-6.
A source study.

684 ------. Notes on the Technique of Milton's Latin Elegies. MP, 37, 1940, 351-6.

685 GOODE, JAMES. Milton and Sannazaro. TLS, Aug. 13, 1931, p. 621.
Borrowings in Milton's Elegy I, 21-2 and Elegy V, 121-2.

686 GOODMAN, PAUL. Milton's On His Blindness: Stanzas, Motion of Thought. Structure of Literature (Chicago: University of Chicago Press, 1954), pp. 192-215.

687 GOTTFRIED, RUDOLF. Milton, Lactantius, Claudian, and Tasso. SP, 30, 1933, 497-503.
On the phoenix passage in Epitaphium Damonis, 185-9.
Rev: L. C. Martin, YWES, 253.

688 GRACE, WILLIAM J. Notes on Robert Burton and John Milton. SP, 52, 1955, 578-91.
On parallels between Burton and Milton in L'Allegro and Il Penseroso and Lycidas.

689 GRAVES, ROBERT. John Milton Muddles Through. NR, May 27, 1957, pp. 17-19.
Animadversions upon L'Allegro.

690 H., C. E. The Pansy Freaked with Jet (Lycidas, 1. 144). NQ, 177, 1939, 98.
Replies by E. H. V(isiak) and by William Jaggard, ibid., 139; by V. R., ibid., 175.

691 HALE, HILDA HANSON. Conventions and Characteristics in the English Funeral Elegy of the Earlier Seventeenth Century. Doctoral diss., University of Missouri, 1956. Abs., DA, 16, 1956, 2149-50.
Discusses Milton's elegies.

692 HALL, BERNARD G. Milton's Shepherd Lad. TLS, Oct. 12, 1933, p. 691.
In Comus.
Rev: L. C. Martin, YWES, 251.

693 HANFORD, JAMES H. Haemony (Comus, 616-48). TLS, Nov. 3, 1932, p. 815.
Rev: L. C. Martin, YWES, 207.

694 ------. Milton's Poem On the Death of a Fair Infant. RES, 9, 1933, 312-15.
On the date of composition (1625).
Rev: L. C. Martin, YWES, 250.

695 HARDY, JOHN E. Reconsiderations; I. Lycidas. KR, 7, 1945, 99-113.

696 HARRELL, KARL P. The Nature of the Grotesque in Milton's Comus. Master's thesis, University of North Carolina, 1951.

697 HARRISON, T. P., JR. The Latin Pastorals of Milton and Castiglione. PMLA, 50, 1935, 480-93.
Rev: L. C. Martin, YWES, 253.

698 - - - - - -. A Note on Lycidas, 91. UTSE, 15, 1935, 22.

699 - - - - - -. The Haemony Passage in Comus Again. PQ, 22,
1943, 251-4.
>On Milton's use of Henry Lyte's New Herbal (1578).
>Rev: L. C. Martin, YWES, 152.

700 - - - - - -. The Pastoral Elegy, an Anthology. English Trans.
by Harry Joshua Leon. Austin: University of Texas
Press, 1939. xii, 312pp.
>Prints the texts of Lycidas and Lament for Damon; com-
>mentary on Milton's pastoral elegies, pp. 289-96.

701 HARVEY, W. J. Milton and the Late Fantastiks. NQ,
N. S., 4, 1957, 523-4.
>Questions Tillyard's view that the Late Fantastiks of At a
>Vacation Exercise are George Herbert and his group.

702 HAUG, RALPH A. They also serve.... NQ, 183, 1942,
224-5.
>Suggests that I Samuel 30 : 24 is the origin of the last line
>of the sonnet On His Blindness.

703 HAUN, EUGENE. An Inquiry into the Genre of Comus.
Essays in Honor of W. C. Curry (Nashville: Vanderbilt
University Press, 1954), pp. 221-39.
>Holds that Comus is not a proper-masque but a transitional
>piece in which the music and dance are secondary to the
>plot.

704 HAVILAND, THOMAS P. Hugh Henry Brackenridge
and Milton's Piedmontese Sonnet. NQ, 176, 1939, 243-4.

705 HELLINGS, PETER. A Note on the Sonnets of Milton.
LL, 64, 1950, 165-9.
>Maintains that speech habits rather than speech rhythms
>form the basis of the grand manner of the sonnets.
>Rev: Arnold Davenport, YWES, 178.

706 HENRY, NATHANIEL H. Who Meant Licence When
They Cried Liberty? MLN, 66, 1951, 509-13.
>On Sonnets 11 and 12. Holds that Milton is referring to the
>"lunatic fringe" of the Independents.
>Rev: Arnold Davenport, YWES, 187.

707 HOELTJE, HUBERT H. L'Allegro, Lines 53-55. PMLA,
45, 1930, 201-3.

708 HOOPES, ROBERT. God Guide Thee Guyon: Nature
and Grace Reconciled in the Faerie Queene, Book II.
RES, N. S., 5, 1954, 14-24.
>Analogies with Comus and Paradise Regained, pp. 23-4.

709 HOWARD, LEON. That Two-handed Egine Once More.
HLQ, 15, 1952, 173-84.
>Rev: Arnold Davenport, YWES, 181.

710 HUGHES, R. E. That Two-handed Engine—Again. NQ, N. S., 2, 1955, 58-9.

711 HUNTER, WILLIAM B., JR. A Note on Lycidas. MLN, 65, 1950, 544.
   On the sheep-rot passage.
   Rev: Arnold Davenport, YWES, 178.

712 JACKSON, ELIZABETH. Milton's Sonnet XX. PMLA, 65, 1950, 328-9.
   Supports and further substantiates Neiman, ibid., 64, 1949, 480-3.
   Rev: Arnold Davenport, YWES, 178.

713 JACKSON, JAMES L., and WALTER E. WEESE. ...Who only Stand and Wait: Milton's Sonnet On His Blindness. MLN, 72, 1957, 91-3.
   Interprets "stand" in the light of Ephesians 6 : 13.

714 JAY, LEMUEL EUGENE. Background and Justification in Pastoral Poetry for the Attack on Church and Clergy in Lycidas. Master's thesis, Duke University, 1942.

715 KANE, ROBERT J. Blind Mouths in Lycidas. MLN, 68, 1953, 239-40.

716 KELLEY, MAURICE. Lycidas: the Two-Handed Engine. NQ, 181, 1941, 273.
   Reply by G. G. Loane, ibid., 320.

717 ------. Milton's Later Sonnets and the Cambridge Manuscript. MP, 54, 1956, 20-5.

718 KEMP, LYSANDER. On a Sonnet by Milton. HR, 6, 1952, 80-3.
   Feels that "When I consider how my light is spent" refers to the exhaustion of the poet's inspiration.

719 KENDALL, LYLE H., JR. Melt with Ruth. NQ, 198, 1953, 145.
   The phrase in Lycidas occurs also in Chaucer and Spenser.

720 KNAPP, C. A. Milton's Eglantine. NQ, 176, 1939, 267. In L'Allegro.

721 LE COMTE, EDWARD S. Lycidas, Petrarch, and the Plague. MLN, 69, 1954, 402-4.

722 ------. Milton: Two Verbal Parallels. NQ, 184, 1943, 17-18.
   The reference to "finny drove" in Comus parallels passages in Spenser and Drayton. Reply by Hibernicus, ibid., 85.
   Rev: L. C. Martin, YWES, 155.

723 - - - - - -. New Light on the Haemony Passage in Comus. PQ, 21, 1942, 283-98.
Rev: L. C. Martin, YWES, 158.

724 - - - - - -. That Two-handed Engine and Savonarola. SP, 47, 1950, 589-606.
Rev: Arnold Davenport, YWES, 178.

725 - - - - - -. That Two-handed Engine and Savonarola: Supplement. SP, 49, 1952, 548-50.

726 - - - - - -. The Veiled Face of Milton's Wife. NQ, N. S., 1, 1954, 245-6.
Milton's "late espoused saint" is Katherine, not Mary.

727 LEGETT, ELVA. The Dramatic Poems of John Milton. Master's thesis, Louisiana State University, 1933.

728 LEISHMAN, J. B. L'Allegro and Il Penseroso in Their Relation to Seventeenth-Century Poetry. E&S, N. S., 4, 1951, 1-36.
Rev: Arnold Davenport, YWES, 186.

729 LEWIS, C. S. Above the Smoke and Stir. TLS, July 14, 1945, p. 331.
Replies by B. A. Wright, ibid., Aug. 4, 1945, p. 36; by Robert Eisler, ibid., Sept. 22, 1945, p. 451; by Lewis, ibid., Sept. 29, 1945, p. 463; by Wright, ibid., Oct. 27, 1945, p. 511. Lewis quotes Henry More as the source of the Spirit in Comus. Wright finds the source in Plato's Phaedo.
Rev: L. C. Martin, YWES, 147.

730 - - - - - -. From the Latin of Milton's De Idea Platonica Quemadmodum Aristoteles Intelexit. Eng., 5, 1945, 195.
Reprints De Idea Platonica..., "probably intended as a mere academic squib; but genius sometimes laughs at authors' intentions."

731 - - - - - -. A Note on Comus. RES, 8, 1932, 170-6.
On Milton's changes in the first five versions of the poem.
Rev: L. C. Martin, YWES, 207.

732 L(OANE), G(ERORGE) G. Milton: Built in th' eclipse (Lycidas, 1. 100). NQ, 179, 1940, 9.
Reply by T. O. Mabbott, ibid., pp. 141-2.

733 - - - - - -. Milton's Eglantine. NQ, 176, 1939, 225.
Milton's use of "eglantine" in L'Allegro reminiscent of Spenser's in The Faerie Queene, 3, 6, 44.

734 LITTLE, MARGUERITE. Milton's Ad Patrem and the Younger Gill's In Natalem Mei Parentis. JEGP, 49, 1950, 345-51.
On the possibility that Milton used Gill's poem as a source.
Rev: Arnold Davenport, YWES, 177.

735 LYNSKEY, WINIFRED. A Critic in Action: Mr. Ransom. CE, 5, 1944, 239-49.
Animadversions on Ransom's criticism of Lycidas.

736 MAAS, P. Hid in, Lycidas, 1. 69. RES, 19, 1943, 397-8.
Believes that the editors should restore the "hid in" of the 1638 edition.
Rev: L. C. Martin, YWES, 152.

737 MABBOTT, THOMAS O. Lycidas and Lycaeus. NQ, 172, 1937, 462.
A reply to McColley, ibid., p. 172.

738 ------. Milton: Built in the eclipse. NQ, 179, 1940, 141-2.
Reply to Loane, ibid., p. 9. On Lycidas, 100.

739 ------. Milton's In Effigei Ejus Sculptorem. Expl., 8, 1950, item 58.
On the meaning of the jest in the epigram.
Rev: Arnold Davenport, YWES, 177.

740 ------. Milton's Latin Poems, TLS, Oct. 27, 1932, p. 790.
Rev: L. C. Martin, YWES, 208-9.

741 ------. Milton's Lycidas, lines 164 and 183-185. Expl., 5, 1947, item 26.

742 MACLEAN, HUGH N. Milton's Fair Infant. ELH, 24, 1957, 296-305.

743 MARILLA, ESMOND L. That Two-handed Engine Finally? PMLA, 67, 1952, 1183-4.

744 MARKS, EMERSON R. Milton's Lycidas. Expl., 8, 1951, item 44.

745 MARTIN, L. C. Thomas Warton and the Early Poems of Milton. Warton Lecture on English Poetry. Proceedings of the British Acad., 20. Oxford: Oxford University Press, 1934. 21pp.
Rev: Eric Gillett, Merc., 30, 1934, 374.

746 MARTZ, LOUIS L. The Poetry of Meditation, a Study in English Religious Literature of the Seventeenth Century. Yale Stud. in Eng., 125. New Haven: Yale University Press, 1954. x, 375pp.
The Nativity Ode discussed, pp. 164-7; other poems, passim.

747 MAXWELL, J. C. The Pseudo-Problem of Comus. Camb. Jour., 1, 1948, 376-80.
The doctrine of virtue.
Rev: L. C. Martin, YWES, 193.

748 MAYERSON, CAROLINE W. The Orpheus Image in Lycidas. PMLA, 64, 1949, 189-207.
> Relates the image to the poet's own conquest of the temp*a*tion to fear and doubt.
> Rev: L. C. Martin, YWES, 163.

749 McCOLLEY, GRANT. Lycidas and Lycaeus. NQ, 172, 1937, 352.
> "Lycidas" may be Milton's poetic transformation of "Lycaeus," a name current at the time of composition of Lycidas.

750 McKENZIE, J. Early Scottish Performances of Comus. NQ, 198, 1953, 158-9.
> On Jan. 7 and 14 and Feb. 1, 1751.

751 - - - - - -. Early Scottish Performances of Comus. NQ, N. S., 1, 1954, 199.
> Additional notices.

752 - - - - - -. Echoes of Dante in Milton's Lycidas. Ital., 20, 1943, 121-6.

753 MITCHELL, CHARLES B. The English Sonnet in the Seventeenth Century, Especially after Milton. Doctoral diss., Harvard University, 1939. Abs., Harvard University, Summaries of Theses, 1942, pp. 239-43.

754 MOLONEY, MICHAEL F. The Prosody of Milton's Epitaph, L'Allegro and Il Penseroso. MLN, 72, 1957, 174-8.
> Argues that for the Epitaph Milton borrows from the funerary art of Jonson but that the poet used a more traditional heptasyllabic and octosyllabic line in the companion pieces.

755 MONTGOMERY, WALTER A. The Epitaphium Damonis in the Stream of the Classical Lament. Studies for William A. Read (Baton Rouge: Louisiana State University Press, 1940), pp. 207-20.

756 MORE, PAUL ELMER. How to Read Lycidas. Amer. Rev., 7, 1936, 140-58. Reprinted in On Being Human (Princeton: Princeton University Press, 1936), pp. 184-202.

757 MUTSCHMANN, H. That Two-Handed Engine at the Door. TLS, Apr. 25, 1936, p. 356.
> Replies by H. L. Savage, ibid., July 25, 1936, p. 616; by Mutschmann, ibid., Aug. 8, 1936, p. 645, and Aug. 15, 1936, p. 664; by A. F. Pollard, ibid., Aug. 29, 1936, p. 697.
> Rev: L. C. Martin, YWES, 189.

758 - - - - - -. That Two-Handed Engine at the Door. NQ, N. S., 2, 1955, 515.

759 MYHR, IVAR L. Milton's Hymn on the Morning of Christ's Nativity, Stanza 8. Expl., 4, 1945, item 16.

760 NEIMAN, FRASER. Milton's Sonnet XX. PMLA, 64, 1949, 480-3.
On the meaning of "spare" (1. 13).
Rev: L. C. Martin, YWES, 164.

761 OMAN, SIR CHARLES. Of Poor Mr. King, John Milton, and Certain Friends. Cornhill, 156, 1937, 577-87.
Reviews the companion pieces of Lycidas.

762 ORAS, ANTS. Metre and Chronology in Milton's Epitaph on the Marchioness of Winchester, L'Allegro, and Il Penseroso. NQ, 198, 1953, 332-3.

763 ------. Milton's Early Rhyme Schemes and the Structure of Lycidas. MP, 52, 1954, 12-22.
Rev: Arnold Davenport, YWES, 139.

764 ------. Milton's Upon the Circumcision and Tasso. NQ, 197, 1952, 314-15.
Rev: Arnold Davenport, YWES, 180.

765 PARKER, WILLIAM R. Milton's Fair Infant. TLS, Dec. 17, 1938, p. 802.
Rev: L. C. Martin, YWES, 177.

766 ------. Milton's Hobson Poems: Some Neglected Early Texts. MLR, 31, 1936, 395-402.
Rev: L. C. Martin, YWES, 188.

767 ------. Milton's Last Sonnet. RES, 21, 1945, 235-8.
Favors Mary Powell as the subject. Reply by T. O. Mabbott, NQ, 189, 1945, 239.

768 ------. Milton's Last Sonnet Again. RES, N. S., 2, 1951, 147-52.
A reply to Pyle, ibid., 25, 1949, 57-60, with further comment by Pyle.
Rev: Arnold Davenport, YWES, 187.

769 ------. Milton's Sonnet: I did but prompt, 6. Expl., 8, 1949, item 3.
Interprets the sonnet as a poetical counterpart of Colasterion.
Rev: L. C. Martin, YWES, 163.

770 ------. Notes on the Chronology of Milton's Latin Poems. A Tribute to G. C. Taylor (Chapel Hill: University of North Carolina Press, 1952), pp. 113-31.

771 ------. Shakespeare and Milton. MLN, 53, 1938, 556.
Addendum to Spencer, ibid., pp. 366-7.

772 - - - - - -. Some Problems in the Chronology of Milton's Early Poems. RES, 11, 1935, 276-83.
Rev: L. C. Martin, YWES, 253.

773 PEPLE, EDWARD C. Notes on Some Productions of Comus. SP, 36, 1939, 235-42.
Supplements Thaler, ibid., 17, 1920, 269-308.

774 POST, MARTIN M. Milton's Twin Lyrics at Three Hundred. EJ, 22, 1933, 567-80.
Uses L'Allegro and Il Penseroso to refute those who feel that Milton has no relation to the modern world.

775 POTTER, JAMES L. Milton's Talent Sonnet and Barnabe Barnes. NQ, N. S., 4, 1957, 447.
Barnes' Sonnets 26 and 28 contain puns on the talents of Matt. 24 : 14-30 and Milton uses the puns in the same way.

776 PYLE, FITZROY. And Old Damaetas Lov'd to Hear Our Song. Hermathena, 71, 1948, 83-92.
Damaetas is William Chappell.
Rev: L. C. Martin, YWES, 193.

777 - - - - - -. Milton's Sonnet on His Late Espoused Saint. RES, 25, 1949, 57-60.
Defends the traditional view that Milton has Katherine Woodstock in mind.
Rev: L. C. Martin, YWES, 164.

778 R. Quotations from Lycidas. NQ, 173, 1937, 393.
Finds seventeen quotations listed in Bartlett (10th ed.).

779 RAINWATER, FRANK P. A Philosophical Study of Milton's Comus. Master's thesis, Vanderbilt University, 1948.

780 RANSOM, JOHN CROWE. A Poem Nearly Anonymous. Amer. Rev., 1, 1933, 179-203, 444-67. Reprinted in The World's Body (New York: Charles Scribner's Sons, 1938), pp. 1-28.
One of the most controversial articles on Lycidas in a generation. A study of the symbolic meaning with the suggestion that "it was written smooth and rewritten rough."

781 - - - - - -. Why Critics Don't Go Mad. KR, 14, 1952, 331-9.
A review article of Brooks and Hardy's edition of the early poems.

782 REISS, EDMUND. An Instance of Milton's Use of Time. MLN, 72, 1957, 410-12.
Shows that in an early poem, Naturam non pati senium, Milton already held that God created time before the world.

783 RINEHART, KEITH. A Note on the First Fourteen Lines of Milton's Lycidas. ÑQ, 198, 1953, 103.
     Believes that Milton consciously approximates the sonnet form to emphasize the two ideas in the first part of the poem.

784 ROBINS, HARRY F. The Key to a Problem in Milton's Comus. MLQ, 12, 1951, 422-8.
     On Comus, 731-5.
     Rev: Arnold Davenport, YWES, 186-7.

785 - - - - - -. Milton's First Sonnet on His Blindness. RES, 7, 1956, 360-6.
     Holds that Sonnet 19 is an expression of "Milton's confidence in his ability to triumph over his affliction and to produce the great poetry toward which his ambition had always been directed."

786 - - - - - -. Milton's Two-Handed Engine at the Door and St. Matthew's Gospel. RES, N. S., 5, 1954, 25-36.

787 ROHR-SAUER, P. V. English Metrical Psalms from 1600 to 1660. A Study in the Religious and Aesthetic Tendencies of that Period. Doctoral diss., Freiburg, 1938. Freiburg: Poppen and Ortmann, 1938. 127pp.
     Milton's Psalms discussed, pp. 39-43.

788 ROSS, MALCOLM M. Milton and the Protestant Aesthetic: the Early Poems. UTQ, 17, 1948, 346-60.
     Milton recalls traditional Christian symbols as he prepares a new and different tradition.
     Rev: L. C. Martin, YWES, 192-3.

789 S., W. W. As taint-worm to the weanling flocks (Lycidas, 1. 45). NQ, 176, 1939, 112-13.
     Author's leter of correction, ibid., 153.

790 ST. CLAIR, F. Y. The Rhythm of Milton's Nativity Ode. CE, 5, 1944, 448.

791 SCHAUS, HERMANN. The Relationship of Comus to Hero and Leander and Venus and Adonis. UTSE, 25, 1946, 129-41.
     Rev: L. C. Martin, YWES, 170.

792 SCHOECK, R. J. Milton and Neaera's Hair. NQ, N. S., 3, 1956, 190-1.
     Believes that Neaera is an echo from the Basia of Joannes Secundus.

793 - - - - - -. That Two-handed Engine yet once more: Milton, John of Salisbury, and the Sword. NQ, N. S., 2, 1955, 235-7.

794 SCHOLDERER, V. Lycidas. TLS, June 28, 1947, p. 323.
Replies by Richard Bell, ibid., July 12, 1947, p. 351; by
Parry Michael, idem., rejoinder by Scholderer, ibid., July 26,
1947, p. 379.
Scholderer believes that Lycidas was written in a single day;
Bell and Michael object.

795 SCHULTZ, HOWARD. A book was writ of late. MLN,
69, 1954, 495-7.
On the meaning of the Tetrachordon sonnet.

796 SEATON, ETHEL. Comus and Shakespeare. E&S, 31,
1946, 68-80.
Echoes of Shakespeare's plays in Comus.
Rev: L. C. Martin, YWES, 170.

797 SENSABAUGH, GEORGE F. The Milieu of Comus. SP,
SP, 41, 1944, 233-49.
Argues that the controversy at the court over the cult of
Platonic love is reflected in the masque.

798 SHAWCROSS, JOHN T. Epitaphium Damonis: Lines
9-13 and the Date of Composition. MLN, 71, 1956,
322-4.

799 - - - - - -. Milton's Fairfax Sonnet. NQ, N. S., 2, 1955,
195-6.

800 - - - - - -. Milton's Sonnet 19: Its Date of Authorship and
Its Interpretation. NQ, N. S., 4, 1957, 442-6.
Late 1655. Interpreted in the light of Isaiah 65.

801 - - - - - -. Milton's Sonnet 23. NQ, N. S., 3, 1956, 202-4.
Agrees with Parker that the deceased wife is Mary Powell.

802 SHEPPARD, JOHN T. Milton's Cambridge Exercises.
Music at Belmont and Other Essays and Addresses
(London: Rupert Hart-Davis, 1951), pp. 152-62.
Rev: TLS, Apr. 18, 1952, p. 266.

803 SHUMAKER, WAYNE. Flowerets and Sounding Seas:
a Study in the Affective Structure of Lycidas. PMLA,
66, 1951, 485-94.
Rev: Arnold Davenport, YWES, 186.

804 - - - - - -. On Milton's Lycidas. Readings for Liberal Education. Ed. by Louis G. Locke et al. (New York: Rinehart,
1948), pp. 47-55.

805 SHUSTER, GEORGE N. Milton and the Metaphysical
Poets. The English Ode from Milton to Keats. Columbia
University Stud. in Eng. and Comp. Lit., 150 (New
York: Columbia University Press, 1940), pp. 64-92.
Rev: Douglas Bush, JEGP, 40, 1941, 304-7.

806 SILLS, KENNETH C. M. Milton's Latin Poems. CJ, 32, 1937, 417-23.
An appreciative essay.

807 SINGLETON, RALPH H. Milton's Comus and the Comus of Erycius Puteanus. PMLA, 58, 1943, 949-57.
A source study.
Rev: L. C. Martin, YWES, 151-2.

808 SMITH, ROLAND M. Spenser and Milton: An Early Analogue. MLN, 60, 1945, 394-8.
Cites parallels between the verse-letter from Spenser to Harvey in 1580 and Milton's sonnet "How soon hath time."

809 SPENCER, THEODORE. Shakespeare and Milton. MLN, 53, 1938, 366-7.
Argues that Milton's Shakespeare was written in imitation of Shakespeare's supposed epitaph on Sir William Stanley.

810 SPITZER, LEO. Understanding Milton. HR, Summer, 1951, pp. 17-25.
On Milton's Sonnet 23 and written in reply to Boas' comments on the poem in The Problem of Meaning in the Arts. Rejoinder by Boas, ibid., 28-30.

811 STAPLETON, LAWRENCE. Milton and the New Music. UTQ, 23, 1954, 217-26.
In the Nativity Ode.
Rev: Arnold Davenport, YWES, 139.

812 STARNES, D. T. More about the Tower of Fame in Milton. NQ, 196, 1951, 515-18.
In Quintum Novembris, 170-3.

813 STAUFFER, DONALD A. Milton's Two-handed Engine. MLR, 31, 1936, 57-60.
Rev: L. C. Martin, YWES, 189.

814 STEADMAN, JOHN M. Milton's Two-Handed Engine and Jehan Gerard. NQ, N. S., 3, 1956, 249-50.

815 ------. William Hog and Milton's Two-Handed Engine. NQ, N. S., 3, 1956, 335.

816 STEPHENSON, EDWARD A. Milton's Materials for Comus. Master's thesis, University of Florida, 1941.

817 STRATHMANN, ERNEST A. Lycidas and the Translation of May. MLN, 52, 1937, 398-400.
On the probability that Milton knew the Latin trans. of Spenser's May eclogue, in which the Protestant pastor is called Lycidas.
Rev: L. C. Martin, YWES, 182.

818 STROUP, THOMAS B. Lycidas and the Marinell Story. SAMLA Studies in Milton (Gainesville: University of Florida Press, 1953), pp. 100-13.

819 STUDLEY, MARIAN H. That Two-Handed Engine. EJ, 26, 1937, 148-51.

820 SVENDSEN, KESTER. Milton's L'Allegro and Il Penseroso. Expl., 8, 1950, item 49.
Maintains that the unity of the poems derives from the "progressive emphasis in both parts on images of sound and music."
Rev: Arnold Davenport, YWES, 177.

821 - - - - - -. Milton's On His Having Arrived at the Age of Twenty-Three. Expl., 7, 1949, item 53.
Rev: Arnold Davenport, YWES, 162.

822 - - - - - -. Milton's Sonnet on the Massacre in Piedmont. Shakespeare Assn. Bull., 20, 1945, 147-55.
On the rhetoric of the sonnet.
Rev: L. C. Martin, YWES, 27, 1946, 171.

823 SYKES, P. M. Sweet Poison (Comus, 47). TLS, July 19, 1934, p. 511.

824 Tercentenary of the First Performance of Milton's Comus, the Occasion for a Historical Pageant at Ludlow Castle. John Ryland's Libr. Bull., 18, 1934, 268-71.

825 THOMPSON, W. LAWRENCE. The Source of the Flower Passage in Lycidas. NQ, 197, 1952, 97-8.
Insists that the passage derives from Jonson's Pan's Anniversary rather than from Shakespeare's Winter's Tale.

826 TILLYARD, E. M. W. The Action of Comus. E&S, 28, 1942, 22-37. Reprinted in Studies in Milton (London: Chatto and Windus, 1951), pp. 82-99.
Rev: L. C. Martin, YWES, 151.

827 - - - - - -. Milton: L'Allegro and Il Penseroso. English Assn. Pamphlet No. 82. Oxford: Oxford University Press, 1932. 19pp. Reprinted in The Miltonic Setting (Cambridge: Cambridge University Press, 1938), pp. 1-28.
Appreciative essay with the suggestion that the poems belong to the Cambridge period.
Rev: L. C. Martin, YWES, 206-7.

828 TILLYARD, PHYLLIS B. What is a Beck? TLS, July 25, 1952, p. 485.
Reply by E. B. C. Jones, ibid., Aug. 8, 1952, p. 517. On L'Allegro, 27-8. To Tillyard, a "beck" is a "nod"; to Jones, "a come hither look."

829 TRUESDALE, CALVIN WILLIAM. English Pastoral
Verse from Spenser to Marvell: A Critical Revaluation.
Doctoral diss., University of Washington, 1956. 342pp.
Abs., DA, 17, 1957, 1087.
Special attention to Lycidas.

830 TURNER, W. ARTHUR. Milton's Two-Handed Engine.
JEGP, 49, 1950, 562-5.
Rev: Arnold Davenport, YWES, 178.

831 TUVE, ROSAMUND, Images and Themes in Five Poems
by Milton. Cambridge: Harvard University Press, 1957.
161pp.
Chapters: The Structural Figures of L'Allegro and Il Penseroso; The Hymn on the Morning of Christ's Nativity;
Theme, Pattern, and Imagery in Lycidas; Image, Form, and
Theme in A Mask.

832 ULLRICH, H. Zu Miltons L'Allegro. Germ.-rom. Mschr.,
18, 1930, 74.
On the "night-raven" of line 7.

833 VERITY, A. W. A Note on Comus (95). TLS, Feb. 26,
1931, p. 154.

834 WAGENKNECHT, EDWARD. Milton in Lycidas. CE,
7, 1946, 393-7.
Interprets the poem as a study of the problem of evil.

835 WALKER, FRED B. Milton's Use of the Bible in His
Shorter English Poems. Master's thesis, University of
Florida, 1947.

836 WALLERSTEIN, RUTH. Iusta Edouardo King. Studies
in Seventeenth Century Poetics (Madison: University of
Wisconsin Press, 1950), pp. 96-114.
Rev: L. C. Martin, MLR, 46, 1951, 486-7; TLS, Sept. 2,
1950, p. 582; NQ, 195, 1950, 528; M. Mincoff, ES, 32,
1951, 38-9; C. T. Harrison, SR, 59, 1951, 698-9; Roy
Daniells, UTQ, 21, 1951, 97-9; L. L. Martz, YR, 40, 1951,
562-5; Allan Gilbert, SAQ, 51, 1952, 177-9; Kathrine
Koller, MLN, 67, 1952, 567-9; Pierre Legouis, RES, 3,
1952, 290-2; J.-J. Denonain, EA, 6, 1953, 155-6; T. A.
Birrell, Neophil., 37, 1953, 123-4.

837 - - - - - -. Rhetoric in the English Renaissance: Two Elegies.
English Institute Essays, 1948, pp. 153-78.
Considers Donne's elegy on Prince Henry and Lycidas.

838 WATSON, SARA R. An Interpretation of Milton's
Haemony. NQ, 178, 1940, 260-1.
Replies by W. W. S., ibid., 321; by T. C. C., ibid., 339.

839 - - - - - -. Milton's Ideal Day: Its Development as a Pastoral
Theme. PMLA, 57, 1942, 404-20.
Rev: L. C. Martin, YWES, 158.

840 - - - - - -. Moly in Drayton and Milton. NQ, 176, 1939,
243-4.
On the influence of Drayton.

841 WHITING, GEORGE W. and ANN GOSSMAN. Milton
and True Love; or Comus, 1741. TLS, Sept. 17, 1954,
p. 591.

842 WILDE, HANS OSKAR. Miltons sonnett On his blind-
ness. Beiträge zur englischen Literaturgeschichte des 17.
Jahrhunderts (Breslau: Priebatsch, 1932), pp. 36-49.
Rev: L. C. Martin, YWES, 209.

843 WITHIM, PHILIP M. A Prosodic Analysis of Milton's
Seventh Sonnet. Bucknell Rev., 6, No. 4, 1957, 29-34.

844 WOODHOUSE, A. S. P. The Argument of Milton's
Comus. UTQ, 11, 1941, 46-71.

845 - - - - - -. Comus Once More. UTQ, 19, 1950. 218-23.
Rev: Arnold Davenport, YWES, 178.

846 - - - - - -. Milton's Pastoral Monodies. Studies in Honor of
Gilbert Norwood (Toronto: University of Toronto Press,
1952), pp. 261-78.
With Lycidas and Epitaphium Damonis the pastoral monody
"becames a powerful outlet for Milton's emotions and an
instrument for transcending his problems...."

COLLECTED PROSE WORKS AND INDIVIDUAL
SELECTIONS: EDITIONS

847 Milton on Education. The Tractate of Education with
Supplementary Extracts from Other Writings from
Milton. Ed. by Oliver Morley Ainsworth. New Haven:
Yale University Press, 1928.
Rev: E. N. S. Thompson, PQ, 8, 1929, 95; Denis Saurat,
RES, 5, 1929, 480; Marjorie Nicolson, MLN, 45, 1930,
197-9; H. F. Fletcher, JEGP, 29, 1930, 464-5.

848 A Brief History of Moscovia and of Other less-known
Countries lying eastward of Russia as far as Cathay.
Gathered from the Writings of Several Eye-witnesses by
John Milton. To which are added other Curious Docu-
ments. Ed. by Prince D. S. Mirsky. London: Blackamore
Press, 1929. 120pp.
Rev: TLS, Dec. 5, 1929, p. 1024; ER, 50, 1930, 523-4.

849 John Milton. Private Correspondence and Academic Exercises. Trans. from the Latin by Phyllis B. Tillyard. With
an Introd. and Commentary by E. M. W. Tillyard.
Cambridge: Cambridge University Press, 1932. xxxix,
143pp.
A trans. of the original 1674 text of Milton's Prolusiones
oratoriae and private letters.
Rev: G. B. Harrison and L. C. Martin, YWES, 202; Spect.,
148, 1932, 460; QR, 258, 1932, 391; NQ, 162, 1932, 162;
C. Saltmarshe, AB, 81, 1932, 319; A. Fremantle, Merc., 26,
1932, 274-5; H. Read, Crit., 11, 1932, 746-7; A. Brandl,
DL, 53, 1932, 835-7; B. A. Wright, MLR, 28, 1933, 259-62;
C. G. Osgood, MLN, 48, 1933, 473-6; Paul Chauvet, RA-A,
10, 1933, 238; Arnold Wilson, NC, 119, 1936, 495-506.

850 John Milton. Areopagitica. New York: Columbia University Press for the Facsimile Text Society, 1934, 1935.
Reproduced from the edition of 1644.

851 Areopagitica by John Milton. Christchurch: Caxton Press,
1941. 55pp.
A limited edition of 150 copies.

852 HAUG, RALPH A. An Annotated Edition of John
Milton's The Reason of Church-Government Urg'd
against Prelaty. Doctoral diss., Ohio State University,
1944. Abs., Ohio State University Abstracts of Diss.,
No. 45, 1943-4, pp. 129-37.

853 John Milton. Prose Selections. Ed. by Merritt Y. Hughes.
New York: Odyssey Press, 1947. cxci, 454pp.
Introd. contains biographical accounts by Aubrey, Edward
Phillips, and the anonymous biographer. Selected biblio-
graphy, pp. cxxv-cxlvii.
Rev: L. C. Martin, YWES, 187.

854 JOCHUMS, MILFORD C., ed. John Milton's An Apology against a Pamphlet.... Doctoral diss., University of Illinois, 1949. 583pp. Illinois Stud. in Lang. and Lit., 35. Urbana: University of Illinois Press, 1950. vi, 255pp.
Rev: Arnold Davenport, YWES, 179; Davis P. Harding, JEGP, 50, 1951, 549-51; A. E. Barker, MLR, 47, 1952, 394-5; D. M. Wolfe, MLN, 68, 1953, 271-2; Ernest Sirluck, MP, 50, 1953, 201-5.

855 STAHL, HERBERT M. An Annotated Edition of The Reason of Church government urg'd against prelaty and Lord Brooke's A discourse opening the nature of that episcopacie which is exercised in England. Doctoral diss., University of Washington, 1950.

856 John Milton. Areopagitica and Of Education, with Autobiographical Passages from Other Prose Works. Ed. by G. H. Sabine. Crofts Classics. New York: Crofts, 1951.

857 BLACKFORD, PAUL W. A Translation and Edition of Joannis Miltoni Angli pro Populo anglicano Defensio contra Claudii Anonymi, alias Salmasii, Defensionam Regiam. Doctoral diss., Northwestern University, 1951. Abs., Summaries of Doctoral Diss., Northwestern University, 18, 1951, 10-14.

858 SMITH, CALVIN C. An Edition of Milton's Prolusiones Oratoriae. Master's thesis, Duke University, 1952.

859 Complete Prose Works of John Milton. Don M. Wolfe, gen. ed. New Haven: Yale University Press, 1953. To be published in 8 vols.
"The purpose of the Complete Prose Works of John Milton is to present annotated texts of Milton's prose in the ascertainable order of its composition, bringing to bear in notes, prefaces, and volume introductions the accumulated scholarship of the past century." In a letter to the compiler, Professor Wolfe states, "It is hoped that Volume II of the Yale Milton will appear in 1958, Volume III in 1959, and Volume IV in 1960. Beyond that we have not made specific plans."

Vol. 1, 1624-1642: Introduction, by Don M. Wolfe (vol. ed.); Prolusions (1628-1632), trans. and prefaces by Phyllis B. Tillyard with notes and prefaces by Kathryn A. McEuen; Private Correspondence (1627-1641), trans., notes, and prefaces by W. Arthur Turner and Alberta T. Turner; Commonplace Book (1630?-1655?), trans., preface, and notes by Ruth Mohl; Of Reformation, preface and notes by Don M. Wolfe and William Alfred; Of Prelatical Episcopacy, preface and notes by J. Max

Patrick; Animadversions, preface by Rudolf Kirk with notes by Rudolf Kirk, assisted by William P. Baker; Reason of Church Government, preface and notes by Ralph A. Haug; An Apology against a Pamphlet, preface and notes by Frederick L. Taft. Appendices: (A) Legal Index, trans. by Ruth Mohl with preface and notes by Maurice Kelley; (B) A Postscript, preface and notes by Don M. Wolfe; (C) The London Petition (Dec. 11, 1640); (D) Constitutions and Canons Ecclesiastical (1640); (E) The Oath Ex-Officio, by Don M. Wolfe; (F) The Legion of Smec, by Frederick L. Taft and Ashur Baizer; (G) The Bishops, by Leo F. Solt, Ashur Baizer, Franklin R. Baruch, and J. Hillis Miller, Jr.; (H) Theme on Early Rising, trans., preface, and notes by Maurice Kelley and Donald Mackenzie; (I) Textual Guide; 1953. xvi, 1073pp.

Rev: Arnold Davenport, YWES, 203-4; D. C. Allen, MLN, 69, 1954, 116-20; TLS, July 30, 1954, p. 484; reply to Allen and TLS reviewer by Arthur Turner, ibid., Sept. 24, 1954, p. 609; Walter Taplin, Spect., June 4, 1954, pp. 690-3; J. Max Patrick et al, SCN, 12, 1954, 1-4, 14-15; J. George, Aberdeen University Rev., 36, 1955, 55-8; F. T. Prince, RES, 6, 1955, 316-18; Barbara Kiefer, Church Hist., 25, 1956, 88-90; I. A. Shapiro, MLR, 51, 1956, 244-6.

Volumes in preparation:

Vol. 2: Ed. by Ernest Sirluck. The Doctrine and Discipline of Divorce, Of Education, The Judgment of Martin Bucer, Areopagitica, Tetrachordon, and Colasterion.

Vol. 3: Ed. by Merritt Y. Hughes. The History of Britain, The Tenure of Kings and Magistrates, Observations upon the Articles of Peace, and Eikonoklastes.

Vol. 4: Ed. by Don M. Wolfe and Alexander M. Witherspoon. A Defence of the English People, A Second Defence, and Defense of Himself.

Vol 5: Ed. by A. S. P. Woodhouse and Arthur Barker. A Treatise of Civil Power, Considerations Touching the Likeliest Means, Letter to a Friend, The Readie and Easie Way, Brief Notes on a Late Sermon, and State Papers.

Vol. 6: Ed. by Maurice Kelley. The Christian Doctrine.

Vol. 7: Ed. by J. Milton French and Maurice Kelley. Accidence Commenced Grammar, Art of Logic, Of True Reigion, A Declaration, or Letters Patent, A Brief History of Moscovia, and Marginalia.

860 AYERS, ROBERT W. A Translation and Critical Edition of the John Phillips-John Milton Johannis Philippi Angli Responsio. Doctoral diss., Rutgers University, 1955. Abs., DA, 15, 1955, 2531.

861 John Milton. Areopagitica and Other Prose Works. Introd. by K. M. Burton. Everyman's Library. New York: Dutton; London: Dent, 1955. xii, 306pp.
    Rev: O. Lutaud, EA, 9, 1956, 162.

862 MOODY, LESTER DEANE, ed. John Milton's Pamphlets on Divorce. Doctoral diss., University of Washington, 1956. Abs., DA, 17, 1957, 855-6.
    Fully annotated.

863 John Milton, Areopagitica. Paris: Aubier, 1956. 241pp.
    Rev: M. Y. Hughes, EA, 10, 1957, 155-6.

PROSE WORKS: CRITICISM

864 ALLEN, JOHN W. Milton's Writings of 1641-1642.
English Political Thought, 1603-1644 (London: Methuen,
1938), 1, 323-38.
Emphasizes Milton's importance as a prose writer of the
period but censures his abusiveness.

865 BARKER, ARTHUR. Christian Liberty in Milton's
Divorce Pamphlets. MLR, 35, 1940, 153-61.
Rev: L. C. Martin, YWES, 173.

866 ------. Milton and the Puritan Dilemma, 1641-1660.
Toronto: University of Toronto Press; London: Milford,
1942. Reprinted, 1956. xxiv, 440pp.
A study of the prose pamphlets and of principles of liberty
in De Doctrina Christiana. The author argues that "Milton's
prose is the record of his effort to develop a theory of
liberty, religious, private, and political, which should reconcile
man's thoughts concerning freedom and those concerning the
spirit of Christianity as an other-worldly religion making
fresh demands for a rigid orthodoxy."
Rev: L. C. Martin, YWES, 24, 1943, 147-9; J. T. McNeill,
AHR, 49, 1943, 96-7; William Haller, SRL, Dec. 18, 1943,
p. 18; Edward Wagenknecht, NYTBR, May 23, 1943, p. 10;
B. M., DR, 23, 1943-4, 484-5; William Haller, JEGP, 43,
1944, 120-4; Louis B. Wright, PRv., 53, 1944, 312-13; B. A.
Wright, RES, 20, 1944, 323-5; H. J. C. Grierson, MLR, 39,
1944, 97-107; G. D., EHR, 61, 1946, 276-7; TLS, Sept. 7,
1956, p. 522.

867 ------. Milton and the Struggle for Liberty. Master's
thesis, University of Toronto, 1934.

868 BERKELEY, DAVID S. Determinate Sentence in Milton's
Of Education. NQ, N. S., 1, 1954, 25-6.
Interprets "determinate" as "definitive" or "conclusive."

869 BOTTKOL, JOSEPH McG. The Holograph of Milton's
Letter to Holstenius. PMLA, 68, 1953, 617-27.
Rev: Arnold Davenport, YWES, 204.

870 BRIET, S. L'Areopagitica de Milton: Historie d'une
traduction par Mirabeau et E. Aignan. RLC, 26, 1952,
446-56.

871 BRYANT, JOSEPH A., JR. Milton and the Art of History:
A Study of Two Influences on A Brief History of
Moscovia. PQ, 29, 1950, 15-30.
Polybius and Bacon.
Rev: Arnold Davenport, YWES, 179.

872 ------. A Reply to Milton's Moscovia not History. PQ,
31, 1952, 221-3.
Answer to Parks, ibid., pp. 218-21.

873 CANDY, HUGH C. H. A Cancel in an Early Milton Tract. Libr., 4th Ser., 16, 1935, 118.
Addendum to Parker, ibid., 15, 1934, 243-6.

874 ------. Milton, N.LL, and Sir. Tho. Urquhart. Libr., 4th Ser., 14, 1934, 470-6.
Reply by J. W. Pendleton, ibid., 15, 1934, 249-50. Concerning the Letters of State.

875 CAWLEY, ROBERT R. Milton's Literary Craftsmanship: A Study of A Brief History of Moscovia, with an Edition of the Text. Princeton Stud. in Eng., 24. Princeton: Princeton University Press, 1941. viii, 103pp.
Rev: H. F. Fletcher, JEGP, 41, 1941, 547-8; J. H. Hanford, Libr. Quar., 12, 1942, 326-7; Douglas Bush, MLN, 58, 1943, 220-2.

876 COOLIDGE, LOWELL W. Milton's Doctrine and Discipline of Divorce (Text of 1643). Doctoral diss., Western Reserve University, 1937.

877 COX, ROBERT. Milton's Areopagitica, an Analytical and Historical Study, with Implications for the College Teacher. Doctoral diss., University of Michigan, 1956. Abs., DA, 17, 1957, 1335-6.

878 CRAIG, HARDIN. An Ethical Distinction by John Milton. The Written Word and Other Essays (Chapel Hill: University of North Carolina Press, 1953), pp. 78-88.
A discussion of Milton's conception of public and private morality in De Doctrina Christiana.

879 D(AVENPORT), A(RNOLD). Milton's Seagull. NQ, 196, 1951, 339.
Milton's reference to Bishop Hall as a seagull in An Apology for Smectymnus is a pun on "sea" (bishop).

880 The Dignity of Kingship Asserted: In Answer to Mr. Milton's Ready and Easie Way to establish a Free Commonwealth. By G. S., a Lover of Loyalty. Reproduced in Facsimile from the Edition of 1660, with an Introduction by William R. Parker. New York: Columbia University Press; London: Milford, 1942. xxi, 315pp.
Rev: TLS, Sept. 26, 1942, p. 476; William Haller, MLN, 58, 1943, 401-2; B. A. Wright, RES, 19, 1943, 217-18.

881 DREW, HELEN L. The Diction of Milton's Prose. Doctoral diss., Cornell University, 1938. Abs., Cornell University Abstracts of Theses...1938, 1939, pp. 29-32.

882 DUHAMEL, P. ALBERT. Milton's Alleged Ramism. PMLA, 67, 1952, 1035-53.

883 DUNCAN-JONES, ELSIE. Milton's Late Court-Poet. NQ, N. S., 1, 1954, 473.
   Identifies Davenant as the poet mentioned in The Ready and Easy Way.

884 EARGLE, MAYRE WALL. Biographical Relationship of Marriage and Divorce in the Thought of John Milton in Selected Works. Master's thesis, University of Alabama, 1951.

885 EISENRING, J. TH. Milton's De Doctrina Christiana: An Historical Introduction and Critical Analysis. Fribourg, Switzerland: Society of St. Paul, 1946. x, 162pp.
   Discusses the history of the text and analyzes the content in the light of Roman Catholic dogma.
   Rev: L. C. Martin, YWES, 174-5.

886 EKFELT, FRED E. The Diction of Milton's Prose. Doctoral diss., University of Iowa, 1942. Abs., (Iowa) Abstracts and References, 3, 1943, 269-76.

887 ------. The Graphic Diction of Milton's English Prose. PQ, 25, 1946, 46-69.
   Rev: L. C. Martin, YWES, 175.

888 ------. Latinate Diction in Milton's English Prose. PQ, 28, 1949, 53-71.
   Rev: L. C. Martin, YWES, 170.

889 EVANS, B. IFOR. The Lessons of the Areopagitica. CR, 166, 1944, 342-6.

890 ------. Milton and the Modern Press. Freedom of Expression. Edited by Herman Ould (London: Hutchinson Intl. Authors, 1945), pp. 26-9.
   Argues that the press and the radio should be regulated, that Milton did not foresee present mass propaganda efforts.

891 Felix Culpa. TLS. Apr. 24, 1943, p. 199.
   Refers to Yule, RES, 19, 1943, 61-6, 409. "There are errors which may claim squatters' rights; and among them none so securely as Milton's eagle mewing her mighty youth."

892 FINK, ZERA S. The Classical Republicans: an Essay in the Recovery of a Pattern of Thought in Seventeenth Century England. Northwestern University Stud. in Humanities, 9. Evanston: Northwestern University Press, 1945. xii, 225pp.
   The study had its inception in an attempt to investigate the classical element in Milton's thinking. Chapter 5, Immortal Government: the Free Commonwealth, pp. 90-122, is a

discussion of Milton's efforts to achieve a mixed state in England. Three appendices are pertinent: B, The Date and Authenticity of Milton's Character of the Long Parliament, pp. 193-4; C, Political Implications in Paradise Regained, pp. 195-6; and D, The Date of Milton's Proposalls for a Firme Government, pp. 197-8.
Rev: L. C. Martin, YWES, 149-50; C. J. Ryan, CQR, 31, 1945, 332-3; A. S. P. Woodhouse, UTQ, 15, 1945, 100-1; D. H. Wilson, SAQ, 45, 1946, 119-20; M. M., QQ, 53, 1946, 106-7; E. S., Greece and Rome, 15, 1946, 79; James Hutton, PRv., 56, 1947, 223-5.

893 ------. The Date of Milton's Proposalls for a Firme Government. MLN, 55, 1940, 407-10.
Between Oct. 20 and Dec. 26, 1659.

894 ------. Venice and English Political Thought in the Seventeenth Century. MP, 38, 1940, 155-72.
Maintains, pp. 165-72, that the contemporary reputation of Venice is reflected in Milton's Ready and Easy Way.

895 FIRTH, SIR C. H. Milton as an Historian. Essays, Historical and Literary (Oxford: Oxford University Press, 1938), pp. 61-102.
A reprint of Stevens' No. 1311.

896 FLETCHER, HARRIS F. Milton's Vicar of Hell. JEGP, 47, 1948, 387-9.
Identifies Sir Francis Bryan as the courtier alluded to in Areopagitica.
Rev: L. C. Martin, YWES, 193.

897 ------. A Note on Two Words in Milton's History of Moscovia. Renaissance Studies in Honor of Hardin Craig (Stanford: Stanford University Press, 1941), pp. 309-19. Printed also in PQ, 20, 1941, 501-11.
On "cursemay" and "rossomakka."

898 ------. The Use of the Bible in Milton's Prose. University of Illinois Stud. in Lang. and Lit., 14, No. 3, Urbana: University of Illinois Press, 1929.
Rev: Israel Baroway, MLN, 46, 1931, 537-9; D. Saurat, RES, 7, 1931, 472-4; M. H. Nicolson, MP, 28, 1931, 381-2; Paul Chauvet, RA-A, 8, 1931, 154; A. Koszul, Rev. critique, 65, 1931, 138-40; S. B. Liljegren, Ang. Bbl., 43, 1932, 377-8; M. Polak, Neophil., 19, 1934, 131-2.

899 FORSTER, EDWARD M. The Tercentenary of the Areopagitica. Two Cheers for Democracy (New York: Harcourt, 1951), pp. 51-5.
There are several other editions of this work.

900 FRENCH, J. MILTON. The Burning of Milton's Defensio in France. MLN, 56, 1941, 275-7.

901 ------. A Comment on A Book Was Writ of Late....
MLN, 70, 1955, 404-5.
Insists that Milton "thought highly of the learning and piety
of the age of Sir John Cheke."

902 ------. The Date of Milton's First Defense. Libr., 5th
Ser., 3, 1948, 56-8.
Feb. 24, 1650/1.
Rev: L. C. Martin, YWES, 30, 1949, 164.

903 ------. Milton as a Historian. PMLA, 50, 1935, 469-79.
The writer of the History of Britain is a man "whose
interests are primarily prosaic—that is, critical, ratiocinative,
scholarly...."

904 ------. Milton as Satirist. PMLA, 51, 1936, 414-29.
In the prose works.

905 ------. Milton, Ramus and Edward Phillips. MP, 47,
1949, 82-7.
Rev: L. C. Martin, YWES, 168-9.

906 FRISSELL, HARRY L. Milton's Art of Logic and Ramist
Logic in the Major Poems. Doctoral diss.,, Vanderbilt
University, 1951. Abs., Bull. of Vanderbilt University,
51, 1951, 22-3. Ann Arbor: U. M., 1952. 250pp.

907 GEORGE, J. An Entry in Milton's Commonplace Book.
NQ, N. S., 1, 1954, 383-4.
Feels that "coitus" is intended for "cujus" in the note (on
fol. 116) beginning "cujus sine amore est frigidus."

908 ------. Milton's The Reason of Church Government.
NQ, N. S., 3, 1956, 157.
Dates the work ca. Nov., 1641.

909 GILBERT, ALLAN H. Milton Quotes from Petrarch.
MLN, 60, 1945, 496.
In Of True Religion (Col. Ed., 6, 167).

910 ------. Ovid's Mulberry in Milton's Pro Se Defensio.
MLN, 63, 1948, 190.
Rev: L. C. Martin, YWES, 193.

911 GILMAN, W. E. Milton's Rhetoric: Studies in His
Defense of Liberty. Doctoral diss., Cornell University,
1937. Abs., Cornell University Abstracts of Theses...
1937, 1938, pp. 67-70. Published as University of
Missouri Stud., 14, No. 3, in condensed and revised
form. Columbia: University of Missouri Press, 1939.
193pp.
Rev: L. C. Martin, YWES, 173; Arthur Barker, MLR, 35,
1940, 560-1; E. N. S. T(hompson), PQ, 19, 1940, 414-15;
Z. S. Fink, JEGP, 40, 1941, 148-9; J. H. McBurney, QJS,
27, 1941, 323; William Haller, MLN, 56, 1941. 636-7.

912 HALL, ALFREDA C. N. A Summary of Milton's Second Defence of the People of England. Part 3 of Master's thesis, McMaster University, 1933.

913 HALLER, WILLIAM. The Compassionate Samaritane. TLS, Mar. 13, 1930, p. 214.

> Wants to examine a copy of the first edition of this anonymous work to determine whether it appeared before or after Areopagitica in 1644.

914 - - - - - -. For the Liberty of Unlicenc'd Printing. Amer. Scholar, 14, 1945, 326-33.

915 - - - - - -. John Fox and the Puritan Revolution. The Seventeenth Century (Stanford: Stanford University Press, 1951), pp. 209-24.

> Relates Milton's Of Reformation to Fox's ideas.
> Rev: Arnold Davenport, YWES, 187.

916 - - - - - -. Liberty and Reformation in the Puritan Revolution. New York: Columbia University Press, 1955. viii, 410pp.

> Milton's activities (1640-9) given a prominent place, passim.
> Rev: Lewis A. Dralle, TT, Nov. 12, 1955, pp. 1474-5; D. A. Roberts, Nat., Aug. 20, 1955, p. 161; W. S. Hudson, JR, 35, 1955, 260-1; Douglas Bush, MLN, 71, 1956, 306-9; Ernest Sirluck, MP, 53, 1956, 278-82.

917 - - - - - -. The Rise of Puritanism; or, The Way to the New Jerusalem as Set Forth in Pulpit and Press from Thomas Cartwright to John Lilburne and John Milton, 1570-1643. New York: Columbia University Press, 1938. vii, 464pp.

> Detailed analyses of Milton's early polemical pamphlets.
> Rev: A. S. P. Woodhouse, AHR, 45, 1939, 123-5; M. M. Knappen, JMH, 11, 1939, 209-11; R. T. F., Pers., 20, 1939, 418-19; Florence Higham, History, N. S., 24, 1939, 147-8; A. E. Barker, UTQ, 8, 1939, 472-7; T. Wilkinson, LQHR, July, 1939, pp. 399-400; H. J. C. Grierson, MLR, 39, 1944, 97-107.

918 - - - - - -, ed. Tracts on Liberty in the Puritan Revolution. New York: Columbia University Press, 1935. 3 vols. 197, 339, and 405pp.

> First vol. contains several commentaries on Milton's prose works. Appendix A is pertinent: Milton's Reputation and Influence, 1643-1647, 1, 128-42.
> Rev: L. C. Martin, YWES, 248, 251-2; A. S. P. Woodhouse, UTQ, 4, 1935, 395-404; R. H. Bainton, Church Hist., 4, 1935, 69-70; G. H. Sabine, PRv., 44, 1935, 391-2; W. Köhler, Historische Zeitschrift, 157, 1937, 163-4.

919 - - - - - -. Two Early Allusions to Milton's Areopagitica. HLQ, 12, 1949, 207-12.

> In John Hall's An Humble Motion to the Parliament, 1649, and The Panegyrike and the Storm, 1659, probably by Richard Watson.

920 ------, and GODFREY DAVIES, eds. The Leveller
Tracts, 1647-1653. New York: Columbia University
Press; London: Milford, 1944. vi, 481pp.
> The emphasis is on Lilburne, of course. Milton, passim.
> A valuable background work.
> Rev: TLS, Apr. 28, 1945, p. 203; C. J. Ryan, CHR, 31,
> 1945, 202-3; W. S. Hudson, JMH, 17, 1945, 87; and Church
> Hist., 14, 1945, 132-3; T. C. Pease, AHR, 50, 1945, 315-16;
> J. E. C. H., EHR, 55, 1945, 273-4; H. N. Brailsford, NSN,
> Oct. 20, 1945, p. 270; A. S. P. Woodhouse, UTQ, 15, 1945,
> 98-9.

921 ------, and MALLEVILLE. The Puritan Art of Love.
HLQ, 5, 1942, 235-72.
> An "account of the teachings of the Puritan pulpit concerning
> love and marriage...during the three or four generations
> before the publication of Milton's first divorce tract, in
> 1643."
> Rev: L. C. Martin, YWES, 159.

922 HARMAN, MARIAN. A Greek Proverb in Milton. CP,
38, 1943, 259-60.
> "When I dye, let the earth be roul'd in flames" appears in
> The Reason of Church Government.
> Rev: L. C. Martin, YWES, 153.

923 HAUG, RALPH A. Milton and Bishop Williams. NQ,
184, 1943, 193.
> Explains an allusion in The Reason of Church Government
> (Col. Ed., 3, 196).
> Rev: L. C. Martin, YWES, 153.

924 ------. Milton and Sir John Harrington, MLQ, 4, 1943,
291-2.
> Notes parallels between The Reason of Church Government
> and Harrington's The Life of Ariosto.
> Rev: L. C. Martin, YWES, 153.

925 HENDRICK, A. L. The Political Writings of John Milton,
1608-1674. Master's thesis, London School of Economics,
1953.

926 HENRY, NATHANIEL H. Milton and Overton. TLS,
Oct. 14, 1949, p. 665.
> Believes that Robert, not Richard, Overton was the author
> of Man's Mortalitie and concludes that Milton's reference
> to Robert in The Second Defence becomes more pointed and
> that Masson's interpretation must be discarded.
> Reply by Earnest A. Payne, ibid., Oct. 25, 1949, p. 697.
> Rev: L. C. Martin, YWES, 164.

927 ------. Milton's Last Pamphlet: Theocracy and Intoler-
ance. A Tribute to G. C. Taylor (Chapel Hill: University of North Carolina Press, 1952), pp. 197-210.

928 HILLWAY, TYRUS. Milton's Theory of Education. CE, 5, 1943-4, 376-9.

929 HUGHES, MERRITT Y. The Historical Setting of Milton's Observations on the Articles of Peace, 1649. PMLA, 64, 1949, 1049-73.
Rev: L. C. Martin, YWES, 164.

930 - - - - - -. Milton's Treatment of Reformation History in The Tenure of Kings and Magistrates. The Seventeenth Century (Stanford: Stanford University Press, 1951), pp. 247-63.
Rev: Arnold Davenport, YWES, 188.

931 - - - - - -. New Evidence on the Charge that Milton Forged the Pamela Prayer in the Eikon Basilike. RES, N. S., 3, 1952, 130-40.
Disavows the charge.
Rev: Arnold Davenport, YWES, 177.

932 IRWIN, HENRY FRANKLIN, JR. Ramistic Logic in Milton's Prose Works. Doctoral diss., Princeton University, 1941.

933 JONES, JOSEPH, Areopagitica: 1644-1944. Libr. Chron. of the University of Texas, 1, No. 2, 1944, 25-31.
Praises the timelessness of the work and describes a copy of the first edition in the University of Texas library.

934 KEETON, G. W. The Tercentenary of the Areopagitica. CR, 166, 1944, 280-6.

935 KELLEY, MAURICE. Additional Texts of Milton's State Papers. MLN, 67, 1952, 14-19.
Prints four letters of state.

936 - - - - - -. Milton's Debt to Wolleb's Compendium Theologiae Christianae. PMLA, 50, 1935, 156-65.
Rev: L. C. Martin, YWES, 255.

937 - - - - - -. This Great Argument: a Study of Milton's De Doctrina Christiana as a Gloss upon Paradise Lost. Princeton: Princeton University Press, 1941. xiv, 269pp.
Reviews listed elsewhere.

938 KLIGER, SAMUEL. The Goths in England, a Study in Seventeenth and Eighteenth Century Thought. Cambridge: Harvard University Press, 1952. 304pp.
Milton's views on the ancient Britons and Anglo-Saxons, pp. 146-53.

939 KRETER, HERBERT. Bildungs- und Erziehungsideale bei
Milton. Studien zur englischen Philologie, 93. Halle:
Niemeyer, 1938. vi, 64pp.
Rev: E. O. Sisson, MLR, 34, 1939, 637; Paul Meissner, DL,
60, 1939, 918-9; H. Mutschmann, Ang. Bbl., 51, 1940, 146-
50; M. Rösler, ESt., 74, 1940, 237-8; W. R. Parker, JEGP,
39, 1940, 599.

940 LASKI, HAROLD J. The Areopagitica after Three
Hundred Years. Freedom of Expression. Ed. by Herman
Ould (London: Hutchinson Intl. Authors, 1945), pp.
168-76.
Feels that the work was unequalled in the range of freedom
it demands until the publication of Mill's Liberty.

941 LE COMTE, EDWARD S. Milton's Attitude Toward
Women in the History of Britain. PMLA, 62, 1947,
977-83.
Rev: L. C. Martin, YWES, 188.

942 LOOTEN, C. Les Débuts de Milton pamphlétaire. EA, 1,
1937, 297-313.

943 MADAN, FRANCIS F. Lord Anglesey and the Eikon
Basilike. TLS, Aug. 31, 1956, p. 511.

944 MAGEALSON, VIOLA. A Study of Syntax in Milton's
Areopagitica. Doctoral diss., University of Pittsburgh,
1934. Abs., Abstracts of Theses, University of Pittsburgh
Bull., 10, 1934, 552-3.

945 MARTIN, L. C. Muing Her Mighty Youth—A Defence.
RES, 21, 1945, 44-6.
Questions Yule, RES, 19, 1943, 61-6, 409.

946 MASON, M. G. Tractate of Education by John Milton.
Education, 74, 1953, 213-24.

947 MAXWELL, J. C. Plato and Milton. MLR, 43, 1948,
409-10.
Milton's statement in Of Education that "The end then of
learning is to repair the ruines of our first parents..." has
as its source the Theaetetus.
Rev: L. C. Martin, YWES, 193.

948 MAYOUX, JEAN-JACQUES. Un Classique de la liberte:
L'Aréopagitique de John Milton. Critique, 118, 1957,
195-207.

949 MERRILL, HARRY G., III. Regii sangunis Clamor ad
Coelum, by Dr. Peter du Moulin the Younger (1652),
Translated into English and with an Introduction.
Doctoral diss., University of Tennessee, 1953.

950 MILLER, SONIA. Two References in Milton's Tenure of Kings. JEGP, 50, 1951, 320-5.
> On Milton's references to Gilby de obedientia and England's Complaint against the Canons.
> Rev: Arnold Davenport, YWES, 188.

951 MINEKA, FRANCIS E. The Critical Reception of Milton's De Doctrina Christiana. UTSE, 22, 1943, 115-47.
> Rev: L. C. Martin, YWES, 158-9.

952 NASH, RALPH. Milton, Jonson, and Tiberius. CP, 41, 1946, 164.
> Believes that Milton may have taken the proverb quoted in The Reason of Church Government from Sejanus.
> Rev: L. C. Martin, YWES, 170.

953 NEUMANN, JOSHUA H. Milton's Prose Vocabulary. PMLA, 60, 1945, 102-20.
> On Milton's contributions to the English language.
> Rev: L. C. Martin, YWES, 150.

954 NICHOLAS, CONSTANCE. Introduction and Notes to Milton's History of Britain. Illinois Stud. in Lang. and Lit., 44. Urbana: University of Illinois Press, 1957. 179pp.
> Written as a companion to Vol. 10 of the Columbia Edition.

955 OLDFATHER, W. A. Pro Joanne Miltonoe Poeta Populum Anglicanum Iterum Defendente. PQ, 19, 1940, 88-9.
> Suggests emendations for a poem in the Second Defence.

956 OSGOOD, CHARLES G. Areopagitica—1644. PAPS, 89, 1945, 495-8.

957 OULD, HERMAN, ed. Freedom of Expression: A Symposium Based on the Conference Called by the London Centre of the Intl. P. E. N. to Commemorate the Tercentenary of the Publication of Milton's Areopagitica: 22-26th August, 1944. London: Hutchinson Intl. Authors, 1945, 184pp.
> Individual articles are listed under their respective authors in this bibliography.
> Rev: A. Closs, Eras., 1, 1947, 157-8.

958 OWEN, EIVION. Milton and Selden on Divorce. SP, 43, 1946, 233-57.
> On Milton's indebtedness.
> Rev: L. C. Martin, YWES, 171.

959 PARKER, WILLIAM R. A Cancel in an Early Milton Tract. Libr., 4th Ser., 15, 1934, 243-6.
> Animadversions.
> Rev: L. C. Martin, YWES, 241.

960 PARKS, GEORGE B. Milton's Moscovia not History. PQ, 31, 1952, 218-21.
    Questions Bryant's conclusions in ibid., 29, 1950, 15-30.
    Rev: Arnold Davenport, YWES, 181-2.

961 - - - - - -. The Occasion of Milton's Moscovia. SP, 40, 1943, 399-404.
    Written "as a guide to diplomatic dealings with Russia."
    Rev: L. C. Martin, YWES, 154.

962 PATRICK, J. MAX. The Date of Milton's Of Prelatical Episcopacy. HLQ, 13, 1950, 303-11.
    June or July, 1641.
    Rev: Arnold Davenport, YWES, 179.

963 PETERSEN, VICT. JUUL. Milton—Akademiet. Et Bland af paedagogiske Syners Historie. Edda, 37, 1937, 35-43.
    Compares Milton and Comenius.
    Rev: L. C. Martin, YWES, 182.

964 PRICE, ALAN F. Incidental Imagery in Areopagitica. MP, 49, 1952, 217-22.
    Rev: Arnold Davenport, YWES, 181.

965 QUINTANA, RICARDO. Notes on English Educational Opinion During the Seventeenth Century. SP, 27, 1930, 265-92.
    Milton's views discussed, pp. 281-3.

966 RAMAGE, SARAH THORPE. Milton's Nationalism as Exemplified in His Early Prose. Doctoral diss., Yale University, 1942.

967 READ, HERBERT. The Areopagitica. A Coat of Many Colors (London: Routledge, 1945), pp. 333-46.
    Appreciative.

968 - - - - - -. On Milton's Areopagitica. Adelphi, 21, 1944, 9-15. Reprinted in Freedom of Expression (London: Hutchinson Intl. Authors, 1945), pp. 122-9.

969 REESING, JOHN. The Materiality of God in Milton's De Doctrina Christiana. HTR, 50, 1957, 159-73.

970 RICE, ELMER. The Supreme Freedom: Three Hundred Years After Milton. Great Expressions of Human Rights. Ed. by R. M. MacIver (New York: Institute for Religious and Social Studies, 1950), pp. 105-25.
    Appreciative. Deplores present strictures on media of communication.

971 RICE, WARNER G. A Note on Areopagitica. JEGP, 40, 1941, 474-81.
    Points out that Milton believes in the restraint of bad men and bad books by the virtuous and the learned.

972 RYAN, CLARENCE J. Theories of Church-State Relationships in Seventeenth Century England. Historical Bull., 27, 1949, 29-30, 36-41.
Milton's views discussed, p. 38.

973 SASEK, LAWRENCE A. Milton's Patriotic Epic. HLQ, 20, 1956, 1-14.
Milton did plan "definitely to celebrate the heroic deeds of his nation in a patriotic work. Although this aim leads one naturally to think of a Virgilian epic, Milton fulfilled it to his own satisfaction in his prose works."

974 SAURAT, DENIS. Milton and Du Moulin. TLS, June 14, 1934, p. 424.
Man's Mortality contains a reference to Pierre du Moulin.

975 SCOTT-CRAIG, T. S. K. The Craftmanship and Theological Significance of Milton's Art of Logic. HLQ, 17, 1953, 1-15.
Rev: Arnold Davenport, YWES, 205.

976 - - - - - -. Milton's Use of Wolleb and Ames. MLN, 55, 1940, 403-7.
In De Doctrina Christiana.

977 SEWELL, ARTHUR. Milton's De Doctrina Christiana. E&S, 19, 1934, 40-65.
Concerning the date of composition and significance of the work as a record of Milton's mature thought.
Replies by Maurice Kelley, TLS, Sept. 6, 1934, p. 604, and by R. E. C. Houghton, ibid., Dec. 6, 1934, p. 875; rejoinder by Sewell, ibid., Nov. 29, 1934, p. 856; rejoinder by Kelley, ibid., Feb. 21, 1935, p. 108.
Rev: L. C. Martin, YWES, 239-40; D. Saurat, MLN, 51, 1936, 263-4.

978 - - - - - -. A Study in Milton's Christian Doctrine. London: Oxford University Press and Milford, 1939. xiii, 214pp.
Rev: L. C. Martin, YWES, 115-16; TLS, Feb. 18, 1939, p. 100; A. S. P. Woodhouse, MLR, 34, 1939, 593-6; D. C. Macgregor, RES, 15, 1939, 479-82; Maurice Kelley, MP, 37, 1939, 102-4; J. E. G., LQHR, Apr., 1939, p. 262; A. H. Gilbert, MLN, 55, 1940, 212-15.

979 SIEBERT, F. S. The Control of the Press During the Puritan Revolution. Freedom of the Press in England, 1476-1776: The Rise and Decline of Government Controls (Urbana: University of Illinois Press, 1952), pp. 165-236.
Places Areopagitica in its historical context, pp. 195-7.
Rev: J. R. Wiggins, AHR, 58, 1953, 349-50.

980 - - - - - -. Regulation of the Press in the Seventeenth
Century; Excerpts from the Records of the Court of the
Stationers' Company. Journalism Quar., 13, 1936, 381-
93.

981 SIRLUCK, ERNEST. Eikon Basilike, Eikon Alethine, and
Eikonoklastes. MLN, 69, 1954, 497-502.
Insists that the Commonwealthsmen were aware of Bishop
G's authorship from the beginning.

982 - - - - - -. Milton Revises The Faerie Queene. MP, 48, 1950,
90-6.
On the reference in Areopagitica to Book II of Spenser's
epic.
Rev: Arnold Davenport, YWES, 176-7.

983 SMITH, G. C. MOORE. A Note on Milton's Art of
Logic. RES, 13, 1937, 335-40.

984 SPITZ, DAVID. Milton's Testament. AR, 13, 1953, 390-
302.
On the timelessness of Areopagitica in view of recent
attempts to suppress ideas.

985 STEDMOND, J. M. English Prose of the Seventeenth
Century. DR, 30, 1950, 269-78.
Remarks on the poetic qualities of the prose works of Milton,
Jeremy Taylor, and Sir Thomas Browne.

986 STRATHMANN, ERNEST A. Note on the Ralegh Canon.
TLS, Apr. 13, 1956, p. 228.
The Cabinet-Council, published by Milton in 1658, not the
work of Ralegh but possibly that of Thomas Beddingfield.

987 SVENDSEN, KESTER. Science and Structure in Milton's
Doctrine of Divorce. PMLA, 67, 1952, 435-45.
Rev: Arnold Davenport, YWES, 181.

988 TAFT, FREDERICK L. Milton and the Smectymnuus
Controversy, 1641-42. Doctoral diss., Western Reserve
University, 1942. 372pp.

989 TAYLOR, GEORGE C. Much Ado about Something.
SAB, 18, 1943, 92-5.
Review article of Kelley's This Great Argument.

990 THOMPSON, E. N. S. Milton's Prose Style. PQ, 14, 1935,
38-53.

991 TIHANY, LESLIE C. Milton's Brief History of Moscovia.
PQ, 13, 1934, 305-6.

992 TREVELYAN, GEORGE MACAULAY. Milton's Areopagitica, 1644. An Autobiography and Other Essays (London: Longmans, 1949), pp. 179-82.
Appreciative.

993 VISIAK, E. H. Milton's Prose as Represented in the Compendious Milton. NC, 123, 1938, 499-508.
Appreciative essay on the polemical tracts.

994 WARNER, CHARLES G. Materials for an Edition of Milton's History of Britain. Doctoral diss., Cornell University, 1941. Abs., Cornell University Abs. of Theses, 1941, pp. 57-8.

995 WHITING, GEORGE W. Milton and Comets. ELH, 4, 1937, 41-2.
On Digby and the reference to comets in Of Reformation.
Rev: L. C. Martin, YWES, 185.

996 ------. Milton and That Learned English Writer. TLS, Jan. 10, 1935, p. 21.
Identifies the writer mentioned in Of Reformation as Sir Francis Bacon.
Rev: L. C. Martin, YWES, 253-4.

997 ------. Milton's Prelatical Pamphlets. TLS, Sept. 5, 1935, p. 552.

998 ------. Milton's Reply to Lord Digby. RES, 11, 1935, 430-8.
Considers Of Reformation an answer to Digby's Speech.
Rev: L. C. Martin, YWES, 253.

999 ------. On the Authorship of Eikon Basilike. NQ, 162, 1932, 134-5.
Supplements Stevens' and Fletcher's references on the subject.
Rev: L. C. Martin, YWES, 211.

1000 ------. A Pseudononymous Reply to Milton's Of Prelatical Episcopacy. PMLA, 51, 1936, 430-5.
A Compendious Discourse (1641).
Rev: L. C. Martin, YWES, 189.

1001 ------. The Satire of Eikonoklastes. NQ, 170, 1936, 435-8.
Addendum to French, PMLA, 51, 1936, 414-29.

1002 ------. The Sources of Eikonoklastes: A Resurvey. SP, 32, 1935, 74-103.
Adds Thomas May's The History of the Parliament of England.
Rev: L. C. Martin, YWES, 254.

1003 WILEY, MARGARET L. The Subtle Knot: Creative Scepticism in Seventeenth-Century England. London: George Allen, 1952. 303pp.

Uses Areopagitica as a basis for a discussion, pp. 257-65, of Milton's relationship to scepticism.

Rev: TLS, Jan. 16, 1953, p. 36; Ernest Sirluck, MP, 51, 1953, 68; F. S. Boas, Eng., 9, 1953, 142-3.

1004 WILLIAMS, ARNOLD. Areopagitica Revisited. UTQ, 14, 1944, 67-74.

1005 WOLFE, DON M. Milton in the Puritan Revolution. New York and London: Nelson, 1941. xvi, 496pp.

Rev: TLS, Oct. 4, 1941, p. 499; J. S. Diekhoff, SR, 49, 1941, 426-8; E. N. S. T(hompson), PQ, 20, 1941, 623-4; Bonamy Dobrée, Spect., Nov. 21, 1941, p. 490; D. A. Roberts, Nat., 153, 1941, 490; A. S. P. Woodhouse, UTQ, 10, 1941, 500, and JEGP, 41, 1942, 102-5; J. T. Wisely, RES, 19, 1943, 86-8; B. A. Wright, RES, 19, 1943, 85-6; Wallace Notestein, MLN, 59, 1944, 142-3; CR, 167, 1945, 256.

1006 WOODHOUSE, A. S. P. Puritanism and Liberty. UTQ, 4, 1935, 395-404.

Review article of Haller's Tracts on Liberty During the Puritan Revolution.

1007 ------. Puritanism and Liberty: Being the Army Debates (1647-9) from the Clarke Manuscripts, with Supplementary Documents. London: J. M. Dent, 1938. 506pp.

Milton mentioned and quoted often, esp. in the Introduction.

Rev: TLS, Dec. 31, 1938; F. Higham, History, 24, 1939, 147-8; F. E. Budd., Eng., 2, 1939, 313-14; E. Barker, UTQ, 8, 1939, 238-41; M. M. Knappen, JMH, 11, 1939, 208-11; J. W. Gough, EHR, 54, 1939, 507-8; W. Haller, AHR, 44, 1939, 855-7; R. N. C. Hunt, CQR, 128, 1939, 152-7.

1008 WRIGHT, NATHALIA. Milton's Use of Latin Formularies. SP, 40, 1943, 390-8.

In his letters.

Rev: L. C. Martin, YWES, 158.

1009 YULE, G. UDNY. The Word "Muing" in Milton's Areopagitica (1644). RES, 19, 1943, 61-6, 409.

Suggests that "muing" is a misprint for "renuing."

Rev. L. C. Martin, YWES, 154.

TRANSLATIONS
Paradise Lost

1010 John Milton. El Paráiso perdido. Edición illustrada. Barcelona: Ediciones Iberia, 1932. 119pp.

1011 John Milton. Il Paradíso Perduto. Trad. di A. Muccioli. Florence: La Nuova Italia, 1933. 457pp.

1012 John Milton. Kadotettu Paratiisi. Trans. by Yrjö Jylhä. Porvoo and Helsinki: Werner Söderström, 1933. 362pp. The first complete metrical translation into Finnish.

1013 John Milton. Il Paradiso Perduto. Trad. di Alessandro Muccioli. Florence: La Nuova Italia, 1933. 459pp.

1014 John Milton. Il Paradiso Perduto. Trad. di Lazzaro. Illus. di Gustave Doré. Milan: Songogno, 1938. 282pp.

1015 John Milton: Il Paradiso Perduto. Trad. di Giuseppe Nicolussi. Naples: Studio di propaganda, 1938.

1016 John Milton. El Paraiso perdido. Santiago de Chile: Ediciones Ercilla, 1940. 310pp.

1017 John Milton. Das Verlorene Paradies. Trans. by B. Pick. Cologne: Kolner Universitatsverl, 1948. 139pp.

1018 John Milton. Il Paradiso Perduto. Trad. di D. Petoello. Turin: Un. Tip. ed. torinese, 1950. 547pp.

1019 John Milton. Rakuen Soshitsu (1-3). Trans. by Takeshi Fugii. Tokyo: Iwanamishoten, 1950. 3 vols. Illus.

1020 John Milton. El paradis perdut. Traducció de Joseph M. Boix i Selva. Barcelona: Aiguaforto de Ramon de Capmany, 1950. 2 vols.

1021 John Milton. Paradis Perdu. Tome I, Livres I à VI. Tome II, Livres VI-XII. Introd., Trad., et Notes de Pierre Messiaen. Paris: Aubier, 1951, 1955, resp. 295, 320pp.
Rev: J. Blondel, EA, 5, 1952, 158-60.

1022 John Milton. El Paraiso Perdido. Trad. per Pablo Laredo. Barcelona: Edit, 1955. 224pp.

1023 John Milton. El paradis perdut. Trad. i notes per J. M. Boix i Selva. Barcelona: Editorial Alpha, 1953. 459pp.
Rev: M. Dole, Arbor., 31, 1955, 150-2.

1024 John Milton. Paráiso Perdido. Trad. por Antonio José Lima Leitão. Brazil, n. d.

The Shorter Poems

1025 John Milton. Lycidas. Trans., notes, and introd. by Amina Mastrostefano. Ascoli Piceno: E. Tassi, 1930. 65pp.

1026 Les Sonnets anglais et italiens de Milton. Traduits en sonnets francais et commentés par E. Saillens. Paris: Fischbacher, 1930. 79pp.
Rev: Paul Chauvet, RA-A, 9, 1932, 336.

1027 Milton: l'Allegro, il Penseroso et Samson Agonistes. Tr. avec une introd. par Floris Delattre. Paris: Aubier, 1937. xcii, 151pp. Reprinted, 1945.
Rev: Paul Dottin, ESt., 72, 1937, 107; Emile Legouis, EA, 1, 1937, 252-3; W. Fischer, Ang. Bbl., 49, 1938, 264.

1028 Milton. Liriche e drammi. Trans. and ed. by Alberto Castelli. Milan: Montuoro, 1941. 228pp.
Includes several sonnets, Samson Agonistes, Lycidas, L'Allegro, and Il Penseroso.

1029 John Milton. Sansone Agonista. A Cura di Marco Lombardi. Milan: Bompiani, 1943. 186pp. Reprinted, 1945.
Also includes translations of Comus and the Italian sonnets. Appendix: I versi italiani di Milton.

1030 Milton. L'Allegro-Il Pensieroso. A cura di Lauro Roberti-Fletcher. Florence: Fussi, 1946. 51pp.

1031 Milton. Sinson der Kampfer. Trans by H. Ulrich and ed. by R. Schneider. Freiburg, 1947.

1032 John Milton. Ode alla Nativita, ad un concerto sacro, Allegro, Penseroso, Arcadi, Como, Licida. Versione col testo a fronte, introduzione e note a cura di Carlo Izzo. Florence: G. C. Sansoni, 1948. xli, 272pp.

1033 John Milton. Sansone agonista, Sonetti. Versione col testo a fronte, introduzione e note a cura di Carlo Izzo. Florence: G. C. Sansoni, 1948. xxxiv, 250pp.

1034 John Milton. Shimson Ha-Gibbor. Trans. by Reuven Avinoam. Tel-Aviv: Massada, 1950.

1035 John Milton. Le Paradis reconquis, Étude critique. Traduction et notes par Jacques Blondel. Paris: Aubier, 1955. 270pp.
Rev: M. Y. Hughes, MLN, 71, 1956, 602-3.

1036 John Milton. Sámson. Trans. by Tihamer Dybas. Budapest: Uj Magyar Kiado, 1955. 111pp. Illus.

1037 John Milton. Ode sur la Nativité. Trans. by Claude Summer. Addis Abada, Ethiopia: University College Press, 1956. 25pp.

Areopagitica

1038 A Translation of Milton's Areopagitica. By Humphrey Lunch. Gaitsford Prize for Greek Prose. Oxford: Blackwell, 1932. 8pp.

1039 John Milton. Areopagitica. Traduzione e prefacione di S. Breglia. Bari: Laterza, 1933. xxxii, 134pp.
Rev: TLS, Feb. 2, 1933, p. 76; Nuova Riv. storica, 17, 1933, 579-80.

1040 John Milton. Om Trykkafrihed. Areopagitica. Trans. by A. C. Krebs. Copenhagen: Berlingske Forlag, 1936.

1041 John Milton. Areopagitica, traducción y prólogo de José Carner. Mexico City: Fondo de cultura economica, 1941. 104pp.
"Primera edicion espaniola, 1941."

1042 John Milton. Areopagitica. Trans. by E. Ganzmann. Basel, 1944.

1043 John Milton. Areopagitica. Rede für die Pressfreiheit und gegen die Zensur. Paris: Aubier, 1945.

1044 John Milton. Shuppan No Jiyû. Trans. by Mitsuo Umezkai et al. Tokyo: Kawade shobô, 1955. 382pp. Illus.
Also contains selections from Locke and Hume and an introduction.

1045 Milton: Areopagitica pour la Liberté d'Imprimer sans Autorisation ni Censure. Ed. and trans. with notes by O. Lutaud. Collection Bilingue des Classiques Etrangers. Paris: Aubier, 1956.

GENERAL CRITICISM

1046 ADAMS, ROBERT M. Empson and Bentley: Something About Milton Too. PR, 21, 1954, 178-89.
Concerning Empson's remarks in Some Versions of Pastoral.

1047 ------. Ikon: John Milton and the Modern Critics. Ithaca: Cornell University Press, 1955. xvii, 231pp.
Intends to clear away some modern misconceptions of Milton. Chapters include Reading Comus, The Devil and Doctor Jung, The Text of Paradise Lost, Empson and Bentley: Scherzo, Milton's Reading, Milton's Verse: Efforts at a Judgment, and Milton and Magnanimity. Chapters 1, 3, and 4, noted elsewhere, are reprints, in altered form, of previous articles.
Rev: Arnold Davenport, YWES, 159; R. O. Evans, SCN, 13, 1955, 41-2; Marvin Mudrick, Hudson Rev., 9, 1956, 126-33; C. M. Coffin, QQ, 63, 1956, 138-44; TLS, June 15, 1956, p. 362; F. T. Prince, RES, 8, 1957, 457-8; Frank Kermode, EIC, 7, 1957, 196-207.

1048 ADDINGTON, MARION H. Milton: Some Parallels. NQ, 164, 1933, 132-3.
The influence of Sylvester and Shakespeare.
Rev: L. C. Martin, YWES, 253.

1049 AGAR, HERBERT. Milton and Plato. Doctoral diss., Princeton University, 1928. Princeton: Princeton University Press, 1928; Oxford: Oxford University Press, 1931. 76pp.
Rev: F. S. Boas, YWES, 12, 1931, 206.

1050 ALDRIDGE, ALFRED O. Milton's and Pope's Conception of God and Man. BS, 96, 1939, 444-58.
"...Milton's approach to the problem of justifying God to man is theological, while Pope's is ethical."

1051 ALLEN, DON CAMERON. The Harmonious Vision: Studies in Milton's Poetry. Baltimore: Johns Hopkins Press, 1954. xx, 125pp.
"Milton, true son of Eve, expended the full powers of his life towards the recapture of the harmonious vision." Chapters include The Search for the Prophetic Strain: L'Allegro and Il Penseroso, The Higher Compromise: On the Morning of Christ's Nativity and A Mask, The Translation of a Myth: The Epicedia and Lycidas, the Idea as Pattern: Despair and Samson Agonistes. Description as Cosmos: The Visual Image in Paradise Lost, Realization and Climax: Paradise Regained.
Rev: Arnold Davenport, YWES, 137-8; Barbara Lpuini, Eng., 10, 1954, 105-6; R. Florence Brinkley, SAQ, 53, 1954, 598; Douglas Bush, MLN, 70, 1955, 58-60; Denis Saurat, EA, 8, 1955, 344-5; L. C. Martin, MLR, 50, 1955, 240-1; J. B. Broadbent, ES, 37, 1956, 276-7; J. C. Maxwell, RES, 7, 1956, 106-7.

1052 - - - - - -. Some Theories of the Growth and Origin of Language in Milton's Age. PQ, 28, 1949, 5-16.
Rev: L. C. Martin, YWES, 170-1.

1053 ALLEN, RALPH K. Milton's Creative Unitarianism. Doctoral diss., University of Washington, 1953. Abs., DA, 13, 1953, 791. Ann Arbor: U. M., 1953. 329pp.

1054 ANAND, MULK RAJ. The Example of Milton. Freedom of Expression. Ed. by Herman Ould (London: Hutchinson, 1945), pp. 142-51.
On Milton, liberty, and the Indian Revolution.

1055 ATKINS, JOHN W. The Last Phase: Jonson and Milton. English Literary Criticism: The Renascence (London: Methuen, 1947; 2nd Edition, New York: Barnes and Noble, 1952), pp. 312-42.
Considers Milton's remarks on rhetoric, the nature and function of poetry, the poet, rhyme, blank verse, and Greek tragedy.
Rev: F. S. Boas, YWES, 106-7; D. C. A(llen), MLN, 63, 1948, 508; E. H. W. Meyerstein, Eng., 7, 1948, 138-9; F. G. Mackarill, LL, 57, 1948, 268-72; G. D. Willcock, RES, 25, 1949, 70-1; M. T. Herrick, JEGP, 48, 1949, 286-9; H. S. Wilson, UTQ, 18, 1949, 402-5.

1056 BAKER, CHARLES E. Milton's Italian Relations. Doctoral diss., Cornell University, 1933. Abs., Ithaca: Cornell University Press, 1933. 3pp.

1057 BAKER, HERSCHEL. The Wars of Truth: Studies in the Decay of Humanism in the Earlier Seventeenth Century. London: Staples Press, 1952. Cambridge: Harvard University Press, 1952. xi, 390pp.
Milton discussed, passim, as the last great exemplar of Renaissance humanism in England.
Rev: Arnold Davenport, YWES, 162; TLS, Mar. 6, 1953, p. 157.

1058 - - - - - -. Where Liberty Lies: Freedom of Conscience in Milton's Day and in Ours. SWR, 41, 1956, 1-13.
On liberty and freedom as dominant themes in Milton's work.

1059 BARKER, ARTHUR E. Seven Types of Milton Criticism. UTQ, 25, 1956, 494-506.
A review of recent criticism.

1060 BARTHOLOMEW, RUTH. Some Sources of Milton's Doctrine of Free Will. Doctoral diss., Western Reserve University, 1945.

1061 BASTIAN, MARGARETHE. Das Problem der Versuchung bei Milton. Doctoral diss., Marburg, 1930. Marburg: Franz Fischer, 1930. 78pp.

1062 BATESON, F. W. Milton. NSN, Aug. 19, 1950, p. 181.
Animadversions on Rex Warner's review (NSN, Aug. 12, 1950, p. 181) of his English Poetry, A Critical Introduction. Defends his comments on Milton.

1063 BATTENHOUSE, HENRY M. Milton. Poets of Christian Thought: Evaluations from Dante to T. S. Eliot (New York: Ronald Press, 1947), pp. 44-62.
A rather sentimental, Victorian interpretation.

1064 BAUGH, ALBERT C., ed. A Literary History of England. New York: Appleton-Century-Crofts, 1950.
Contains three chapters on Milton, written by Tucker Brooke: Milton, The Last Elizabethan, pp. 673-80; Milton's Latin Poems and Prose Works, pp. 681-88; Milton in the Restorian, pp. 689-98.
Rev: De Lancey Ferguson, NYHTBR, May 2, 1948, p. 11; Charles Duffy, NYTBR, May 23, 1948, p. 25; TLS, Mar. 26, 1949, p. 202; J. J. Parry, JEGP, 48, 1949, 147-9; René Wellek, MP, 47, 1949, 39-45.

1065 BENTLEY, J. A. Undergraduate Disparagement of Milton. DR, 26, 1945-46, 421-32.
Deplores the present neglect of Milton.

1066 BETHELL, S. L. The Cultural Revolution of the Seventeenth Century. London: Denis Dobson, 1951. 161pp.
Passim.
Rev: Arnold Davenport, YWES, 170.

1067 - - - - - -. Essays on Literary Criticism and the English Tradition. London: Denis Dobson, 1948.
Classifies poetry as the Shakespeare-Donne type and the Spenser-Milton-Tennyson type.
Rev: Ethel Seaton, YWES, 20.

1068 BISHOP, SANFORD D. Milton's Attitude Toward Women. Master's thesis, Atlanta University, 1945.

1069 BITTING, MARY E. Contempt of the World in the Poetry of John Milton: A Study in Milton's Changing Personal and Artistic Emphases. Master's thesis, University of North Carolina, 1937.

1070 BLAKE, WILLIAM. Seconds livres prophetiques, contenant Milton. Trad. de l'anglais avec une introduction par Pierre Berger. Paris: Rieder, 1930. 256pp.
Rev: TLS, June 1, 1933, p. 376.

1071 BLISSETT, WILLIAM F. The Historical Imagination in the English Renaissance, Studied in Spenser and Milton. Doctoral diss., University of Toronto, 1950. Abs., University of Toronto...Final Oral Examinations for the Degree of Doctor of Philosophy, Session 1949-50.

1072 BRILL, MARY C. Milton and Ovid. Doctoral diss., Cornell University, 1935. Abs., Cornell University Abstracts of Dissertations. Ithaca: Cornell University Press, 1935. 6pp.

1073 BRINKLEY, ROBERTA F. Milton and the Arthurian Story. Arthurian Legend in the Seventeenth Century. Johns Hopkins Monographs in Literary History, 3 (Baltimore: Johns Hopkins University Press, 1932), pp. 126-41.
> Rev: TLS, July 21, 1932, pp. 521-2; A. G. van Kranendonk, ES, 15, 1933, 69-71; J. J. Parry, MLN, 48, 1933, 267-8; C. B. Millican, RES, 10, 1934, 101-2; H. Marcus, Ang. Bbl., 45, 1934, 50-2.

1074 BROADBENT, J. B. Links Between Poetry and Prose in Milton. ES, 37, 1956, 49-62.
> In his poetry, Milton often repeats ideas that he has stated in the prose. "A knowledge of the repetitions will occasionally help us to elucidate a passage in the poems by reference to the prose...."

1075 BROADUS, EDMUND K. John Milton and the Puritans. The Story of English Literature (Revised Edition. New York: Macmillan, 1931), pp. 196-228.
> Rev: TLS, April 28, 1932, 314; G. H. C., QQ, 39, 1932, 572-4.

1076 BRODRIBB, C. W. Milton and Buchanan. NQ, 158, 1930, 185.
> Similarities between Buchanan's Latin poems and the poetry of Milton.

1077 - - - - - -. Milton and Two Latin Poets. NQ, 159, 1930, 129.
> Milton's indebtedness to Manlius and Statius.

1078 - - - - - -. Milton's Bellman. NQ, 182, 1942, 273.
> Dekker's Bell-man (1608) "bears very closely on Milton's words."

1079 BROOKS, CLEANTH. Milton and Critical Re-Estimates. PMLA, 66, 1951, 1045-54.
> A paper read before the Milton group of MLA, Dec. 28, 1950.
> Rev: Arnold Davenport, YWES, 184-5.

1080 ------. Milton and the New Criticism. SR, 59, 1951, 1-22.
Milton not radically different from Donne in his use of metaphor.
Rev: Arnold Davenport, YWES, 185.

1081 BROWN, CALVIN S. Music and Literature. A Comparison of the Arts. Athens: University of Georgia Press, 1948. xi, 287pp.
Considers the influence of music on Milton's poetry.
Rev: Ethel Seaton, YWES, 11.

1082 BROWN, STUART G. A Note on Poetry and Prophecy. SR, 49, 1941, 107-15.
Remarks on Grierson's concept of prophetic poetry in his Milton and Wordsworth.

1083 BRUNNER, HILDEGARDE. Miltons persönliche und ideelle Welt in ihrer Beziehung zum Aristokratismus. Bonner Studien zur engl. Philologie, 19. Bonn: Hanstein, 1933. 50pp.
Rev: W. Milch, Die Literatur, 36, 1933, 52; Lit. Zentralblatt, 84, 1933, 694; A. Brandl, Archiv, 164, 1933, 135; Paul Chauvet, RA-A, 11, 1934, 256-7; G.-K. Bauer, GRM, 22, 1934, 249-50. H. F. F(letcher), JEGP, 33, 1934, 338; J. H. Hanford, MLN, 51, 1936, 53-4; W. Schmidt, Literaturblatt, 57, 1936, 34-5.

1084 BRYANT, JOSEPH A., JR. The Evolution of Milton's Conception of History. Doctoral diss., Yale University, 1948.

1085 ------. Milton's Views on Universal and Civil Decay. SAMLA Studies in Milton (Gainesville: University of Florida Press, 1954), pp. 1-19.

1086 ------. A Note on Milton's Use of Machiavelli's Discorsi. MP, 47, 1950, 217-21.
Milton did not know Machiavelli's important critical writings until late in his career.
Rev: Arnold Davenport, YWES, 177.

1087 BURKE, KENNETH. Responses to Pressure. Poetry, 51, 1937-8, 37-42.
Review article on Grierson's Wordsworth and Milton.

1088 BUSH, DOUGLAS. Classical Influences in Renaissance Literature. Martin Classical Lectures, Oberlin College, 13. Cambridge: Harvard University Press, 1952. 60pp.
Passim.
Rev: Rudolf Gottfried, MLN, 68, 1953, 505-6; Northup Frye, RN, 6, 1953, 47-8; Hardin Craig, JEGP, 52, 1953, 255-6.

1089 - - - - - -. The Critical Significance of Biographical Evidence: John Milton. English Institute Essays, 1946, pp. 5-19.

Biographical evidence is often abused in the case of Milton, but often it is useful in re-creating circumstances of composition and in throwing light on the text.

1090 - - - - - -. Milton. English Literature in the Earlier Seventeenth Century. Oxford History of English Literature, 5. Edited by F. P. Wilson and Bonamy Dobreé (Oxford: Oxford University Press, 1945), 359-98.

Interprets Milton as a Christian humanist. Contains a Milton bibliography, pp. 567-71.
Rev: L. C. Martin, YWES, 132-4; Geoffrey Tillotson, Eng., 6, 1946, 28-30; DUJ, N. S., 7, 1946, 66-7; J. H. P. P., Libr., 5th Ser., 1, 1946, 79-81; C. J. Sisson, MLR, 41, 1946, 432-3; H. B. Charlton, MGW, 54, 1946, 49; H. J. C. Grierson, Spect., Jan. 18, 1946, p. 68; J. F. Macdonald, Canadian Forum, 26, 1946, 187; B. M., DR, 26, 1946, 387-8; C. R. T., QQ, 53, 1946, 397-9; ES, 27, 1946, 62; L. C. Martin, RES, 23, 1947, 167-9; M. E. Prior, MP, 45, 1947, 139-42; L. L. Martz, YR, 36, 1947, 568-70; H. F. Fletcher, JEGP, 46, 1947, 315-17; Rafael Koskimies, Eras., 1, 1947, 288-90; Arthur Barker, UTQ, 16, 1947, 206-10; S. C. Chew, NYHTBR, Mar. 30, 1947, p. 6; R. Kirk, MLQ, 9, 1948, 108-9; M. Y. Hughes, MLN, 63, 1948, 190-4.

1091 - - - - - -. English Poetry. The Main Currents from Chaucer to the Present. New York: Oxford University Press, 1952. 222pp.

Milton discussed, pp. 68-79.

1092 - - - - - -. Milton. Mythology and the Renaissance Tradition in English Poetry (Minneapolis: University of Minnesota Press; London: Oxford University Press, 1932), pp. 248-86. Reprinted, Library of Literary History and Criticism, No. 3, New York: Pageant Book Co., 1957.

Studies influences exerted by Ovid et al.

1093 - - - - - -. Notes on Milton's Classical Mythology. SP, 28, 1931, 259-72.

Rev: F. S. Boas, YWES, 206.

1094 - - - - - -. Milton. The Renaissance and English Humanism (Toronto: University of Toronto Press, 1939; reprinted, 1941), pp. 101-34.

Milton is the last great exponent of Christian humanism in its historical continuity.
Rev: W. G. Rice, UTQ, 9, 1940, 238-42; A. Walker, RES, 16, 1940, 337-8; R. V. Cram, Classical Weekly, 33, 1940, 212-13; TLS, Jan. 18, 1941, p. 32; B. E. C. Davis, MLR, 36, 1941, 256-8.

1095 - - - - - -. Science and English Poetry, a Historical Sketch,
1590-1950. The Patten Lectures, Indiana University,
1949. New York: Oxford University Press, 1950.
> Milton discussed in a chapter entitled The New Science and
> Seventeenth Century Poets, pp. 27-50.
> Rev: Geoffrey Bullough, YWES, 12-13.

1096 - - - - - -. Virgil and Milton. CJ, 47, 1952, 178-82, 203-4.

1097 BUTLER, P. R. Rivers of Milton and Spenser. QR, 291,
1953, 373-84.
> "Let rivers, then, and streams be our business, as two great
> poets mention them...."

1098 BUXTON, CHARLES R. Prophets of Heaven and Hell.
Virgil, Dante, Milton, Goethe. An Introductory Essay.
Cambridge: Cambridge University Press, 1945. xv, 115pp.
> Discusses, i. a., the poems as works of art, the historical
> value of the poems, the moral and intellectual effect of the
> poems, and the poems as documents expressing the basic
> ideas of Western civilization.
> Rev: L. C. Martin, YWES, 143; TLS, Aug. 25, 1945, p.
> 406; DUJ, 7, 1945, 31-2; NQ, 189, 1945, 131-2; V. de S.
> Pinto, Eng., 5, 1945, 207-10; A. D. Lindsay, MGW, Oct. 5,
> 1945, p. 178; B. Ifor Evans, CR, 159, 1946, 60-1; B. A.
> Wright, MLR, 41, 1946, 76-7; J. S. Collis, FR, 945, 1946,
> 146-7; L. C. Martin, RES, 22, 1946, 243-4.

1099 CAMPBELL, LILY B. The Christian Muse. HLB, No. 8,
1935, pp. 29-70.
> Milton represents the culmination of a movement which
> opposed the "paganizing and secularizing of literature
> throughout the Renaissance."
> Rev: L. C. Martin, YWES, 250.

1100 CANDY, HUGH C. H. Milton's Early Reading of Browne.
NQ, 158, 1930, 310-12.

1101 - - - - - -. Milton's Early Reading of Sylvester. NQ, 158,
1930, 93-5.

1102 CARTER, HELEN P. Milton's Attitude Toward Classical
Mythology and Philosophy. Master's thesis, University
of Alabama, 1941.

1103 CARVER, P. L. The Sources of Macaulay's Essay on
Milton. RES, 6, 1930, 49-62.
> Rev: H. J. C. Grierson and A. M. Clark, YWES, 222.

1104 CAWLEY, ROBERT R. Milton and the Literature of
Travel. Princeton Studies in English, 32. Princeton:
Princeton University Press, 1951.
> Rev: Arnold Davenport, YWES, 185; J. H. Hanford, YR,
> 41, 1951-2, 634-6; Allan Gilbert, SAQ, 51, 1952, 465-6;
> H. F. Fletcher, JEGP, 51, 1952, 294; A. I. Carlisle, RES,
> 4, 1953, 288-9; J. Blondel, EA, 6, 1953, 359-60.

1105 CHAFFURIN, LOUIS. Milton. Les Langues modernes, 36, 1938, 441-7.

1106 CHAMBERS, R. W. Poets and Their Critics: Langland and Milton. Warton Lecture on English Poetry. Proceedings of the British Academy, 27, London: Milford, 1942. 48pp.
Rev: TLS, Aug. 22, 1942, p. 419; William R. Parker, MLN, 59, 1944, 205-6.

1107 CHESTERTON, GILBERT K. Milton and Merry England. The Man Who Was Chesterton. Comp. and ed. by R. T. Bond (New York: Dodd, 1937), 631-46.
Reprint of Stevens' No. 2482. Discusses Milton's grand style.

1108 ------. Taste for Milton. Handful of Authors (New York: Sheed and Ward, 1953), pp. 75-7.
A reprint of an 1908 essay, apparently unnoticed by Stevens or Fletcher.

1109 CHEW, AUDREY. Joseph Hall and John Milton. ELH, 17, 1950, 274-95. Published also in pamphlet form.
Similarities and differences in ideas.
Rev: Arnold Davenport, YWES, 169.

1110 CHRISTENSEN, PARLEY A. On Liberty in Our Time. Milton and Mill. WHR, 6, 1952, 110-18.

1111 CLARK, EVERT M. Milton and the Warfare of Peace, SAQ, 45, 1946, 195-208.
Milton long ago realized that the ultimate guarantees of world peace are neither political nor military but moral.

1112 ------. Milton's English Poetical Vocabulary. SP, 53, 1956, 220-38.
On the size and origins of Milton's vocabulary.

1113 CLARK, G. N. The Seventeenth Century. Oxford: Oxford University Press, 1929. 384pp.
Passim.

1114 COHEN, WILLIAM H. Romantic Criticism of Milton. Master's thesis, University of Florida, 1954.

1115 COLERIDGE, SAMUEL T. Coleridge on the Seventeenth Century. Ed. by Roberta F. Brinkley. Introd. by Louis I. Bredvold. Durham: Duke University Press, 1955.
Reproduces Coleridge's lectures, comments, and marginalia on Milton, passim, but there are two main chapters: Milton/Prose, pp. 471-3; Milton/Poetry, pp. 541-611.
Rev: J. M. Raines, BA, 30, 1956, 89; Lucyle Werkmeister, Pers., 37, 1956, 314-15; Roland M. Frye, SAB, 22, 1956, 14-15; George Whalley, UTQ, 25, 1956, 259-62; G. B. Evans, JEGP, 55, 1956, 337-8.

1116 COLIN CLOUT. Milton's "Two Men I Honour...." NQ, 185, 1943, 45.
Reproduces a letter to Benedetto Buonmattei dated Sept. 10, 1638, expressive of Milton's interest in the purity of the mother tongue.

1117 CONDEE, RALPH W. The Formalized Openings of Milton's Epic Poems. JEGP, 50, 1951, 502-8.
Analysis indicative of Milton's attempt to imitate both Homer and Virgil.

1118 CONIBEAR, MABEL RUTH. Milton's Attitude Toward the Bible as Reflected in His Poetry and Prose Works, and in His Letters. Master's thesis, Alberta University, 1932. 260pp.

1119 CONKLIN, GEORGE N. Biblical Criticism and Heresy in Milton. New York: King's Crown Press, 1949.
Rev: L. C. Martin, YWES, 165; H. F. Fletcher, JEGP, 49, 1950, 254-5; W. S. Hudson, Rev. of Religion, 15, 1950, 60-2; T. S. K. Scott-Craig, MLN, 65, 1950, 567-8; C. Smyth, CQR, 150, 1950, 266-8; E. L. Allen, RES, 2, 1951, 281-2.

1120 COOPER, LANE. Abyssinian Paradise in Coleridge and Milton. Late Harvest (Ithaca: Cornell University Press, 1952), pp. 59-64.
Milton's and Coleridge's use of Purchas' Pilgrimage (1617). Reprint of Stevens' No. 2268.

1121 CORMICAN, L. A. Milton's Religious Verse. Guide to English Literature, 3, 1956, 173-92.

1122 CRAIG, HARDIN, ed. A. History of English Literature. New York: Oxford University Press, 1950.
Milton discussed, pp. 322-39.

1123 CRAMER, MARJORIE LEE. Milton and the Levellers. Master's thesis, Dalhousie University, 1945, 74pp.

1124 CRINO, ANNA MARIA. Le Opere di Milton a Firenze nel Seicento. Italia, 28, 1951, 108-10.

1125 CURRY, WALTER C. Milton's Dual Concept of God as Related to Creation. SP, 47, 1950, 190-210.
Rev: Arnold Davenport, YWES, 179-80.

1126 ------. Milton's Ontology, Cosmogony, and Physics. Lexington: University of Kentucky Press, 1957. 226pp.
Chapters: Milton's Dual Concept of God as Related to Creation; Milton's Chaos and Old Night; The Consistence and Qualities of Chaos; The Genesis of Milton's World; The Lordship of Milton's Sun; Some Travels of Satan and the Road to Hell; Milton's Scale of Nature. Appendix:

Milton's Light Exhaling from Darkness: A Study in Symbols. The Lordship of Milton's Sun and the appendix are here printed for the first time; the other chapters are revisions of earlier articles.
Rev: W. B. Hunter, Jr., SCN, 15, 1957, 29.

1127 DAMBRIN, M. L'Art de Milton. Diss. in progress, Paris, 1938.

1128 DANE, NATHAN. Milton's Callimachus. MLN, 56, 1941, 278-9.
Milton used a 1514 text.

1129 DANIELLS, ROY. Baroque Form in English Literature. UTQ, 14, 1945, 393-408.
Milton, pp. 406-8. The recognition of a baroque period might be the means of establishing the unity of seventeenth-century literature.

1130 D(AVENPORT), A(RNOLD). Possible Echoes from Sidney's Arcadia in Shakespeare, Milton, and Others. NQ, 194, 1949, 554-5.

1131 DAWSON, GRACE G. Milton's Conception of Woman. Master's thesis, University of South Carolina, 1937.

1132 DE SELINCOURT, ERNEST, ed. Milton. English Poets and the National Ideal (Oxford: Clarendon Press, 1940), pp. 34-60.
Milton and liberty. A reprint of a 1915 essay.

1133 DE SOET, F. D. Puritan and Royalist Literature in the Seventeenth Century. Doctoral diss., Amsterdam, 1932. Amsterdam: Gedrukt, 1932. 163pp.
Milton discussed, pp. 10-56. Concerned with Milton's political and religious views.

1134 DICKSON, DAVID W. D. Milton's Use of Light. Doctoral diss., Harvard University, 1949.

1135 DIEKHOFF, JOHN S. Critical Activity of the Poetic Mind: John Milton. PMLA, 55, 1940, 748-72.
On Milton's method of composition. Points up the consciousness of the poet's artistry.

1136 ------. Milton's Craftsmanship as Revealed by the Revisions of the Poems of the Trinity College Manuscript. Doctoral diss., Western Reserve University, 1937.

1137 DOBRÈE, BONAMY. Milton and Dryden: A Comparison and Contrast in Poetic Ideas and in Poetic Method. ELH, 3, 1936, 83-100.
Printed also in the Johns Hopkins Alumni Magazine, 25, 1937, 125-44.

1138 DUBBELL, S. EARL. Leisure at Horton. SAQ, 36, 1937, 163-70.
    On the benefits of a retirement such as Milton's.

1139 DURRETT, R. W. Do the Epic Poets Reveal Themselves to Us by Their Failures? CJ, 25, 1930, 500-6.
    Milton failed to some extent, but "the good in him far outweighs the bad."

1140 DWORSKY, BESA R. Milton and the Rabbinical Bible. TLS, Apr. 25, 1935, p. 272.
    Reply by Theodor Gaster, ibid., May 9, 1935, p. 301.
    Rev: L. C. Martin, YWES, 256.

1141 EASTLAND, ELIZABETH W. Milton's Ethics. Doctoral diss., Vanderbilt University, 1941. Abs., Bull. of Vanderbilt University, 41, No. 10, 1941, 17-19. Published in summary form, Nashville: Vanderbilt University Press, 1946.

1142 EASTMAN, FRED. John Milton. Men of Power: Sixty Minute Biographies (Nashville: Cokesbury Press, 1938), 2, 137-84.

1143 EGLE, A. Milton und Italien. Doctoral diss., Freiburg im Breisgau, 1940, 147pp.

1144 EISIG, K. T. Moral Criteria in Renaissance Literary Criticism, with Special Reference to Milton. Master's thesis, University of London, 1952.

1145 ELIOT, T. S. Milton. Annual Lecture on a Master Mind. Henriette Hertz Trust of the British Academy. Oxford: Oxford University Press, 1947. 19pp. Reprinted in SR, 56, 1948, 185-209, and in On Poetry and Poets (London: Faber, 1957), pp. 165-83.
    Still does not like Milton the man but retracts somewhat from his 1936 position that Milton's influence has been bad.
    Rev: L. C. Martin, YWES, 185-6; TLS, Dec. 13, 1947, p. 65; Desmond McCarthy, Sun. Times, Nov. 9, 1947, p. 3; B. A. Wright, MLR, 43, 1948, 530-2; W. Weintraub, Kultura, 4, 1948, 129-31.

1146 ------. A Note on the Verse of John Milton. E&S, 21, 1936, 32-40. Reprinted in On Poetry and Poets (London: Faber, 1957), pp. 156-64.
    Milton's rhetoric is "not necessarily bad in itself" but "is likely to be bad in its influence; and it may be considered bad in religion to the historical life of a language as a whole."
    Rev: L. C. Martin, YWES, 187-8.

1147 ------. What is a Classic? London: Faber, 1945. 32pp.
> An address delivered before the Virgil Society on Oct. 16,
> 1944. Argues that Milton's style is not a classic style because
> "it is a style of a language still in formation, the style of a
> writer whose masters were not English, but Latin and to a
> less degree Greek."

1148 ELLIOTT, G. R. Milton and Miss Moore. SRL, 6, 1929, 30.
> Disparages Miss Moore's romantic notions of Milton made
> in her criticism of his review of Spurgeon's Keats's Shake-
> speare (SRL, 5, 1929, 1105).

1149 ------. Milton and the Present State of Poetry. The
Cycle of Modern Poetry (Princeton: Princeton University Press; London: Milford, 1929), pp. 135-94.
> Milton should be our guide in the development of modern
> poetry.
> Rev: TLS, June 20, 1929, p. 491; Norman Foerster, AL,
> 1, 1929, 331-4, and AB, 70, 1929, 214-15; H. H. Clark,
> SRL, Aug. 17, 1929, p. 52; Irving Babbitt, Forum, 82, Oct.,
> 1929, xviii, xx, xxii, xxiv.

1150 ------. Revival of the Poet of Hope. AB, 72, 1930, 341-9.
> Milton the greatest poet of human hope in English and
> perhaps in all secular literature.

1151 EMPSON, WILLIAM. Milton and Bentley. Some Versions
of Pastoral (London: Chatto and Windus, 1935), pp.
149-94.
> Uses Bentley's criticism of Paradise Lost as a springboard
> for his own remarks on the poetry.
> Rev: TLS, Nov. 30, 1935, p. 798; reply by Empson, ibid.,
> Dec. 7, 1935, p. 838; D. Hawkins, Spect., Nov. 15, 1935,
> p. 828.

1152 FERRAÙ, ANTONIO. Milton rivoluzionario. Rassegna
italiana, 34, 1933, 716-22.

1153 FINDLEY, MARGARET K. Women in Milton's Writings
and in His Life. Master's thesis, University of Pittsburgh,
1931. Abs., University of Pittsburgh Bull., 28, 1931, 334.

1154 FINK, ZERA S. Milton and the Theory of Climatic
Influence. MLQ, 2, 1941, 67-80.

1155 ------. The Theory of the Mixed State and the Development of Milton's Political Thought. PMLA, 57, 1942,
705-36.
> Emphasizes Milton's belief in the superiority of the mixed
> state.
> Rev: L. C. Martin, YWES, 159.

1156 ------. Milton's Retirement to Horton and Renaissance
Literary Theory. ES, 22, 1940, 137-8.

1157 ------. Immortal Government: The Free Commonwealth. The Classical Republicans (Evanston: Northwestern University Press, 1945), pp. 90-122.
An account of Milton's efforts to achieve a mixed state in England.

1158 FIORE, AMADEUS P., O. F. M. The Problem of 17th-Century Soteriology in Reference to Milton. FS, 15, 1955, 48-59, 257-82.
Considers the redemptive element in De Doctrina Christiana, Paradise Lost, and Paradise Regained in relation to the Renaissance milieu.

1159 FISHER, PETER F. Milton's Theodicy. JHI, 17, 1956, 28-53.
Milton's theory concerning matter.

1160 FISHER-SHORT, W. John Milton and the Problems of Literary Criticism—an Examination of Some Twentieth-Century Critics of Milton. Master's thesis, Manchester University, 1952.

1161 FLETCHER, HARRIS F. Milton's Copy of Gesner's Heraclides, 1544. JEGP, 47, 1948, 182-87.

1162 ------. Milton's Homer. JEGP, 38, 1939, 229-32.
The 1560 edition by Eustathius.

1163 ------. Milton (Index Politicus)—The Theatrum Poetarum by Edward Phillips. JEGP, 55, 1956, 35-40.

1164 ------. Milton's Rabbinical Readings. Urbana: University of Illinois Press, 1930. 344pp.
Rev: H. J. C. Grierson and A. M. Clark, YWES, 226-7; TLS, Jan. 1, 1931, p. 14; J. A. Montgomery, JEGP, 30, 1931, 291-3; E. C. Baldwin, MLN, 66, 1931, 536-7; S. B. Liljegren, Ang. Bbl., 43, 1932, 373-7; Paul Chauvet, RA-A, 9, 1932, 240-1; G. W. Whiting, NQ, 162, 1932, 344-7; G. W. Whiting, RES, 8, 1932, 450-3; Zu Miltons rabbinischen Studien, Beiblatt, 44, 1933, 154-9.

1165 ------. Milton's Semitic Studies. Chicago: University of Chicago Press, 1926.
Rev: E. C. Greenlaw, MLN, 44, 1929, 263.

1166 FOERSTER, DONALD M. Homer, Milton, and the American Revolt Against Epic Poetry: 1812-1860. SP, 53, 1956, 75-100.

1167 FOGEL, EPHIM G. Milton and Sir Philip Sidney's Arcadia. NQ, 196, 1951, 115-17.
The Leonatus episode is the source of the first lines in Samson Agonistes. Milton's use of the passage illustrates his method of composition.

1168 FOSTER, WILLIAM. Milton and India. TLS, Apr. 6, 1933, p. 248.
Milton knew how to pronounce Indian names properly.
Rev: L. C. Martin, YWES, 253.

1169 FREEDMAN, MORRIS. A Note on Milton and Dryden as Satirists. NQ, N. S., 1, 1954, 26-7.
Points out neglected resemblances.

1170 ------. Milton and Dryden. Doctoral diss., Columbia University, 1953. Abs., DA, 14, 1954, 109. Ann Arbor: U. M., 1954. 203pp.

1171 FREITAG, WOLFGANG. Milton und seine Zeitgenossen in ihrem Verhaltnis zur Musik. Doctoral diss., Freiburg, 1949. 218pp.

1172 FRENCH, J. MILTON. Chips from Milton's Workshop. ELH, 10, 1943, 230-42.
Changes made by Milton in his workbook reveal his method of writing poetry.
Rev: L. C. Martin, YWES, 158.

1173 ------. John Milton's Songs of Experience. SCN, 15, 1957, 6-7.
A speech delivered before the Milton Society at its annual dinner on Dec. 28, 1956. Insists that Milton's life experiences contributed to the texture of Paradise Lost, Paradise Regained, and Samson Agonistes.

1174 ------. Milton's Annotated Copy of Gildas. Harvard Stud. and Notes, 20, 1938, 76-80.
Rev: L. C. Martin, YWES, 179.

1175 ------. Some Notes on Milton. NQ, 188, 1945, 52-5.
Discusses the following points: Milton's alleged misconduct in Italy, editions of Salmasius' Responsio, Salmasius' reward for writing his Responsio, the burning of Milton's Defensio abroad, Milton's connection with John Phillips' Responsio of 1652; Milton Taunted with Blindness, and the effect of Milton's Defensio on More.

1176 FRISSELL, HARRY L. Milton's Art of Logic and Ramist Logic in the Major Poems. Doctoral diss., Vanderbilt University, 1951. Abs., Bull. of Vanderbilt University, 51, 1951, 22-3. Ann Arbor: U. M., 1952. 250pp.

1177 FRYE, ROLAND M. Milton and the Modern Man. QR, 288, 1950, 373-9.
Suggests that we turn to Milton for strength and guidance.

1178 ------. The Teachings of Classical Puritanism on Conjugal Love. Stud. in the Renaissance (Ren. Soc. of America), 2, 1955, 148-59.

1179 GÄCKLE, OSKAR. Die unsichtbare Welt in Miltons Denken und ihre Wirkung auf seinen Freiheitsbegriff. Doctoral diss., Heidelberg, 1944. 208pp.

1180 GAINES, ERVIN J. Merchant and Poet: a Study of Seventeenth Century Influences. Doctoral diss., Columbia University, 1953. Abs., DA, 14, 1954, 110.
Considers Milton's anti-Utopian ideas.

1181 GASTER, THEODOR. Milton and the Rabbinical Bible. TLS, May 9, 1935, p. 301.
Rev: L. C. Martin, YWES, 256.

1182 GERRIETTS, JOHN S. A Study of the Imaginal Qualities of Poetry, Based on Descriptive Passages of Milton and Coleridge. Doctoral diss., Loyola University (Chicago), 1954.

1183 GIBBS, PAUL T. Milton's Use of the Law of Nature. Doctoral diss., University of Washington, 1938. Abs., University of Washington Abstracts of Theses, 3, 1938, 319-21.

1184 GILBERT, ALLAN H. Milton's Defense of Bawdry. SAMLA Studies in Milton (Gainesville: University of Florida Press, 1953), pp. 54-71.
Draws passages from many of Milton's works to illustrate the poet's attitude toward obscenity.

1185 ------. Some Critical Opinions on Milton. SP, 33, 1936, 523-33.
Discusses recent Milton scholarship.

1186 GOODE, JAMES. Milton and Longinus. TLS, Aug. 21, 1930, p. 668.

1187 GRAVES, ROBERT. The Ghost of Milton. The Common Asphodel: Collected Essays on Poetry, 1922-1949 (London: Hamish Hamilton, 1949), pp. 315-25.
"I have included 'The Ghost of Milton' as a minority report justifying my dismay at the recent revival of Milton-worship. To me, Milton has always been a monster and a renegade...."

1188 GRAY, F. CAMPBELL. Milton's Counterpoint: Classicism and Romanticism in the Poetry of John Milton. SR, 43, 1935, 134-45.

1189 GREENE, D. J. Sooth in Keats, Milton, Shakespeare, and Dr. Johnson. MLN, 65, 1950, 514-17.

1190 GRIERSON, SIR HERBERT J. C. Criticism and Creation: Essays and Addresses. London: Chatto and Windus, 1949.

Contains two articles on Milton: The Metaphysics of Donne and Milton, pp. 35-48; Milton and Political Liberty, pp. 71-94.
Rev: TLS, Feb. 17, 1950, p. 106; Janet Smith, NSN, Feb. 18, 1950, pp. 196, 198; M. H. M. MacKinnon, Canadian Forum, 30, 1950, 214.

1191 ------. John Milton: The Man and the Poet. Cross Currents in English Literature of the Seventeenth Century, or, the World, the Flesh, and the Spirit, Their Action and Relations. Being the Messenger Lectures on the Evolution of Civilization, Cornell University, 1926-27 (London: Chatto and Windus, 1929), pp. 232-73. See also passim.
Rev: Sherard Vines, Nat. and Athen., 46, Dec., 1929, 10, 252; Sat. Rev. 148, 1929, 680-2; TLS, Jan. 16, 1930, p. 41; G. Saintsbury, Bookman, 77, 1930, 330; J. S., Oxf. Mag., Feb. 6, 1930, p. 447; M. Praz, ES, 12, 1930, 117-19; W. K. Fleming, LL, 4, 1930, 133-41; Marjorie Nicolson, MLN, 46, 1931, 205-6; D. A. Roberts, SRL, 8, 1931, 218.

1192 ------. John Milton: l'homme et le poete. RA-A, 6, 1929, 19-36, 97-114.

1193 ------. Milton and Liberty, MLR, 39, 1944, 97-107.

1194 ------. Milton and Wordsworth: Poets and Prophets. A Study of Their Reactions to Political Events. Cambridge: Cambridge University Press; New York: Macmillan, 1937. x, 185pp.
Rev: TLS, Mar. 6, 1937, p. 167; NQ, 172, 1937, 252; E. G. G., CR, 151, 1937, 154-7; J. Kooistra, ES, 19, 1937, 122-5; B. de Selincourt, Obs., Mar. 7, 1937; E. Muir, Merc., 35, 1937, 83-4; E. Sackville-West, NSN, Jun. 5, 1937, p. 936; M. Praz, Crit., 17, 1937, 154-7; E. G. C., CW, 145, 1937, 752-3; P. Hutchinson, NYTBR, Jun. 20, 1937, p. 6; I. E., Jour. of Philosophy, 34, 1937, 639-40; C. A. Hawley, Unity, 120, 1937, 100; M. Van Doren, Nat., 145, 1937, 22-3; K. Burke, Poetry, 51, Oct., 1937, 37-42; QR, 268, 1937, 368; N. C. Smith, Eng., 1, 1937, 435; J. Veldkamp, Neophil., 23, 1937, 63-5; Emile Legouis, EA, 1, 1937, 330-1; E. C. Batho, MLR, 33, 1938, 70-1; D. Saurat, RES, 14, 1938, 225-8; reply by Grierson, ibid., 458-60; F. R. Leavis, Scr., 7, 1938, 104-14; H. F. B. B. - S., Oxf. Mag., Mar. 10, 1938, pp. 526-7; E. M. W. Tillyard, MLN, 53, 1938, 381-3; W. H., ELH, 5, 1938, 24; George Williamson, MP, 36, 1938, 77-9; W. Mann, Ang. Bbl., 50, 1939, 206-9; S. G. Brown, SR, 49, 1941, 107-15.

1195 ------, and J. C. SMITH. Milton. A Critical History of English Poetry (London: Chatto and Windus, 1944. New York: Oxford University Press, 1946), pp. 172-86.
Rev: Gwyn Jones, LL, 43, 1944, 170, 172, 174; TLS, Dec. 2, 1944, pp. 582-3; Raymond Mortimer, NSN, Nov. 11, 1944, pp. 324-5; Sheila Shannon, Spect., Nov. 24, 1944, pp. 484,

486; B. I. Evans, MGW, Feb. 23, 1945, p. 107; Herman Peschmann, Eng., 5, 1945, 192; Babette Deutsch, NYHBTR, Dec. 1, 1946, p. 46; Leonard Bacon, SRL, Dec. 7, 1946, p. 70; F. A. Pottle, YR, 36, 1947, 731-4; D. C. A(llen), MLN, 62, 1947, 360; Earl Daniels, CE, 8, 1947, 443-4.

1196 GUIDI, AUGUSTO. La Figure di Cristo nel poema di Milton. Humanitas, 1, 1946, 403-6.
From the Nativity Ode to Samson Agonistes.

1197 ------. John Milton. Brescia: Morcelleana, 1940. 195pp.
Topics: Poesie giovanili, Il Paradiso Perduto, Le ultime opere.

1198 GULLETTE, GEORGE A. Methodology in Milton's Source Studies. Doctoral diss., University of Michigan, 1945. Abs., DA, 6, No. 2, 1945, 53-5. Ann Arbor: U. M., 1945. 279pp.

1199 ------. Some Inadequacies of Method in the Study of Milton's Sources. Papers Mich. Acad., 32, 1948 for 1946, 447-56.
Reply by Arnold Williams, ibid., p. 707.

1200 HALLECK, REUBEN P. John Milton. The Story of English Literature. Revised Edition (New York: American Book Co., 1937), pp. 238-52.

1201 HALLER, WILLIAM. The Future of Milton Studies. SCN, 15, 1957, 5-6.
A speech delivered before the Milton Society at its annual dinner on Dec. 28, 1956.

1202 ------. Hail Wedded Love. ELH, 13, 1946, 79-97.
The background of Milton's ideas concerning marriage and divorce.
Rev: L. C. Martin, YWES, 171.

1203 ------. Poet of the Devil's Party, and God's. SRL, 32, Nov. 19, 1949, p. 22.
Review article of Hanford's John Milton, Englishman.

1204 HANFORD, JAMES H. A Milton Handbook. New York: Appleton-Century-Crofts, 1926. x, 304pp. Revised Edition, 1933. Third Edition, 1939. Fourth Edition, 1946. Reprinted, 1954.
Chapters: Materials for Milton's Biography, The Prose Works, The Minor Poems, Paradise Lost, Paradise Regained and Samson Agonistes, Milton's Style and Versification, Milton's Fame and Influence. Appendices: Milton and the Universities, Milton's "Biographia Literaria," The Milton Portraits, Milton's Private Library, Milton and His Printers, Milton in Italy. There is a bibliography, pp. 421-48, Fourth Edition.

Rev: L. C. Martin, YWES, 14, 1933, 169; Commonweal, 17, 1933, 588; W. Fischer, Ang. Bbl., 46, 1935, 243-4; W. R. Parker, MLN, 56, 1941, 392-3; L. C. Martin, YWES, 27, 1946, 169.

1205 ------. Milton in Current Criticism. EJ, 28, 1939, 342-8.
Discusses the criticism of Eliot, Grierson, Tillyard, Haller, and others.

1206 ------. That Shepherd Who First Taught the Chosen Seed: A Note on Milton's Mosaic Inspiration. UTQ, 8, 1939, 403-19.
On Milton's belief in his divine inspiration.
Rev: L. C. Martin, YWES, 114.

1207 HARASHIMA, YOSHIMORI. Milton's Taste and Doctrine of Music. Stud. in Eng. Lit. (Eng. Lit. Soc. Japan), 18, 1938, 531-43.
Milton and music and Milton's views on the celestial harmony.

1208 HARBESON, GERALDINE M. Nature in the Poetry of Milton and Spenser. Master's thesis, Florida State College for Women, 1944.

1209 HARDELAND, GERTRUD. Miltons Anschauungen von Staat, Kirche, Toleranz. Doctoral diss., Göttingen, 1934. Studien zur englischen Philologie, 81. Halle: Niemeyer, 1934. 175pp.
Rev: H. Scherpbier, ES, 16, 1934, 224-6; W. F. Schirmer, Dt. Litzt, 55, 1934, 2180-2; A. B(randl), Archiv, 166, 1934, 139; H. F. Fletcher, JEGP, 34, 1935, 120-1; H. O. Wilde, Ang. Bbl., 46, 1935, 240; L. C. Martin, YWES, 238-9; D. Saurat, MLN, 51, 1936, 263-4; W. Schmidt, LGRP, 57, 1936, 35-6; A. Koszul, RC, 69, 1936, 211-12.

1210 HARDING, DAVIS P. Milton and Ovid: A Study of the Influence of Ovid and his Renaissance Editors and Commentators on Milton's Poetry. Doctoral diss., University of Illinois, 1943. Published as Milton and the Renaissance Ovid. University of Illinois Studies in Lang. and Lit., 30, No. 4. Urbana: University of Illinois Press, 1946. 105pp.
Rev: L. C. Martin, YWES, 169-70; Michael Krouse, MLN, 62, 1947, 135-8; Douglas Bush, CP, 62, 1947, 132-3; A. M. Clark, CR, 61, 1948, 128-9; A. N. Jeffares, ES, 27, 1948, 182-5; M. Y. Hughes, MLQ, 10, 1949, 113-15.

1211 HARDY, J. E. Critical Pretense. SR, 62, 1954, 509-19.
A review article of Stein's Answerable Style.
"...we begin to get, in this book, a Milton criticism to match the new Milton influence."

1212 HARRIS, VICTOR. All Coherence Gone. Chicago: University of Chicago Press, 1949.
    Concerned with the controversy on the decay of nature. Milton's views discussed, pp. 160-3.

1213 HARRISON, T. P. They Tell of Birds: Chaucer, Spenser, Milton, Drayton. Austin: University of Texas Press, 1956. xviii, 159pp.
    Milton, pp. 85-108. Concludes that "for Milton the bird world was largely useful in providing symbols of despicable human beings."

1214 HAUG, RALPH A. Milton and Archbishop Ussher. NQ, 185, 1943, 66-7.
    Evidence shows that Ussher was unaware of the tracts Milton wrote against him. Replies by E. H. Visiak, ibid., p. 146, and T. O. M(abbott), ibid., pp. 293-4.
    Rev: L. C. Martin, YWES, 153.

1215 HAVILAND, THOMAS P. John Milton—Religious Liberal. Christian Register, 118, 1939, 261-3.

1216 HEINRICH, HELLMUT. John Miltons kirchenpolitik, puritanische ideen zum problem staat und kirche. Berlin: Junker and Dünnhaupt, 1942. 132pp.

1217 HENRY, NATHANIEL H. Milton and Hobbes: Mortalism and the Intermediate State. SP, 48, 1951, 234-49.
    Milton's mortalism in the Socinian tradition.
    Rev: Arnold Davenport, YWES, 187.

1218 ------. Milton's Official Translations. TLS, Aug. 17, 1933, p. 549.
    Rev: L. C. Martin, YWES, 252.

1219 ------. Milton's Puritanism: A Study of the Theological Implications of his Thought. Doctoral diss., University of North Carolina, 1942. Abs., University of North Carolina Record, Research in Progress, No. 383, 1942, pp. 74-5.

1220 HESSE, ERNST. John Miltons mystisch-theistisches Weltbild. Mit ein anh.: Miltons Gedanken über Jugenderziehung. Doctoral diss., Leipzig, 1934. Dresden: Gittel, 1934. 64pp.
    Summaries the sources and the nature of Milton's ideas.
    Rev: Lit. Zentralblatt, 85, 1934, 1135.

1221 HESSELBERG, ARTHUR K. A Comparative Study of the Theories of Ludovicus Molina, S. J., and John Milton. Doctoral diss., Catholic University, 1952. Abs., Catholic University Studies in Politics, Government, and International Law, Abstract Series, 2. Washington: Catholic University Press, 1952. 26pp.

1222 HIBBITTS, JOHN B. Milton's Heresy. Master's thesis, Dalhousie University, 1946. 204pp.

1223 HIGHET, GILBERT. The Classical Tradition. Greek and Roman Influences on Western Literature. New York: Oxford University Press; Oxford: Clarendon Press, 1949. xxxviii, 763pp.
   Almost all of Milton's works discussed, passim, in the light of the classical background.
   Rev: H. W. Garrod, Spect., Sept. 30, 1949, pp. 424, 426; G. F. Whicher, NYHTBR, Dec. 18, 1949, p. 7; TLS, Jan. 6, 1950, p. 12; F. C. G., Anglican Theological Rev., 32, 1950, 244; F. M. Cambellack, CL, 2, 1950, 376-9; A. C., Dublin Mag., 25, 1950, 2, 44-6; G. Romilly, NSN, Feb. 11, 1950, pp. 171-2; C. A. Robinson, Jr., SRL, Mar. 4, 1950, p. 21.

1224 HINDLEY, DOUGLAS. Milton and Christian Humanism. Doctoral diss., Stanford University, 1950. Abs., Abstracts of Diss., Stanford University, 25, 1950, 130-3.

1225 HINES, MARY M. Literary and Philosophical Aspects of the Theme of Good and Evil in Milton's Poetry. Master's thesis, University of North Carolina, 1941.

1226 HIRSCH, FRANZ. Die Rolle der klassischen Mythologie in der geistigen Entwicklung Miltons. Doctoral diss., Wien, 1944. 107pp.

1227 HOVEY, R. BENNETT. Milton's Attitude Toward Science. Isis, 35, 1944, 32.

1228 HOWARTH, R. G. Milton and Camoens. Southerly (Sidney, Australia), 11, 1950, 57-8.
   Believes that Milton could have read Camoens in the original.

1229 HUGHES, MERRITT Y. A Meditation on Literary Blasphemy. JAAC, 14, 1955, 106-15.
   Attacks on Shakespeare and Milton.

1230 ------. Milton and the Sense of Glory. PQ, 28, 1949, 107-24.
   Rev: L. C. Martin, YWES, 169.

1231 ------. Studies in Milton. Doctoral diss., Edinburgh University, 1951.

1232 HUNT, E. L. Reading for Honors and Common Sense. School and Society, 42, 1935, 726-32.
   Milton's writings on education from the standpoint of practical citizenship.

1233 HUNTER, WILLIAM B., JR. Milton and Thrice Great Hermes. JEGP, 45, 1946, 327-36.
   On Milton's conception of the life principle.
   Rev: L. C. Martin, YWES, 174.

1234 ------. Milton on the Nature of Man; a Study in Late Renaissance Psychology. Doctoral diss., Vanderbilt University, 1946. Abs., Bull. of Vanderbilt University, 47, No. 11, 1947, 13-14. Summary, Nashville: Joint University Libraries, 1946. 33pp.

1235 ------. Milton's Materialistic Life Principle. JEGP, 45, 1946, 68-76.
> The life principle inherent in the sun as the source of all life-giving energy.
> Rev: L. C. Martin, YWES, 174.

1236 ------. Milton's Power of Matter. JHI, 13, 1952, 551-62.
> Milton's theory Aristotelian, not Augustinian.

1237 ------. New Words in Milton's English Poems. Essays in Honor of W. C. Curry (Nashville: Vanderbilt University Press, 1954), pp. 241-59.
> Contrary to accepted opinion, Milton "has enriched our vocabulary in a number of ways."

1238 IGLESIAS, ANTONIO. An Open Letter to Milton— Formidable Pamphleteer. SRL, Aug. 23, 1952, pp. 20-1, 33-4.
> Relates Milton's efforts to achieve liberty to the recent struggle of liberals against the "professed defenders of personal freedom."

1239 JEFFREY, LLOYD N. Virgil and Milton. Class. Outlook, 31, 1954, 69-70.

1240 JONAS, LEAH. John Milton. Divine Science: The Aesthetic of Some Representative Seventeenth-Century English Poets. Columbia University Stud. in Eng. and Comp. Lit., 151 (New York: Columbia University Press, 1940), pp. 166-200.
> On Milton and his theory of poetry and how he disciplined himself to become a great poet.

1241 JONES, MARY B. Milton's Attitude Toward Basic Catholic Dogma. Master's thesis, North Carolina College, 1953.

1242 KEENE, THELMA B. Biographers and Critics on Milton's Opinions of Woman. Master's thesis, Duke University, 1940.

1243 KELLEY, MAURICE. "J" and "I" in Milton's Script. MLR, 44, 1949, 545-7.
> Holds that the principle of banishing "J" and the consonantal "I" from the text of the Latin poems is still valid.
> Rev: L. C. Martin, YWES, 171.

1244 ------. Milton and Miracles. MLN, 53, 1938, 170-2.
Argues that Milton accepts miracles.

1245 ------. Milton and the Third Person of the Trinity. SP, 32, 1935, 221-34.
Rev: L. C. Martin, YWES, 255.

1246 ------. Milton, Ibn Ezra, and Wollebius. MLN, 49, 1934, 506-7.

1247 ------, and SAMUEL D. ATKINS. Milton's Annotations of Aratus. PMLA, 70, 1955, 1090-1106.
An index to Milton's intellectual development.

1248 KELLY, F. JOSEPH. Milton and Dante: A Few Points of Contrast. CW, 132, 1930, 170-3.

1249 KENRICK, EDWARD F. The Origin and Development of Milton's Thought on the Trinity: First Period, 1608-1625. Doctoral diss., Fordham University, 1951. Abs., Fordham University Diss., 18, 1952, 60-3.

1250 KIRKCONNELL, WATSON. Some Latin Analogues of Milton, with a Chronological Checklist. TRSC, 3rd. Ser., 40, 1946, 173-89.

1251 KIRKLAND, E. C. A Collection and Explanation of the Folklore in Milton's English Poems. Doctoral diss., Northwestern University, 1934. Abs., Northwestern University, Summaries of Ph.D. Diss., 2, 1934, 5-11.

1252 KNIGHT, G. WILSON. The Frozen Labyrinth: An Essay on Milton. The Burning Oracle: Studies in the Poetry of Action (London: Milford; Oxford: Oxford University Press, 1939), pp. 59-113.
Rev: TLS, Sept. 2, 1939, pp. 514, 516; H. I'A. Fausset, MGW, Sept. 8, 1939, p. 194; A. C., SRL, Sept. 16, 1939, p. 20; G. G. Sedgwick, UTQ, 9, 1940, 246-8; Wilfrid Gibson, Eng., 3, 1940, 35-6; B. E. C. Davis, MLR, 35, 1940, 268-9; K. Tillotson, RES, 17, 1941, 245-6; G. H. C., QQ, 48, 1941, 88-90.

1253 ------. Chariot of Wrath: the Message of John Milton to Democracy at War. London: Faber and Faber, 1942. 194pp.
Relates passages in the major poems and in Milton's other works to the struggle of the democratic nations against totalitarianism.
Rev: L. C. Martin, YWES, 163-4; NQ, 182, 1942, 336; TLS, May 30, 1942, p. 271; B. S., MGW, July 31, 1942, p. 65; S. Addleshaw, CQR, 134, 1942, 121-3; E. E. Kellett, NSN, Aug. 29, 1942, p. 146; Geoffrey Tillotson, Eng., 4, 1943, 130-1; F. O. Mathiessen, NR, 108, 1943, 674-5.

1254 KOEHLER, GEORGE S. Milton and the Roman Elegists. Doctoral diss., Princeton University, 1942. Ann Arbor: U. M., 1952. 208pp.

1255 KURTH, BURTON O. Milton and the English Traditions of Biblical Heroic Narrative. Doctoral diss., University of California (Berkeley), 1955.

1256 LARSON, MARTIN A. Milton and Puritanism—Clarified. PQ, 9, 1930, 308-11.
Milton stood alone, a heretic.
Reply by E. N. S. Thompson, ibid., pp. 311-12.
Rev: H. J. C. Grierson and A. Melville Clark. YWES, 229-30.

1257 LATIMER, ROSA C. Milton's Views on Religion. Master's thesis, Atlanta University, 1938.

1258 LEAVIS, F. R. The Common Pursuit. London: Chatto and Windus, 1952.
Contains two reprints o articles on Milton: Mr. Eliot and Milton, pp. 9-32; In Defense of Milton, pp. 33-43. The first article, occasioned by Eliot's 1947 recantation, originally appeared in SR, 57, 1949, 1-30, and contains a restatement of the author's case against Milton's style. The second article first appeared in Scr., 7, 1938, 104-14.
Rev: F. Y. Thompson, YWES, 16; Dudley Fitts, NR, Apr. 21, 1952, pp. 18-19; M. C. Bradbrook, Shakespeare Survey, 6, 1953, 153; Henry Fluchere, EA, 6, 1953, 73-5; David Stanford, CR, 183, 1953, 161.

1259 - - - - - -. Milton's Verse. Scr., 2, 1933, 123-36.
Reprinted in Revaluation: Tradition and Development in English Poetry (London: Chatto and Windus, 1936), pp. 42-67.

1260 LE COMTE, EDWARD S. Yet Once More: Verbal and Psychological Pattern in Milton. New York: Liberal Arts Press, 1954. ix, 192pp.
A study of Milton's borrowing from himself.
Rev: Arnold Davenport, YWES, 140; E. W. Robbins, MLN, 70, 1955, 141-3; Kester Svendsen, BA, 30, 1956, 222-3; TLS, Jan. 20, 1956, p. 38; reply by Le Comte, ibid., Mar. 9, 1956, p. 149.

1261 LEGOUIS, EMILE. Milton. A History of English Literature. By Emile Legouis and Louis Cazamian. Trans. by W. D. MacInnes (London: Macmillan, 1927), pp. 589-612. Revised editions, 1933, 1957.
Rev: TLS, Aug. 3, 1933, p. 526; B. de Selincourt, Obs., July 23, 1933; L. Abercrombie, Spect. 151, 1933, 130.

1262 - - - - - -. Milton. A Short History of English Literature. Trans. by V. F. Boyson and J. Coulson (Oxford: Clarendon Press, 1934), pp. 165-70.

1263 LEGOUIS, PIERRE. Les Amours de Dieu chez Collins et Milton. RA-A, 8, 1931, 136-8.

1264 LEVINSON, RONALD B. Milton and Plato, MLN, 46, 1931, 85-91.

1265 LEWIS, C. S. Variation in Shakespeare and Others. Rehabilitations and Other Essays (Toronto: Macmillan, 1936), pp. 159-80.
   Discusses the differences between Shakespeare's and Milton's uses of variation.

1266 LILJEGREN, S. B. Some Notes on Milton Criticism. UEIES, 16, 1956, xx-xxv.
   Animadversions on R. W. Chambers, L. B. Wright, and other Miltonists.

1267 - - - - - -. Supplementary Note on H. F. Fletcher, Milton's Rabbinical Readings, Ang. Bbl., 45, 1934, 20-3.
   An attack on Fletcher's studies and on his claims to scholarship in general.

1268 LOANE, GEORGE G. Milton and Chapman. NQ, 175, 1938, 456-7.

1269 LOOTEN, C. C. J. Milton quelques aspects de son génie. Paris: Desclée de Brouwer, 1938. 247pp.
   Animadversions on Tillyard's, Saurat's, and Belloc's interpretations of Milton. Discusses Milton the pamphleteer, Milton the republican and regicide, Milton the historian, Milton and the idea of the poet, Milton and music, Paradise Lost, and the theolgy of Milton.

1270 - - - - - -. Milton et la musique. RA-A, 8, 1931, 393-408.
   Rev: F. S. Boas, YWES, 207.

1271 - - - - - -. Milton et l'idée du Poète. RA-A, 9, 1931, 1-15.

1272 LOVE, CHRISTOPHER C. The Scriptural Latin Plays of the Renaissance and Milton's Cambridge Manuscript. Doctoral diss., University of Toronto, 1950. Abs., University of Toronto...Final Oral Examinations for the Degree of Doctor of Philosophy, Session 1949-50.

1273 LUMIANSKY, ROBERT M. Milton's English Again. MLN, 55, 1940, 591-4.
   Argues against the belief in the alien character of Milton's vocabulary.

1274 MACKELLAR, WALTER, Milton and Pindar. TLS, Dec. 3, 1931, p. 982.

1275 MACKENZIE, PHYLLIS. Milton's Visual Imagination: an Answer to T. S. Eliot. UTQ, 16, 1946, 17-29.
   Rev: L. C. Martin, YWES, 28, 1947, 185.

1276 MACKINNON, MALCOLM H. M. Milton's Theory and Practice of the Epic, Examined in Relation to Italian Renaissance Literary Criticism. Doctoral diss., University of Toronto, 1948.

1277 MACKLEM, MICHAEL. Love, Nature, and Grace in Milton. QQ, 56, 1949, 534-47.

1278 MADSEN, WILLIAM G. The Idea of Nature in Milton's Poetry. Doctoral diss., Yale University, 1952.

1279 MANUEL, M. The Seventeenth-Century Critics and Biographers of Milton. Doctoral diss., University of Wisconsin, 1956. Abs., DA, 16, 1956, 2166-7.

1280 MARILLA, E. L. Milton and Bacon: a Paradox. ES, 36, 1955, 106-11.
Milton agrees that fruitless speculation is undesirable and approves Bacon's concern for scientific advancement as a means for man's material improvement; he differs from Bacon by regarding such mastery as an instrument of man's purpose in life.
Rev: Arnold Davenport, YWES, 161.

1281 MARTIN, PATRICIA. Milton as a Humanist. Master's thesis, Stetson University, 1938.

1282 MAXEY, CHESTER C. Voices of Freedom. Political Philosophies (New York: Macmillan, 1938), pp. 236-64.
Milton discussed, pp. 237-46. An account of his political career and comments on polemical prose.

1283 McCOLLEY, GRANT. Milton's Technique of Source Adaptation. SP, 35, 1938, 61-110.
Milton sometimes utilizes ideas in his sources in their original order and sometimes in reverse order.
Rev: L. C. Martin, YWES, 177-8.

1284 ------. The Seventeenth-Century Doctrine of the Plurality of Worlds. Annals of Science, 1, 1936, 385-430.
Rev: L. C. Martin, YWES, 183-4.

1285 ------. The Theory of a Plurality of Worlds as a Factor in Milton's Attitude Toward the Copernican Hypothesis. MLN, 47, 1932, 319-25.
Rev: L. C. Martin, YWES, 210.

1286 McDAVID, RAVEN I., JR. Milton as a Political Thinker. Doctoral diss., Duke University, 1935.

1287 McDILL, JOSEPH M. Milton and the Pattern of Calvinism. Doctoral diss., Vanderbilt University, 1939. Nashville: The Author, 1942. xxiii, 432pp.

1288 McLACHLAN, H. The Religious Opinions of Milton, Locke, and Newton. Manchester: Manchester University Press, 1941. vii, 221pp.
Rev: C. J. Cadoux, HJ, 40, 1941, 111-12; TLS, July 19, 1941, p. 344; H. J. L., MGW, July 25, 1941, p. 58; Denis Saurat, NSN, July 12, 1941, pp. 111-12; Lee Atkinson, LQHR, Oct., 1941, pp. 491-2; E. H. W. Meyerstein, Eng., 4, 1942, 23-4; R. W. Battenhouse, Church Hist., 11, 1942, 257-8; F. M. Higham, Hist., N. S., 27, 1942; 87-8.

1289 McLEOD, FRANCES R. Milton's View of Women as Shown by His Life and Writings. Master's thesis, Alabama Polytechnic Institute, 1945.

1290 MEGROZ, RODOLPHE L. Milton Agonistes. Thirty-One Bedside Essays (Hadleigh, Essex: Tower Bridge Publications, 1951), pp. 99-102.
Comments on Visiak's Milton Agonistes. Agrees that Milton has been unjustly maligned and neglected.

1291 MENZIES, W. Milton: The Last Poems. E&S, 24, 1938, 80-113.
Rev: L. C. Martin, YWES, 117.

1292 MERTNER, EDGAR. Die Bedeutung der kosmischen Konzeption in Miltons Dichtung. Ang., 69, 1950, 105-34.

1293 MILLER, MILTON. Milton's Imagination and the Idyllic Solution. WR, 13, 1948, 35-43.

1294 MILLER, VIRGINIA. Milton's Conception of Liberty. Master's thesis, University of Georgia, 1938.

1295 Milton Bombarded. TLS, Nov. 9, 1940, p. 567; Nov. 16, 1940, p. 579.
Refers to L. P. Smith's Milton and His Modern Critics. Holds that the present detraction may be due to the decline of classical learning.

1296 Milton e l'ortografia. La Cultura, 12, 1934, 726-7.

1297 A Milton Tercentenary. TLS, Sept. 22, 1945, p. 451.

1298 Milton without the Epic. TLS, Sept. 2, 1955, 501-2.
Milton's poetic career is a progress from one great form to another; Samson Agonistes is not an ebb tide.

1299 MIMS, EDWIN. John Milton, Dissenter and Heretic. The Christ of the Poets (New York: Abingdon-Cokesbury Press, 1948), pp. 100-18.

1300 ------. Milton and the Modern World. Golden Book, April, 1931, pp. 87-9.
On the relevance of Milton's ideas today.

1301 MÖLLER, ALFRED. Zu Miltons rabbinischen Studien. Ang. Bbl., 44, 1933, 154-9.
Comments prompted by Liljegren's attack on Fletcher's scholarship.

1302 MONTGOMERY, SARA DRAKE. John Milton—Alexander Pope, A Study in Contrast. Master's thesis. University of Georgia, 1938.

1303 MORAND, PAUL PHELPS. De Comus à Satan: L'oeuvre poetique de John Milton expliquee par sa vie. Paris: Didier, 1939. 262pp.
Rev: E. N. S. T(hompson), PQ, 19, 1940, 223; E. M. W. Tillyard, MLN, 55, 1940, 635-6.

1304 MOUNTS, CHARLES E. "Sooth" in De La Mare, Keats, and Milton. MLN, 62, 1947, 271-2.
To Milton the word means "truth," while to Keats and De La Mare it means "smooth."

1305 MULLEN, CECIL. Milton's Poetry, Viewed in the Light of Catholic Doctrine. Master's thesis, Ottawa University, 1935. 112pp.

1306 MURDOCH, WALTER. On Two Poets. 72 Essays (Sydney: Angus and Robertson, 1947), pp. 317-21.
Contrasts the temperaments of Shakespeare and Milton.

1307 MURRAY, JOHN F. Milton's Conception of Original Justice and of Original Sin. Doctoral diss., University of New Mexico, 1957. Abs., DA, 18, 1958, 583.

1308 MURRY, JOHN MIDDLETON. Heaven—and Earth. London: Cape, 1938. 383pp.
Contains three chapters on Milton: Milton: I Am That Satan, pp. 147-57; Milton: Lear Without Cordelia, pp. 158-67; Milton: Tendering the Whole, pp. 168-83. Quite unsympathetic.

1309 - - - - - -. John Milton. Heroes of Thought (New York: Julian Messner, 1938), pp. 142-77.
Argues that Milton has no charity.

1310 MUTSCHMANN, H. Die Beweggründe zu Miltons Festlandreise. Beiblatt, 50, 1939, 278-82.
Rev: L. C. Martin, YWES, 113-14.

1311 MYHR, IVAR L. The Evolution and Practice of Milton's Epic Theory. Doctoral diss., Vanderbilt University, 1940. Abs., Bull. of Vanderbilt University, 40, No. 10, 1940, 14-15. Published in summary form. Nashville: Joint University Libraries, 1942. 53pp.

1312 NAZARI, EMILIO. Problemi Miltoniani. Palermo: A. Priulla, 1951. 250pp.
Chapter topics: Milton's trip to Italy and his religious uncertainties, classical and Italian elements in Paradise Lost, and some considerations on the life and personality of Milton.

1313 NEILSON, WILLIAM A. On Milton's Conception of Poetry. Studies in the History of Culture: The Disciplines of the Humanities (Menasha, Wash.; George Banta, 1942), pp. 156-60.

1314 NICHOLAS, CONSTANCE. The Editions of the Early Church Historians Used by Milton. JEGP, 51, 1952, 160-2.
He probably used the Historiae Ecclesiasticae Scriptores Graeci, Geneva, 1612.
Rev: A. Davenport, YWES, 178.

1315 ------. Milton's Medieval British Readings. Doctoral diss., University of Illinois, 1951. Abs., Urbana: University of Illinois Press, 1951.

1316 NICOLSON, MARJORIE HOPE. The Breaking of the Circle: Studies in the Effect of the New Science upon Seventeenth Century Poetry. The Norman Wait Harris Lectures Delivered at Northwestern University, July, 1949. Evanston: Northwestern University Press, 1950.
Milton discussed passim and pp. 160-6. "In the astronomy of Paradise Lost Milton, whether he realized it or not, broke the Circle of Perfection."
Rev: Samuel Mintz, Isis, 43, 1952, 98-100; Joan Bennett, RES, 3, 1952, 178-80; William Blackburn, SAQ, 51, 1952, 469-70; H. J. C. Grierson, MLR, 47, 1952, 390-2.

1317 ------. The Microscope and English Imagination. Smith College Stud. in Modern Lang., 16, 4. Northampton, Mass.: Banta, 1935, 92pp.
A background study.
Rev: L. I. Bredvold, PQ, 15, 1936, 167-8; W. J. Schmidt, Ang. Bbl., 47, 1936, 250; A. B., Archiv., 169, 1936, 137; F. R. Johnson, MLN, 52, 1937, 229-31.

1318 ------. Milton and the Telescope. ELH, 2, 1935, 1-32.
Rev: L. C. Martin, YWES, 250-1.

1319 ------. The Telescope and Imagination. MP, 32, 1935, 233-60.
Rev: L. C. Martin, YWES, 250-1.

1320 NOTT, KATHLEEN. Old Puritan Writ Large. The Emperor's Clothes (Bloomington: Indiana University Press, 1954), pp. 159-93.
Agrees with the New Critics that "Milton the poet was the portentous and comet-like cause which accounted for much of the devastation in poetic language."

1321 NOYES, ALFRED. A French View of Milton. The
Opalescent Parrot (London: Sheed and Ward, 1929),
pp. 55-70.
Censures Taine and Saurat for their criticism of Milton.

1322 O'BRIEN, GORDON W. The Avatars of Dignity: A
Study in the Imagery of Humanism. Doctoral diss., Ohio
State University, 1951. Abs., DA, 18, 1958, 1789-91.
Shows how Milton employs certain images and themes to set
forth his conception of the dignity of man.

1323 O'CONNOR, JOHN J. A Note on the Meaning of the
Word Novel in the Seventeenth Century. NQ, 198, 1953,
477-8.
Milton's De Doctrina Christiana not the first work in which
the word appeared signifying "a fictitious prose narrative or
tale of considerable length."

1324 OGDEN, H. S. V. The Principles of Variety and Contrast
in Seventeenth Century Aesthetics, and Milton's Poetry.
JHI, 10, 1949, 159-82.
Rev: L. C. Martin, YWES, 170.

1325 ORAS, ANTS. Notes on Some Miltonic Usages: Their
Background and Later Development. Acts et Commen-
tationes Universitatis Tartuensis, Dorpatensis, B. 43, 3.
Tartu: Kruger, 1938. 133pp.
Rev: W. Héraucourt, Ang. Bbl., 50, 1939, 198-200; P.
Meissner, DL, 60, 1939, 919-20; H. Scherpbier, Neophil.,
24, 1939, 312.

1326 - - - - - -. Spenser and Milton: Some Parallels and Contrasts
in the Handling of Sound. Sound and Poetry, English
Institute Essays, 1956 (New York: Columbia University
Press, 1957), pp. 109-33.
Feels that Spenser's approach is pre-Neo-Aristotelian, while
Milton's reflects an absorption of Renaissance principles and
points beyond them.

1327 ORSINI, NAPOLEONE. La lingua poetica inglese: Note
storiche. Anglica, 1, 1946, 139-48, 193-203, 241-52.
Includes remarks on Milton and Shakespeare.

1328 - - - - - -. Studii sul Rinascimento italiano in Inghilterra.
Con alcuni testi inglese inediti. 5, Milton's Machiavelli
Studies. Florence: Sansoni, 1937. 141pp.
Rev: A. Zanco, Rivista italiana del dramma (Rome), Jan.
15, 1938.

1329 OSBORNE, LAWRENCE J. Changes in Milton's Theology
from The Nativity Ode through Of True Religion.
Doctoral diss., Stanford University, 1952.

1330 OSGOOD, CHARLES G. Milton. Poetry as a Means of Grace: Studies in Dante, Spenser, Milton and Johnson. (Princeton: Princeton University Press, 1941), pp. 80-105.
> General remarks addressed to theological students.
> Rev: Douglas Bush, MLN, 58, 1943, 222.

1331 ------. Virgil and the English Mind. The Tradition of Virgil (Princeton: Princeton University Press, 1930), 23-40.
> Especially concerned with Virgil and Milton.

1332 ------. Milton. The Voice of England: A History of English Literature (New York: Harper and Bros., 1935; Second Edition, 1952), pp. 237-51.

1333 PARKER, WILLIAM R. The Trinity Manuscript and Milton's Plans for a Tragedy. JEGP, 34, 1935, 225-32.
> Rev: L. C. Martin, YWES, 254.

1334 PARKINSON, MABEL B. Milton. The Drama and the Theatre. Master's thesis, University of Alabama, 1939.

1335 PARSONS, EDWARD S. Milton's Seasonal Inspiration. MLN, 49, 1934, 46.
> Cites a parallel from Cowper, who says that he writes best during the winter.

1336 PATRICK, J. MAX, ed. SAMLA Studies in Milton. Essays on John Milton and His Works by Members of the South Atlantic Modern Language Association. Foreward by James H. Hanford. Gainesville: University of Florida Press, 1953.
> Each essay is entered separately in this bibliography under its appropriate classification.
> Rev: R. Wood, MLN, 70, 1955, 448-50; Arnold Davenport, YWES, 199-200.

1337 PETER, JOHN. Reflections on the Milton Controversy. Scr., 19, 1952, 2-15.
> On Leavis and his adversaries.
> Rev: Arnold Davenport, YWES, 183.

1338 PETIT, HERBERT H. Milton, Aristotle, and the Modern Critics. Class. Bull., 25, Nov., 1948, 8-10.

1339 POWYS, JOHN C. Milton. The Enjoyment of Literature (New York: Simon and Schuster, 1938), pp. 238-75.
> General laudatory remarks.

1340 PRAZ, MARIO. Milton and Poussin. Seventeenth Century Studies Presented to Sir Herbert Grierson (Oxford: Clarendon Press, 1938), pp. 192-210.
> On the connection between Milton's stylistic development and the painting of his age.

1341 ------. Milton e Poussin. Gusto Neoclassico (Florence: Sansoni, 1940), pp. 9-34.

1342 ------. John Milton. Storia della Letterature Inglese (Florence: Sansoni, 1937), pp. 155-65.

1343 ------. Rapporti tra la letteratura italiana e la letteratura inglese. Letterature Comparate (Milan: Marzorati, 1948), pp. 145-96.
Considers Milton's relations with Italy in general, pp. 167-9.

1344 PRIEST, HAROLD M. Tasso in English Literature, 1575-1675. Doctoral diss., Northwestern University, 1933. Abs., Summaries of Diss., Northwestern University, 1, 1933, 5-9.
Considers Milton as the second great English poet to be influenced profoundly.

1345 PRINCE, F. T. The Influence of Tasso and Della Casa on Milton's Diction. RES, 25, 1949, 222-36.
Rev: L. C. Martin, YWES, 169.

1346 ------. The Italian Element in Milton's Verse. Oxford: Clarendon Press, 1954. xv, 183pp.
"My endeavor has been to show that this Italian influence on Milton's verse is deeper than it had been thought to be, especially as it affects the epic poetry."
Rev: Arnold Davenport, YWES, 138; TLS, Mar. 5, 1954, p. 152; CE, 16, 1954, 75; Sergio Baldi, Riv. di. Let. Mod., 5, 1954, 308-10; K. M. Lea, RES, 6, 1955, 203-4; Denis Saurat, EA, 8, 1955, 344-5; Wilhelmina Gordon, QQ, 63, 1956, 312-13.

1347 PRITCHARD, JOHN P. The Fathers of the Church in the Works of John Milton. CJ, 33, 1937, 79-87.

1348 PURCELL, JAMES M. Milton y los siete tipos de ambigüedad. Estudios (Duquesne University), 1, 1953, 23-9.

1349 QUILLER-COUCH, SIR ARTHUR T. Milton. Cambridge Lectures (London: Dent, 1943), pp. 207-58.
A reprint of Stevens' No. 2496.

1350 RADER, KATHERINE. The Soliloquy in Milton's English Poems. Doctoral diss., University of Oklahoma, 1952.

1351 RAJAN, B. Simple, Sensuous, and Passionate. RES, 21, 1945, 289-301.
Milton's aesthetic credo.

1352 RALLI, AUGUSTUS. Milton. Poetry and Faith (London: John Lane, 1951), pp. 131-43.
Appreciative.
Rev: TLS, Apr. 27, 1951, p. 640

1353 RANSOM, JOHN CROWE. Mr. Empson's Muddles. Southern Rev., 4, 1938, 322-39.
Comments on Empson's Bentley and Milton.

1354 RASCOE, BURTON. Milton the Conscience. Titans of Literature: From Homer to the Present (New York: Putnam, 1932), pp. 276-296.
Repeats all the old charges against Milton.
Rev: A. Colton, SRL, 9, 1932, 252, 357-60; M. Godwin, NR, 73, 1932, 134-5; C. H. Grattan, Scribner's, 93, 1932, 7-8.

1355 RAY, DON E. Milton and the Elizabethan Tradition of Christian Learning. Doctoral diss., Rice Institute, 1957.

1356 READ, HARLAN E. A Great Poet Whose Contributions to Freedom Were Written in Prose. Fighters for Freedom: The Story of Liberty Throughout the Ages (New York: McBride, 1946), pp. 164-7.
Laudatory.

1357 REBORA, PIERO. Milton a Firenze. Nuova Antologia, 459, 1953, 147-63.

1358 RECK, JOSEF. Das Prinzip der Freiheit bei Milton. Erlangen: Dörres, 1931, 55pp.

1359 REESING, JOHN P., JR. Milton's Philosophical View of Nature. Doctoral diss., Harvard University, 1954.

1360 REWIS, HELEN S. The Conflict between Humanism and Puritanism: Milton and His Predecessors. Master's thesis, Emory University, 1937.

1361 RICHARDS, I. A. The Places and the Figures. KR, 11, 1949, 17-30.
Critical comment on Clarke's John Milton at St. Paul's School.

1362 RICHTER, WALTER. Der Hiatus im englischen Klassizismus (Milton, Dryden, Pope). Freiburg i. Br. Schramberg: Gatzer and Hahn, 1934. 139pp.

1363 RILEY, EDGAR H. Milton's Tribute to Virgil. SP, 26, 1929, 155-65.
Brings together Milton's scattered references to Virgil.

1364 ROBERTS, DONALD R. The Music of Milton. PQ, 26, 1947, 328-44.
Relates Milton's verse to the music of his era.
Rev: L. C. Martin, YWES, 185.

1365 ROBERTS, E. A. Essays on Milton, with Selections from His Works. King's Treasuries of Literature. London: Dent, 1930.

1366 ROSS, MALCOLM M. Milton and the Protestant
Aesthetic. Poetry and Dogma: the Transfiguration of
Eucharistic Symbols in Seventeenth-century English
Poetry (New Brunswick: Rutgers University Press, 1954),
pp. 183-204.
> The Christian symbols in Milton's poetry are externalized,
> but they cease to be ritualistic in the Protestant context of
> Milton's thought.

1367 - - - - - -. Milton and Sir John Stradling. HLQ, 14, 1951,
129-46.
> Suggests several parallels between Stradling's Divine Poems
> (1625) and Milton's poems.
> Rev: Arnold Davenport, YWES, 191.

1368 - - - - - -. Milton's Royalism: A Study of the Conflict of
Symbol and Idea in the Poems. Doctoral diss., Cornell
University, 1941. Published as Cornell Stud. in Eng., 34.
Ithaca: Cornell University Press, 1943. xiii, 150pp.
> Rev: Maurice Kelley, MLN, 59, 1944, 578-9; H. F. Fletcher,
> JEGP, 43, 1944, 253-4; TLS, May 27, 1944, p. 263; B. A.
> Wright, RES, 21, 1945, 66-8; W. R. Parker, MLQ, 6, 1945,
> 106-7; Arthur Barker, Canadian Forum, 24, 1944, 189;
> Kirby Neill, CHR, 31, 1945, 241-2; Louise Brown, JMH,
> 17, 1945, 89.

1369 ST. CLAIR, FOSTER Y. The Myth of the Golden Age
from Spenser to Milton. Doctoral diss., Harvard University, 1931. Abs., Summaries of Theses, Harvard University, 1931, pp. 242-4.

1370 SAINTSBURY, GEORGE. Milton. The Cambridge History of English Literature (Cambridge: Cambridge University Press; New York: Macmillan, 1933), 7, 108-61.
> A reprint of Stevens' No. 2379.

1371 SALTMARSHE, C. John Milton, Letter Writer. Bookman
(London), 81, 1932, 319-20.

1372 SAMARIN, R. M. K voprosu o teorii eposa u Miltona.
Doklady i soobsheheniia filol. Fakul'tetov, Moscow,
Universitet. Soobsheheniia, 5, 1948, 47-51.
> Concerning Milton's theory of the epic.

1373 SAMPSON, GEORGE. Milton. The Concise Cambridge
History of English Literature (Cambridge: Cambridge
University Press, 1941), pp. 357-70.
> Rev: L. B. Wright, MLQ, 3, 1942, 493; Edith J. Morley,
> RES, 18, 1942, 375-8.

1374 SAMUEL, IRENE. Milton on Learning and Wisdom.
PMLA, 64, 1949, 708-23.
> In Paradise Lost and Paradise Regained Milton expands, not
> retracts, what he has said earlier about studies.

1375 ------. Milton's References to Plato and Socrates. SP, 41, 1944, 50-64.
Early poems contain references to the philosophers, while the later poems incorporate Platonic theories.

1376 ------. Platonism in the Poetry of John Milton. Doctoral diss., Cornell University, 1940. Abs., Cornell University Abstracts of Theses, 1940, pp. 44-7. Published as Plato and Milton. Cornell Stud. in English, 35. Ithaca: Cornell University Press, 1947. xii, 182pp.
Rev: TLS, June, 14, 1947, p. 299; J. M. French, MLN, 63, 1948, 280-2; C. R. T., QQ, 55, 1948, 109; L. C. Martin, YWES, 185-6; Lionel Stephenson, Pers., 30, 1949, 207-8.

1377 SANDERFORD, PATRICIA B. Milton on War. Master's thesis, Duke University, 1956.

1378 SAUNDERS, J. W. Milton, Diomede, and Amaryllis. ELH, 22, 1955, 254-86.
Milton's relationship to his audience.

1379 SAURAT, DENIS. Milton et le materialisme chretien en Angleterre. Paris: Rieder, 1928. 243pp.
Stevens' No. 2609.
Rev: Paul Chauvet, RA-A, 6, 1929, 172-4; C. B., Rev. historique, 54, 1929, 407-8; André Leroy, Rev. d'histoire de la philosophie, 2, 1929, 427-9; René Pruvost, Rev. de synthese historique, N. S., 21, 1929, 125; R. S. Crane, MP, 27, 1930, 361-4; B. Fehr, Ang. Bbl., 42, 1931, 161-9.

1380 ------. Milton: Man and Thinker. London: Jonathan Cape; New York: Dial Press, 1925. Second Edition, London: Dent, 1944; reprinted, 1946. xiv, 291pp.
Rev: B. Fehr, Ang. Bbl., 42, 1931, 161-9; TLS, Sept. 16, 1944, p. 451; Joan Bennett, NSN, Sept. 2, 1944, pp. 156-7; Charles Williams, Spect., Aug. 18, 1944, p. 154; E. M. Forster, La France libre, Oct. 16, 1944, pp. 449-50; A. S. P. Woodhouse, Time and Paradise Lost, UTQ, 15, 1946, 200-5.

1381 SAYERS, DOROTHY L. Dante and Milton. Further Papers on Donte (New York: Harper, 1957), pp. 148-82.
A comparison of their careers.

1382 SCHIRMER, WALTER F. Die epische Dichtung und John Milton. Geschichte Der englischen Literatur von den Anfängen bis zur Gegenwart (Halle: Niemeyer, 1937), pp. 322-41.
Rev: H. S. V. Jones, JEGP, 36, 1937, 617-18; H. Lüdeke, ES, 20, 1938, 219-23; M. Wildi, DL, 59, 1939, 702-8; W. E. Süskind, Die Literatur, 40, 1939, 758; F. Brie, ESt., 72, 1939, 283-6; H. G. Fiedler, Eng., 2, 1939, 247-9; W. Fischer, Ang. Bbl., 51, 1940, 49-54; S. B. Liljegren, SN, 13, 1940, 154-8.

1383 SCHNEIDER, R. Milton zwischen Politik und Geschichte. Die Literatur, 38, 1936, 314-18.

1384 SCHORK, W. Die Dramenpläne Miltons. Freiburg i. Br. Quakenbrück: Trute, 1934. 92pp.
Rev: H. O. Wilde, Ang. Bbl., 46, 1935, 239; J. H. Hanford, JEGP, 36, 1937, 584-6; A. B., Archiv, 167, 1935, 141; L. C. Martin, YWES, 236.

1385 SCHULTZ, HOWARD. Milton and Forbidden Knowledge. MLA Revolving Fund Series, 17. New York: Modern Language Assn. of America, 1955. vii, 309pp.
Rev: Arnold Davenport, YWES, 159-60; Donald Howard, SCN, 13, 1955, 43-4; D. C. Allen, MP, 54, 1956, 138-9; H. F. Fletcher, JEGP, 55, 1956, 322-3; J. I Cope, MLN, 71, 1956, 529-32; H. L. Short, HJ, 55, 1956, 405-6; Frank Kermode, EIC, 7, 1957, 196-207; B. O. Kurth, Pers., 37, 1957, 102-3; B. K. Lewalski, Rev. of Religion, 22, 1957, 198-202; Ernest Sirluck, Church Hist., 26, 1957, 189-92; Kenneth Muir, RES, 8, 1957, 443-4.

1386 SCHULTZ, JOHN H. Obscurantism in Milton and the Humanistic Tradition. Doctoral diss., Harvard University, 1940. Abs., Harvard University, Summaries of Theses, 1940, pp. 356-60.

1387 SCOTT-CRAIG, T. S. K. Miltonic Tragedy and Christian Vision. The Tragic Vision and the Christian Faith. Ed. by Nathan A. Scott, Jr. (New York: Association Press, 1957), pp. 99-122.
Argues against Johnson and holds that in Paradise Lost and Paradise Regained "we have almost ideal examples of tragic vision illuminated by biblical faith, and of biblical faith transforming the tragic vision of life."

1388 SENIOR, JOHN. Milton and Eliot. Nat., 161, 1945, 186-7.

1389 SEWELL, ARTHUR. Milton and the Mosaic Law. MLR, 30, 1935, 12-18.
Rev: L. C. Martin, YWES, 255-6.

1390 SHAFER, ROBERT. Milton and Pindar. TLS, Dec. 3, 1931, p. 982.

1391 SIEBERT, THEODOR. Wahrheit und Wahrhaftigkeit bei Milton. ESt., 64, 1929, 53-64.

1392 SIEBERT, THOMAS. Untersuchungen über Miltons Kunst vom psychologischen Standpunkt aus. Ang., N. F., 42, 1930, 67-82.

1393 SIEGEL, PAUL N. Milton and the Humanist Attitude toward Women. JHI, 15, 1950, 42-53.
Rev: Arnold Davenport, YWES, 176.

1394 SILVER, HELEN. The Significance of Milton's Political Theories. Master's thesis, McGill University, 1933.

1395 SIRLUCK, ERNEST. Milton's Political Thought: A Survey Preliminary to the Investigation of the Classical Influence. Master's thesis, University of Toronto, 1941. 226pp.

1396 - - - - - -. Milton and the Law of Nature. Doctoral diss., University of Toronto, 1949.

1397 - - - - - -. Milton's Critical Use of Historical Sources: An Illustration. MP, 50, 1953, 226-31.
Sarpi, in Areopagitica.
Rev: Arnold Davenport, YWES, 204.

1398 SISTER MARGARET TERESA. A Paradise Remembered. Th., 22, 1947, 483-94.
Considers the influence of Dante and Italy on Milton.

1399 SMITH, LOGAN PEARSALL. Milton and His Modern Critics. London: Oxford University Press, 1940. 88pp.
A reply to Milton's twentieth-century detractors.
Rev: L. C. Martin, YWES, 171-2; NQ, 189, 1940, 360; John Hayward, Spect., Nov. 8, 1940, pp. 482-4; H. I'A. F., MGW, Nov. 22, 1940, p. 390; Peter Quennell, NSN, N. S., Nov. 16, 1940, pp. 496-9; E. Johnson, NR, 104, 1941, 800-1; T. M., CW, 153, 1941, 760-1; C. I. W., NEQ, 14, 1941, 604-5; A. M. Witherspoon, SRL, July 12, 1941, p. 8; D. A. Roberts, NYTBR, May 25, 1941, p. 5; B. A. Wright, MLR, 36, 1941, 407; W. R. Parker, RES, 17, 1941, 346-7; W. Gibson, Eng., 4, 1941, 189-90; Orlo Williams, Natl. Rev., 116, 1941, 236-41; F. A. Voight, NC, 130, 1941, 211-21; Theodore Maynard, CW, 153, 1941, 760-1.

1400 SPENCER, TERENCE. Milton, the First English Philhellene. MLR, 47, 1952, 553-4.
Assembles various passages to show that Milton hoped the Greeks could overthrow the Turks.
Rev: Arnold Davenport, YWES, 177.

1401 SPENCER, T. J. B. Longinus in English Criticism: Influences before Milton. RES, N. S., 8, 1957, 137-43.
Shows that Milton's allusion to Longinus in Of Education is not the first recognition of that critic in England and argues that Milton had no real knowledge of Longinus.

1402 STARNES, D. T. The Hesperian Gardens in Milton. UTSE, 31, 1952, 42-51.
A consideration of Stephanus and Natalis Comes as sources of Milton's identification of the garden with the Elysian Field and the Isles of the Blest.

1403 - - - - - -. Proper Names in Milton: New Annotations. A
Tribute to G. C. Taylor (Chapel Hill: University of
North Carolina Press, 1952), pp. 38-61.
> Argues "that the reference books, especially the lexicons and
> dictionaries known to Milton and his contemporaries, are
> often the best guides to the author's meaning."

1404 - - - - - -, and ERNEST W. TALBERT. Milton and the
Dictionaries. Classical Myth and Legend in Renaissance
Dictionaries: A Study of Renaissance Dictionaries in
Their Relation to the Classical Learning of Contem-
porary English Writers (Chapel Hill: University of North
Carolina Press, 1955), pp. 226-39.
> Milton probably used the Thesaurus of Robert Stephanus
> and the Dictionarium of Charles Stephanus.

1405 - - - - - -. John Milton and Renaissance Dictionaries. UTSE,
1943, pp. 50-65.
> Rev: L. C. Martin, YWES, 157-8.

1406 STEIN, ARNOLD. Milton and Metaphysical Art: an
Exploration. ELH, 16, 1949, 120-34.
> Rev: L. C. Martin, YWES, 170.

1407 STILLMAN, DONALD G. Milton as Proof Reader.
MLN, 54, 1939, 353-4.
> Rev: L. C. Martin, YWES, 115.

1408 STOLL, ELMER E. Criticisms Criticized: Spenser and
Milton. JEGP, 41, 1942, 451-77.
> A review of recent criticism. Latter portion reprinted in
> From Shakespeare to Joyce, pp. 413-21.

1409 - - - - - -. From Shakespeare to Joyce: Authors and Critics,
Literature and Life. New York: Doubleday, 1944. xx,
442pp.
> Contains three articles on Milton, which are noted in their
> appropriate sections.
> Rev: Mark Schorer, NYTBR, Feb. 6, 1944, p. 7; G. W.
> Stonier, NSN, June 10, 1944, pp. 390-1; J. T. S., AB, 1,
> 1944, 127; Louis Kronenberger, Nat., Feb., 19, 1944, pp.
> 229-31.

1410 - - - - - -. Milton Classical and Romantic. PQ, 23, 1944,
222-47.

1411 - - - - - -. Milton a Romantic. RES, 8, 1932, 425-36.
> Reprinted in From Shakespeare to Joyce, pp. 389-412.
> Rev: L. C. Martin, YWES, 211-12.

1412 - - - - - -. Milton, Puritan of the Seventeenth Century.
Poets and Playwrights (Minneapolis: University of
Minnesota Press, 1930), pp. 241-95.
> Rev: H. J. C. Grierson and A. Melville Clark, YWES, 228-9.

1413 STROUP, THOMAS B. Implications of the Theory of Climatic Influence in Milton. MLQ, 4, 1943, 185-9.
Believes that the theory influenced Milton's interpretation of the universe and had a bearing on his attitude toward his own work.
Rev: L. C. Martin, YWES, 158.

1414 SVENDSEN, KESTER. Cosmological Lore in Milton. ELH, 9, 1942, 198-223.
Rev: L. C. Martin, YWES, 161.

1415 ------. Milton and the Encyclopedias of Science. SP, 29, 1942, 303-27.
Rev: L. C. Martin, YWES, 161.

1416 ------. Milton and Medical Lore. BHM, 13, 1943, 158-84.
Rev: L. C. Martin, YWES, 157.

1417 ------. Milton and Science. Cambridge: Harvard University Press, 1956. viii, 304pp.
"What is proposed here, then, is a comprehensive study of natural science in Milton, based on the medieval and Renaissance encyclopedias of science in the vernacular but extending to popular learning in any form and occasionally including documents in new science as these are relevant."
Rev: Stephen Merton, SCN, 15, 1957, 3-4; W. B. Hunter, MLN, 72, 1957, 620-2; F. R. Johnson, RN, 10, 1957, 201; W. R. Gilman, QJS, 43, 1957, 90-1; Wilhelmina Gordon, QQ, 64, 1957, 621-2; E. M. Clark, BA, 31, 1957, 198-9; Douglas Bush, Isis, 48, 1957, 494-5; M. G. Parks, DR, 37, 1957, 302-8; V. de S. Pinto, NQ, N. S., 4, 1957, 273-4.

1418 ------. Milton's Use of Natural Science, with Special Reference to Certain Encyclopedias of Science in English. Doctoral diss., University of North Carolina, 1940. Abs., University of North Carolina Record, No. 359, 1943, pp. 85-7.

1419 SWEDENBERG, H. T., JR. The Theory of the Epic in England, 1650-1800. University of California Pubs. in Eng., 15. Berkeley: University of California Press, 1944. 396pp.
Milton discussed, passim, but the study contains no detailed analysis of the poet's epic theory.

1420 TATE, ALLEN. Notes on Milton. NR, 68, 1931, 266-8.
A review article of Patterson's edition of the works plus critical remarks on Milton. "It is high time that the modern poets, who feel strongly other seventeenth century influences, came to a better view of Milton's significance and style."

1421 TAYLOR, DICK, JR. Grace as a Means of Poetry: Milton's Pattern for Salvation. Tulane Stud. in Eng., 4, 1954, 57-90.

Milton believed that salvation came only by God's grace but that man had to prove himself eligible by trial and temptation. This provides an organizing pattern for the major poems.
Rev: Arnold Davenport, YWES, 140.

1422 TAYLOR, GEORGE C. Milton on Mining. MLN, 45, 1930, 24-7.
Rev: H. J. C. Grierson and A. Melville Clark, YWES, 222.

1423 ------. Milton's English. NQ, 178, 1940, 56-7.
Milton's vocabulary does not favor Latin rather than native English words.

1424 ------. Some Patristic Conventions Common to Shakespeare and Milton. SP, 28, 1931, 652-6.
Points out that Shakespeare and Milton held many opinions in common and holds that source hunters forget the commonplaceness of many of the ideas of the age.

1425 TAYLOR, IVAN E. John Milton's Views on the Teaching of Foreign Languages. MLJ, 33, 1949, 528-36.

1426 TERVO, ESTHER F. Milton's Conception of Liberty. Master's thesis, University of British Columbia, 1943. 69pp.

1427 THALER, ALWIN. Shakespeare's Silences. Cambridge: Harvard University Press, 1929.
Contains two articles on Milton: The Shakespearean Element in Milton, pp. 139-208; Milton in the Theatre, pp. 209-56. Both are reprints of Stevens' Nos. 2566 and 487, resp. The first is supplemented by Thaler in his Shakespeare and Milton Once More (SAMLA Studies in Milton, pp. 80-99).

1428 (THOMPSON, E. N. S.) Studies in Milton: Essays in Memory of Elbert N. S. Thompson. PQ, 27, No. 1, 1949. 236pp.
Each article is noted under its appropriate classification.

1429 THOMPSON, HARLEY S. Cicero's Influence on Milton. Doctoral diss., Yale University, 1947.

1430 THOMPSON, J. A. K. The Classical Background of English Literature. London: Allen and Unwin, 1948. 272pp.
Milton discussed, pp. 192-8.
Rev: Gilbert Murray, Spect., Mar. 5, 1948, p. 290; V. de Sola Pinto, Eng., 7, 1948, 139-40.

1431 THOMPSON, WHITNEY M. Two Milton Essays. (a) The Aesthetic of Milton. (b) Puritanism and Anglicanism in the Age of Milton. Master's thesis, McMaster University, 1931. 35pp.

1432 THORPE, JAMES, ed. Milton Criticism: Selections from Four Centuries. New York: Rinehart, 1950. 376pp.
Part One contains essays and excerpts from critics ranging from Addison to C. S. Lewis and T. S. Eliot; in Part Two Thorpe presents excerpts and brief comments from critics from Marvell to Arnold.
Rev: Arnold Davenport, YWES, 175-6; CE, 11, 1950, 471; T. B. Stroup, SCN, 8, 1950, 2; TLS, Sept. 28, 1951, p. 613; G. S. Fraser, NSN, Oct. 27, 1951, pp. 468-9.

1433 THWAITES, MICHAEL. Milton Blind. London: Blackwell, 1938. 8pp.
The year's Nedwigate poem. On Milton's ability to inspire modern man to trust God.
Rev: TLS, June 4, 1938, p. 377.

1434 TILLYARD, E. M. W. John Milton (1608-74). Chambers's Encyclopaedia. (New Edition. London: George Newnes, 1955), 9, 416-19.

1435 - - - - - -. The Metaphysicals and Milton. London: Chatto and Windus, 1956. 87pp.
Proposes to examine the supposed opposition of the metaphysicals to Milton.
Rev: TLS, Dec. 27, 1956, p. 10, Oct. 26, p. 633; NSN, Nov. 3, 1956, pp. 565-6; Christopher Hill, Spect., Nov. 23, 1956, pp. 751-2; Kenneth Muir, London Mag., 4, No. 8, 1957, pp. 8, 70ff; M. Poirier, EA, 10, 1957, 257-8; Max Patrick, SCN, 15, 1957, 29.

1436 - - - - - -. Milton. London: Longmans for the British Council, 1952. 54pp.
Brief comments on many of the works.
Rev: Arnold Davenport, YWES, 179.

1437 - - - - - -. Milton and the Classics. Essays by Diverse Hands: Being the Transactions of the Royal Society of Literature of the United Kingdom, N. S., 26, 1953, 59-72.
Milton indebted but not to the extent indicated by many of the source hunters.

1438 - - - - - -. Milton and Longinus. TLS, Aug. 28, 1930, p. 684.

1439 - - - - - -. The Miltonic Setting: Past and Present. Cambridge: Cambridge University Press; New York: Macmillan, 1938. Second Impression, 1947. xii, 208pp.
Several chapters are reprints. Chapters: L'Allegro and Il Penseroso, Milton and Keats, Milton and Primitive Feeling, Milton and Prophetic Poetry, Milton and Protestantism, Milton's Visual Imagination, Milton's Style, Milton and the English Epic Tradition, the Growth of Milton's Epic Plans.
Rev: L. C. Martin, YWES, 175-6; QR, 271, 1938, 182; Denis Saurat, FR, 144, 1938, 367-8, and RES, 14, 1938, 473-4; T. O. Mabbott, Com., 28, 1938, 190; A. M. Witherspoon, SRL, June 18, 1938, p. 16; G. W. Whiting, MP, 36,

1938, 215-17; D. A. Roberts, Nat., 147, 1938, 272; TLS, Mar. 12, 1938, p. 169; F. R. Leavis, Scr., 7, 1938, 104-14; Merc., May, 1938, p. 82; Charles Williams, Crit., 17, 1938, 738-40; NQ, 174, 1938, 252; B. A. Wright, MLR, 35, 1939, 236-8; A. Brandl, DL, 59, 1939, 1496-9; W. R. Parker, MLN, 55, 1940, 215-18; R. Stamm, ESt., 75, 1942, 250-2; TLS, June 26, 1947, p. 380; H. B. C., MGW, June 20, 1947, p. 10.

1440 ------. Poetry Direct and Oblique. London: Chatto and Windus, 1934. 286pp.

Milton's works cited in a number of instances to illustrate the differences between direct and implied meaning in poetry.
Rev: TLS, Apr. 26, 1934, p. 298; K. John, NSN, 7, 1934, 678; B. de Selincourt, Obs., Apr. 15, 1934; M. Roberts, Spect., 153, 1934, 23; D. W. H., Scr., 3, 1934, 89; F. Kendon, FR, 142, 1934, 123-4; D. Verschoyle, Crit., 14, 1934, 152-6.

1441 ------. Studies in Milton. London: Chatto and Windus, 1951. 176pp.

A number of chapters are reprints. Chapters: Arnold on Milton; the Crisis of Paradise Lost; Satan; Satan, Gabriel, and the Plowman; Adam and Eve in Paradise; Milton's Humour; the Action of Comus; the Christ of Paradise Regained and the Renaissance Heroic Tradition; Private Correspondence and Academic Exercises; Theology and Emotion in Milton. Appendices: Milton and Statius; Milton and Philostratus.
Rev: L. C. Martin, YWES, 116-17; M. C. Bradbrook, NSN, Aug. 4, 1951, pp. 133-4; F. S. Boas, FR, 1016, 1951, 564-5; Hugh I'A. Fausset, MGW, July 19, 1951, p. 12; TLS, July 27, 1951, p. 464; Bonamy Dobrée, Spect., Aug. 3, 1951, pp. 166-8; M. G., Twentieth Century, 150, 1951, 171-2.

1442 TOUSLEY, MARION. Milton as Mythmaker. Master's thesis, Louisiana State University, 1939.

1443 TURNER, AMY L. The Visual Arts in Milton's Poetry. Doctoral diss., Rice Institute, 1955.

1444 TUVESON, ERNEST L. Millenium and Utopia: A Study in the Background of the Idea of Progress. Berkeley: University of California Press, 1949.

On the rise of the idea that a millenium was being brought about by God. Milton, passim.
Rev: G. N. Conklin, RN, 3, 1950, 47-8; G. R. Stephenson, NYTBR, Mar. 5, 1950, p. 18.

1445 USSERY, ANNIE W. Milton on Marriages and the Character of Women. Master's thesis, Emory University, 1943.

1446 VALENTE, LEONE. Milton. La poesia inglese ad il suo contributo alla conoscenza dello spirito (Firenze: Vallecchi, 1947), pp. 97-130.

1447 VECHTMAN-VETH, A. C. E. A Guide to English Studies: Suggestions for the Study of Milton and Dryden. ES, 11, 1929, 137-40.

1448 VISIAK, E. H. The Animus Against Milton. Derby, England: The Grasshopper Press, 1945. 9pp.
Notices several aspects of anti-Miltonic criticism.
Rev: NQ, 188, 1945, 176.

1449 - - - - - -. Notes on Milton. NQ, 174, 1940, 184-6, 276-8, 311-14, 453-4.
Topics discussed, resp., are Milton's development towards Quakerism, Samson Agonistes, Milton's Egotism, and Milton's personality.

1450 - - - - - -. Notes on Milton. NQ, 180, 1941, 133-4, 313, 316.
The subjects include Milton's genius, and Milton's idea of chastity, resp.

1451 - - - - - -. Notes on Milton. NQ, 183, 1942, 250.
On familiarized phrases and their sources.

1452 VIVANTE, LEONE. John Milton, 1608-1674. English Poetry and Its Contribution to the Knowledge of a Creative Principle (London: Faber, 1950), pp. 61-75.
On Milton and light.

1453 VOGT, KARL F. Milton als Publizist. Eine Untersuchung über die puritanische Auffassung von der Sendung Englands in 17. Jahrhundert. Doctoral diss., Tübingen. Würzburg: R. Mayr, 1933. 100pp.
Rev: A. B(randl). Archiv, 166, 1934, 139-40; L. C. Martin, YWES, 15, 1934, 239; H. O. Wilde, Ang. Bbl., 46, 1935, 241.

1454 VOIGT, F. A. Milton Thou Shouldst be Living.... NC, 130, 1941, 211-21.
A review of recent books.

1455 VOLTAIRE, FRANCOIS. Essay on Milton. Ed. by Desmond Flower. Cambridge: Cambridge University Press, 1954. xiv, 29pp.

1456 WARNER, REX. John Milton. London: Max Parrish, 1949. 112pp.
Rev: Arnold Davenport, YWES, 173; TLS, Apr. 28, 1950, p. 255; letter by E. M. W. Tillyard, ibid., May 5, 1950, p. 277; NSN, Mar. 11, 1950, p. 284; P. Russell, NER, 135, 1950, 72-4.

1457 WARREN, KATHRYN L. Milton's Concept of the Creation and Nature of Man: An Inquiry into Their Origins. Master's thesis, University of South Carolina, 1951.

1458 WATKINS, WALTER B. C. An Anatomy of Milton's Verse. Baton Rouge: Louisiana State University Press, 1955, x, 151pp.

> Chapters: Sensation, Creation, Temptations. In Sensation, Watkins discusses the sensory elements in the poetry; in Creation and in Temptation, he traces those themes in poems ranging from Comus to Samson Agonistes.
> Rev: Marvin Mudrick, Hudson Rev., 9, 1956, 126-33; Charles M. Coffin, QQ, 63, 1956, 138-44; TLS, Jan. 20, 1956, p. 38; D. C. Allen, MLN, 71, 1956, 532-3; R. W. Condee, CE, 18, 1956, 176; Kester Svendsen, BA, 30, 1956, 331; E. H. Emerson, SCN, 15, 1957, 28.

1459 WATSON, SARA R. Milton's Use of Phineas Fletcher's Purple Island. NQ, 180, 1941, 258.

1460 WEDDELL, FITZ-JOHN. References to Nature in the English Poems of John Milton. Master's thesis, Columbia University, 1932. 100pp.

1461 WEDGWOOD, C. V. John Milton. Seventeenth Century English Literature. Home University Library (Oxford: Oxford University Press, 1950), pp. 108-19.

> Rev: TLS, Oct. 6, 1950, p. 626; H. R. Charlton, MGW, Nov. 2, 1950, p. 11; R. G. Cox, Scr., 18, 1951, 56-9.

1462 WESEMAN, FRIEDRICH. Milton and das Naturrecht. Versuch eines Beitrages zur Geschichte der Menschenrechte. Doctoral diss., Hamburg, 1949. 151pp.

1463 WHITING, GEORGE W. The Father to the Son. MLN, 65, 1950, 191-3.

> Milton follows the Greek Fathers and St. Ambrose in believing that in creating man the Son was the external efficiency of God.

1464 - - - - - -. Milton and Cockeram's Dictionarie. NQ, 193, 1948, 555-8.

> This work (1623) useful in determining the meaning of Milton's words.
> Rev: L. C. Martin, YWES, 197.

1465 - - - - - -. Milton in The Classical Tradition. NQ, 197, 1952, 556-60.

> i.e., the book by Gilbert Highet.
> Rev: Arnold Davenport, YWES, 178.

1466 - - - - - -. Milton's Literary Milieu. Chapel Hill: University of North Carolina Press; London: Oxford University Press, 1939. xii, 401pp.

> "The definite purpose of this volume is to compare ideas in Milton's poetry and prose with those in contemporary writing, hexaemeral, historical, cartographical, phychological, theological, poetical, and controversial."

Rev: L. C. Martin, YWES, 168; B. A. Wright, MLR, 35, 1940, 393-4; E. N. S. T(hompson), PQ, 19, 1940, 414-15; Douglas Bush, JEGP, 39, 1940, 418-20; A. R. Benham, MLQ, 1, 1940, 558-9; A. M. Witherspoon, SRL, Jan. 20, 1940, p. 7; A. S. P. Woodhouse, UTQ, 10, 1941, 502-4; P. L. Carver, RES, 20, 1944, 163-6.

1467 - - - - - -. Milton's Rules for -ed. MLN, 49, 1934, 166-8.
Rev: L. C. Martin, YWES, 238.

1468 - - - - - -. Notes on Milton's Rabbinical Readings. NQ, 162, 1932, 344-6.
On the study by Harris F. Fletcher.

1469 - - - - - -. Pareus, the Stuarts, Laud, and Milton. SP, 50, 1953, 215-29.
On Milton and Pareus' doctrine of royal responsibility.
Rev: Arnold Davenport, YWES, 205.

1470 WILDE, HANS-OSKAR. Miltons geistesgeschichtliche Bedeutung. Heidelberg: Winter, 1933. 144pp.
Rev: L. C. Martin, YWES, 249; Lit. Zentralblatt, 84, 1933, 790; J. H. Hanford, MLN, 51, 1936, 53-4.

1471 - - - - - -. Miltons personliche und ideele Welt in ihrer Beziehung zum Aristokratismus. Bonn: Hanstein, 1933. 50pp.
Rev: L. C. Martin, YWES, 250.

1472 WILLEY, BASIL. The Seventeenth Century Background: Studies in the Thought of the Age in Relation to Poetry and Religion. London: Chatto and Windus, 1934. viii, 315pp.
Milton discussed, pp. 69-76 (on Scriptural interpretation), pp. 219-63 (the heroic poem in a scientific age), and passim. There have been several reprints of this study, including paperback editions.
Rev: TLS, Apr. 19, 1934, p. 269; H. J. C. Grierson, Scr., 3, 1934, 294; G. Burgess, Spect., 152, 1934, 466; T. O. Beachcroft, Crit., 13, 1934, 692-6; P. Meissner, ES, 17, 1935, 34-7; Walter Graham, JEGP, 42, 1943, 468-9; Arthur Barker, PRv., 52, 1943, 413-14; D. C. Allen, MLN, 59, 1944, 437-8.

1473 WILLIAMS, ARNOLD. Conservative Critics of Milton. SR, 49, 1941, 90-106.
On the criticism of Eliot, Grierson, and Tillyard.

1474 - - - - - -. Methods and Achievements in the Use of Milton's Sources: a Defense. Papers of the Mich. Acad., 32, 1948 for 1946, 471-80.
A reply to Gullette, ibid., pp. 447-56.

1475 - - - - - -. Milton and the Renaissance Commentaries on Genesis. MP, 37, 1940, 263-78.

1476 WILLIAMS, CHARLES. Milton. The English Poetic
Mind (Oxford: Clarendon Press, 1932), pp. 110-52.
Interprets Milton's poetry as a battle between gods and false
gods.
Rev: TLS, June, 16, 1932, p. 443; B. E. C. Davis, MLR,
28, 1933, 112-13; K. Arns, ESt., 68, 1933, 119-20.

1477 ------. The New Milton. Merc., 36, 1937, 225-61.
Favors a kindlier interpretation.

1478 WILLIAMSON, GEORGE. Milton and the Mortalist
Heresy. SP, 32, 1935, 553-79.
Rev: L. C. Martin, YWES, 254-5.

1479 WILSON, ARNOLD. New Light on Milton. NC, 119,
1936, 495-506.
On the contributions of Belloc, Skeat, Visiak and P. B. and
E. M. W. Tillyard. Censures Belloc for his attitude toward
Milton the man.

1480 WITHERSPOON, A. M. Milton Complete. SRL, Aug. 8,
1931, pp. 33-5.
Reviews the first two volumes of the Columbia Edition and
makes appreciative remarks about Milton.

1481 WOLFE, DON M., ed. Leveller Manifestoes of the Puritan
Revolution. Foreward by Charles A. Beard. New York
and London: Nelson, 1944. xvi, 440pp.
Rev: H. N. Brailsford, NSN, Aug. 26, 1944, pp. 140-1;
E. N. S. Thompson, PQ, 23, 1944, 287; William Haller,
MLN, 60, 1945, 135-6; H. J. C. Grierson, MLR, 40, 1945,
138-40; J. R. Roberts, MLQ, 6, 1945, 105-6; T. C. Pease,
AHR, 50, 1945, 315-16; W. S. Hudson, Church Hist., 14,
1945, 132-3; A. S. P. Woodhouse, UTQ. 15, 1945, 99-100;
Godfrey Davies, Pol. Sci. Quar. 60, 1945, 155-6.

1482 ------. Milton and Hobbes: a Contrast in Social Temper.
SP, 41, 1944, 410-26.

1483 ------. Milton and the Theory of Democracy. Doctoral
diss., University of Pittsburgh, 1930. Abs., University of
Pittsburgh, Abstracts of Theses, 6, 1930, 206-12.

1484 ------. Milton, Lilburne, and the People. MP, 31, 1934,
253-72.
Rev: L. C. Martin, YWES, 239.

1485 ------. Milton's Conception of the Ruler. SP, 33, 1936,
253-72.

1486 ------. Milton under Glass. TLS, May 18, 1956, p. 304.
A defense of recent Milton scholarship.

1487 WOLFF, SAMUEL L. Milton's Advocatum Nescio Quem:
Milton, Salmasius, and John Clark. MLQ, 2, 1941,
559-600.

1488 WOODHOUSE, A. S. P. The Approach to Milton: a Note on Practical Criticism. TRSC, 38, 1944, 201-13.
Censures the New Critics and defends the "conservative or solid" type of criticism.

1489 ------. Background for Milton. UTQ, 10, 1941, 504-5.
A review of recent Milton studies.

1490 ------. The Historical Criticism of Milton. PMLA, 66, 1951, 1033-44.
A paper read before the Milton group of MLA on Dec. 28, 1950.
Rev: Arnold Davenport, YWES, 184-5.

1491 ------. Milton and His Age. UTQ, 5, 1935, 130-9.
Comments on studies by Hanford, Sewell, Willey, Saurat, Powicke, and Cassirer.

1492 ------. Milton the Poet. Sedgewick Memorial Lecture, University of British Columbia. Toronto: J. M. Dent, 1955. 30pp.
Attacks Eliot, Brooks, Empson, and Bodkin and considers six distinctive marks of Milton the poet.

1493 ------. Milton, Puritanism, and Liberty. UTQ, 4, 1935, 483-513.

1494 ------. Notes on Milton's Early Development. UTQ, 13, 1943, 66-101.
On the dates and interrelations of the early poems.
Rev: L. C. Martin, YWES, 150.

1495 ------. Notes on Milton's Views on the Creation: the Initial Phase. PQ, 28, 1949, 211-36.
Rev: L. C. Martin, YWES, 165-6.

1496 WRENN, C. L. The Language of Milton. Studies in English Language and Literature Presented to Karl Brunner on the Occasion of His Seventieth Birthday. Ed. by S. Korniger. Weiner Beiträge zur Englischen Philologie, 65 (Wein-Stuggart: Wilhelm Braumuller, 1957), pp. 252-67.
Appreciative.

1497 WYLD, H. C. The Significance of -'n and -en in Milton's Spelling. ESt., 70, 1935, 138-48.
Rev: L. C. Martin, YWES, 256.

1498 ZAGARIA, R. Serafino da Salandra, Inspiratore di Milton. Bari: Resta, 1950. 86pp.

1499 ZAGORIN, PEREZ. John Milton. A History of Political Thought in the English Revolution (London: Routledge, 1954), pp. 106-20.
"The vast amount of writing that has appeared...serves, I think, to obscure the fact that as a political theorist and systematic thinker, he was not of the first order."

BIOGRAPHY

1500 ADAMS, BOWN, and RICHARD ARMOUR. To These Dark Steps. A Play in Three Acts Suggested by the Life of John Milton. New York: New York Institute for the Education of the Blind, 1943. 72pp.

1501 ALLEN, DON CAMERON. Dr. Gui Patin Looks at England. SAQ, 42, 1943, 179-84.
Views from letters on Englishmen, esp. Milton and Bacon.

1502 ANDERSON, PAUL B. Anonymous Critic of Milton: Richard Leigh? or Samuel Butler? SP, 44, 1947, 504-18.
Assigns three anonymous tracts to Butler.
Rev: L. C. Martin, YWES, 192.

1503 ASHLEY, MAURICE. John Wildman: Plotter and Postmaster. A Study of the English Republican Movement of the Seventeenth Century. London: Cape, 1947. 319pp.
Passim.

1504 AUBREY, JOHN. Aubrey's Brief Lives. Ed. by Oliver Lawson Dick. London: Secker and Warburg, 1949. cxiv, 408pp.
Milton, pp. 199-203, and passim.

1505 BAILEY, JOHN. Milton. Home University Library. Revised Edition. New York: Henry Holt; London: Williams and Norgate, 1930.
Stevens' No. 2417.

1506 BAINTON, ROLAND H. The Bard of Speech Unbound: John Milton. The Travail of Religious Liberty: Nine Biographical Studies (Philadelphia: Westminster Press, 1951), pp. 179-207.
An account of Milton's political activities.
Rev: L. A. Loetscher, Church Hist., 21, 1952, 82-3; Robert Friedmann, Mennonite Quar. Rev., 26, 1952, 324-5; Theodore Hoyer, Concordia Theological Monthly, 23, 1952, 781-2.

1507 BALDWIN, RUTH M. Alexander Gill, the Elder, High Master of St. Paul's School: An Approach to Milton's Intellectual Development. Doctoral diss., University of Illinois, 1955. Abs., DA, 15, 1955, 1862.

1508 BARKER, ARTHUR. Milton's Schoolmasters. MLR, 32, 1937, 517-36.

1509 BELLER, ELMER A. Milton and Mercurius Politicus. HLQ, 5, 1942, 479-87.
Denies that Milton wrote any of the editorials in this journal.

1510 BELLOC, HILAIRE. Milton. London: Cassell; Philadelphia: Lippincott, 1935. 336pp.
> A biased account of Milton the man but penetrating criticism of the works.
> Rev: L. C. Martin, YWES, 252; TLS, Apr. 4, 1935, p. 225; Bonamy Dobrée, Merc., May, 1935, pp. 70-1; E. Shanks, FR, 143, 1935, 633-4; A. M. Witherspoon, SRL, 11, 1935, 646-7; Blanche Kelly, CW, 141, 1935, 368-70; E. M. W. Tillyard, Spect., 154, 1935, 576; LL, 12, 1935, 105-6; P. Hutchinson, NYTBR, Mar. 24, 1935, pp. 4, 16; E. Wagenknecht, VQR, 11, 1935, 601-6; E. Ryan, CHR, 21, 1936, 458-60; Arnold Wilson, NC, 119, 1936, 495-506.

1511 BENHAM, ALLEN R. The So-Called Anonymous or Earliest Life of Milton. ELH, 6, 1939, 245-55.
> Argues against the view that Wood used the anonymous life and favors a date later than Wood's account, Reaffirms this view in Reply to Dr. Parsons, ELH, 9, 1942, 116-17.

1512 BLOCK, EDWARD A. Milton's Gout. BHM, 28, 1954, 201-11.
> Rev: Arnold Davenport, YWES, 137.

1513 BRENNECKE, ERNEST, JR. John Milton the Elder and His Music. Columbia University Stud. in Musicology, 2. New York: Columbia University Press, 1938. xiii, 324pp.
> Rev: L. C. Martin, YWES, 176; W. G. Hill, JEGP, 38, 1939, 618-20; J. A. W., ML, 20, 1939, 197-8; T. M. Pearce and D. F. Smith, New Mex. Quar., 9, 1939, 67-8; C. S. Smith, MLN, 54, 1939, 628-9; TLS, Apr. 15, 1939, p. 222.

1514 BRODRIBB, C. W. Milton at St. Paul's School. TLS, Oct. 10, 1929, p. 794.

1515 B(RODRIBB), C. W. A portrait of Milton by Mytens. NQ, 164, 1933, 389.

1516 BROWN, ELEANOR G. Milton's Blindness. Doctoral diss., Columbia University, 1934. New York: Columbia University Press; London: Milford, 1934. 167pp.
> Rev: L. C. Martin, YWES, 234; TLS, Aug. 23, 1934, p. 579; A. H. Gilbert, SAQ, 33, 1934, 316-17; E. N. S. Thompson, PQ, 13, 1934, 318; B. A. Wright, MLR, 30, 1935, 231-3; H. O. Wilde, Ang. Bbl., 46, 1935, 241-3; W. H. Wilmer, MLN, 50, 1935, 402-3; G. W. Whiting, MP, 33, 1935, 92-5; D. Saurat, MLN, 51, 1936, 263-4.

1517 CAMERON, KENNETH W. Milton's Library. TLS, Oct. 24, 1936, p. 868.
> Concerning the discovery of an unrecorded Milton autograph. See note by Maurice Kelley, ibid., Dec. 19, 1936, p. 1056.
> Rev: L. C. Martin, YWES, 190.

1518 CANDY, HUGH C. H. Milton as Translator. NQ, 161, 1931, 129-30.
Holds that the English version of May's Breviary of the History of the Parliament of England (1650) was really the work of Milton.
Rev: F. S. Boas, YWES, 208.

1519 ------. Milton Autographs Established. Libr., N. S., 13, 1932, 192-200.
On marginal corrections in Lycidas
Rev: L. C. Martin, YWES, 208.

1520 ------. Milton's Prolusio Script. Libr., 4th Ser., 15, 1934, 330-9.
On Milton's early handwriting.

1521 CARD, WILLIAM M. Milton's Coming of Age. Doctoral diss., University of Wisconsin, 1936. Abs., Summaries of Doctoral Diss., University of Wisconsin, 1, 1938, 273-5.
A study of the develpoment of Milton's character and literary interests to his twenty-first year.

1522 Charles Diodati. NQ, 175, 1938, 145.
A biographical account.

1523 CHESTER, ALLAN G. Milton, Latimer, and the Lord Admiral. MLQ, 14, 1953, 15-20.
Concerning Milton's charge that Latimer was the creature of the politicians.
Rev: Arnold Davenport, YWES, 204.

1524 CHIFOS, EUGENIA. Milton's Letter to Gill, May 20, 1628. MLN, 62, 1947, 37-9.
Dates the letter May 20, 1630.
Rev: L. C. Martin, YWES, 186.

1525 CLARK, DONALD L. John Milton and William Chappell. HLQ, 18, 1955, 329-50.

1526 ------. John Milton at St. Paul's School, a Study of Ancient Rhetoric in English Renaissance Education. New York: Columbia University Press, 1948. x, 269pp.
Chapters: The Trivium, Milton as a Schoolboy, St. Paul's School, Milton's Schoolmasters, The Course of Study at St. Paul's School, Textbooks, Authors for Imitations, Exercises for Praxis.
Rev: L. C. Martin, YWES, 192; H. F. Fletcher, JEGP, 47, 1948, 308-9; W. A. Turner, JMH, 20, 1948, 367; VQR, 24, 1948, lxxxiii; F. M. Krouse, MLN, 64, 1949, 130-2; A. H. Gilbert, SAQ, 48, 1949, 486-7; L. C. Martin, RES, 25, 1949, 362-3; C. T. Harrison, SR, 57, 1949, 709-14; H. W. Wilson, UTQ, 19, 1949, 103-5; I. A. Richards, KR, 11, 1949, 17-30; Lionel Stephenson, Pers., 30, 1949, 207-8.

1527 ------. Milton's Schoolmasters: Alexander Gill and His Son Alexander. HLQ, 9, 1946, 121-47.
Rev: L. C. Martin, YWES, 175.

1528 CLARK, WILLIAM S. Milton and the Villa Diodati.
RES, 11, 1935, 51-7.
On the improbability of Milton's having stayed there during
his Italian trip.
Rev: L. C. Martin, YWES, 256.

1529 CLYDE, WILLIAM M. Parliament and the Press, 1643-7.
Libr., 4th Ser., 13, 1933, 399-424; 14, 1933, 39-58.
Milton and the 1643 ordinance, pp. 408-15.

1530 COOLIDGE, LOWELL W. At Any Hour the Italian
Tongue. NQ, 194, 1949, 537.
On Milton's method of learning Italian.
Rev: L. C. Martin, YWES, 163.

1531 DAICHES, DAVID. Milton. London and New York:
Hutchinson's University Library, 1957. 254pp.
Rev: TLS, Oct. 25, 1957, p. 642.

1532 DARBISHIRE, HELEN. The Chronology of Milton's
Handwriting. Libr., 4th Ser., 14, 1933, 229-35.
Rev: L. C. Martin, YWES, 251.

1533 - - - - - -, ed. The Early Lives of Milton. London: Constable,
1932. lxi, 353pp.
Contains the six contemporary accounts.
Rev: L. C. Martin, YWES, 205-6; TLS, Dec. 1, 1932, p.
918; R. Macaulay, Spect., 149, 1932, 835; B. A. Wright,
MLR, 28, 1933, 518-25; L. L. Irvine, Obs., Feb. 12, 1933;
Dublin Rev., 193, 1933, 301-4; G. C. M. S., EHR, 48, 1933,
699-700; H. Agar, ER, 56, 1933, 98-100; K. M. L., Oxf.
Mag., May 4, 1933, p. 613; Paul Chauvet, RA-A, 10, 1933,
521.

1534 DAVIES, GODFREY. Milton in 1660. HLQ, 18, 1955,
351-63.

1535 DE BEER, E. S. The Site of Diodati's House. RES, 14,
1938, 78.

1536 DIEKHOFF, JOHN S., ed. Milton on Himself: Milton's
Utterances upon Himself and His Works. New York:
Oxford University Press, 1939. xxxvi, 307pp.
A collection of autobiographical passages accompanied by
editorial comments.
Rev: L. C. Martin, YWES, 113; M. L. Zisowitz, SRL, June
17, 1939, p. 18; D. Roberts, NYTBR, June 4, 1939, p. 2;
TLS, June 10, 1939, p. 346; W. R. Parker, MLN, 55, 1940,
215-18; Z. S. Fink, JEGP, 39, 1940, 286-7; D. C. Macgregor,
RES, 16, 1940, 114-15.

1537 DORIAN, DONALD C. Charles Diodati at Geneva.
PMLA, 59, 1944, 589-91.

1538 - - - - - -. The English Diodatis. A History of Charles
Diodati's Family and His Friendship with Milton.
Doctoral diss., Columbia University, 1950. New Bruns-
wick: Rutger's University Press, 1950. xvii, 365pp.
> Rev: Arnold Davenport, YWES, 174-5; NQ, 195, 1950, 374;
> Marguerite Little, JEGP, 49, 1950, 585; E. G. Midgley,
> MLR, 46, 1951, 90-1; A. H. Gilbert, SAQ, 50, 1951, 435-6;
> D. C. A(llen), MLN, 66, 1951, 570-1; A. E. Barker, UTQ,
> 20, 1951, 430-2; H. W. Donner, ES, 33, 1952, 35-7.

1539 DOS PASSOS, JOHN R. Liberty to Speak to Print. The
Ground We Stand On (New York: Harcourt, 1941),
pp. 85-100.
> An account of Milton's activities prior to 1640.

1540 DUNCAN-JONES, ELSIE. Milton and Marvell. TLS,
July 31, 1953, p. 493.
> The "learned man" in Milton's letter to Henry Oldenburg
> (Aug. 1, 1657) is Andrew Marvell.

1541 ELLWOOD, THOMAS. Davideis. Ed. by Walther
Fischer. Heidelberg: Winter, 1936.
> The epic written by Milton's friend.

1542 ENGLAND, SYLVIA L. The Site of Diodati's House.
RES, 13, 1937, 73-6.

1543 EVANS, WILLA M. Henry Lawes: Musician and Friend
of Poets. MLA Revolving Fund Series, 11. New York:
Modern Language Association; London: Oxford University Press, 1941. 250pp.
> Rev: J. T. Wisely, RES, 19, 1943, 86-8; H. E. Rollins,
> MLN, 58, 1943, 317-18; John Butt, MLR, 38, 1943, 51-2;
> E. N. S. Thompson, PQ, 22, 1943, 284-5.

1544 FALCONER, J. P. E. A Portrait-Miniature of John
Milton. NQ, 194, 1949, 142-3.
> Rev: L. C. Martin, YWES, 171.

1545 FISCHER, WALTHER. Ein wenig bekanntes Autogramm
Miltons. Ang., 57, 1933, 221-4.
> Rev: L. C. Martin, YWES, 252.

1546 FLETCHER, HARRIS F. Education of a Literary Genius.
Phi Delta Kappan, 35, 1954, 243-6.

1547 - - - - - -. The Intellectual Development of John Milton.
Vol. 1: The Institution to 1625: From the Beginnings
Through Grammar School. Urbana: University of Illi-
nois Press, 1956. iii, 459pp.
> The first of a projected several volumes designed to trace
> Milton's mental growth to 1654.
> Rev: W. R. Parker, MLN, 72, 1957, 447-51; D. L. Clark,
> JEGP, 56, 1957, 633-6; TLS, Jan. 25, 1957, p. 50; J. Max
> Patrick, SCN, 15, 1957, 9.

1548 - - - - - -. Milton's E Nostro Suburbano. JEGP, 51, 1952, 154-9.

> Argues against the assumption of Milton's retirement to Horton.
> Rev: Arnold Davenport, YWES, 177.

1549 - - - - - -. Milton's Private Library—An Additional Title. PQ, 28, 1949, 72-6.

> Bernardo Davanzati's Scisma d'Inghilterra con altre Operette (1638).
> Rev: L. C. Martin, YWES, 171.

1550 FRANK, JOSEPH. The Levellers. A History of the Writings of Three Seventeenth-Century Social Democrats: John Lilburne, Richard Overton, and William Walwyn. Cambridge: Harvard University Press, 1955. viii, 345pp.

> A background study.

1551 FREEDMAN, MORRIS. Dryden's Memorable Visit to Milton. HLQ, 18, 1955, 99-108.

> The connection between the visit and the rhymed couplet-blank verse controversy.

1552 FRENCH, J. MILTON. An Action Against Milton. TLS, Dec. 21, 1935, p. 879.

> Sir Robert Pye's complaint, Feb. 11, 1646/7.
> Rev: L. C. Martin, YWES, 256-7.

1553 - - - - - -. An Action Against Milton. TLS, Mar. 14, 1936, p. 224.

> Milton's reply to Pye's complaint.
> Rev: L. C. Martin, YWES, 190.

1554 - - - - - -. The Autographs of John Milton. ELH, 4, 1937, 300-30.

> Rev: L. C. Martin, YWES, 186.

1555 - - - - - -. The Baptism of Milton's Daughter Mary. MLN, 63, 1948, 264-5.

> Rev: L. C. Martin, YWES, 196.

1556 - - - - - -. The Date of Milton's Blindness. PQ, 15, 1936, 93-4.

> About 1651/2.
> Rev: L. C. Martin, YWES, 190.

1557 - - - - - -, ed. The Life Records of John Milton. Rutgers Stud. in Eng., 7. New Brunswick: Rutgers University Press, 1949-58.

> Five volumes: 1, 1608-1639, 1949, x, 446pp.; 2, 1639-1651, 1950, vi, 395pp.; 3, 1651-1654, 1954, 470pp.; 4, 1655-1669, vi, 482pp.; 5, 1670-1674, 1958, 568pp.

Of inestimable value to future biographers.
Rev: D. C. Dorian, Rutgers Alumni Monthly, Apr., 1950,
pp. 18-19; TLS, Apr. 14, 1950, p. 232, and Oct. 5, 1956,
p. 583; NQ, 195, 1950, 198; Dora N. Raymond, AHR, 55,
1950, 970-1; H. F. Fletcher, JEGP, 49, 1950, 416-21;
Wilhelmina Gordon, QQ, 57, 1950, 136-7; A. H. Gilbert,
SAQ, 49, 1950, 418-19; D. A. Roberts, Nat. (N. Y.), Aug. 5,
1950, pp. 132-3, May 12, 1951, p. 448, and Feb. 5, 1955,
p. 181; B. A. Wright, RES, 2, 1951, 179-81, Ernest Sirluck,
MP, 48, 1951, 273-4; H. W. Donner, ES, 33, 1952, 33-5,
and 37, 1956, 18-19; A. S. P. Woodhouse, UTQ, 21, 1952,
193-6; M. M. Mahood, MLR, 47, 1952, 393-4; Ralph W.
Condee, CE, 17, 1955, 126; W. B. Hunter, MLN, 70, 1955,
531-2, and 72, 1957, 618-19; NQ, N. S., 2, 1955, 276; L. C.
Martin, MLR, 51, 1956, 102-3; Ruth Mohl, SCN, 14, 1956,
3-4; J. B. Broadbent, MLR, 52, 1957, 627; NQ, N. S., 4,
1957, 90.

1558 ------. John Milton, Scrivener, the Temples of Stowe,
and Sir John Lenthall. HLQ, 4, 1941, 303-7.
Three documents concerning the elder Milton.

1559 ------. Milton and the Politicians. PQ, 15, 1936, 94-5.

1560 ------. The Miltonic Epitaph on Mazarin. NQ, 168,
1935, 445.
Questions Milton's authorship.

1561 ------. Milton in Chancery; New Chapters in the Lives
of the Poet and His Father. MLA Monograph Series,
10. New York: Modern Language Association; London:
Milford, Oxford University Press, 1939. x, 428pp.
Rev: L. C. Martin, YWES, 112-13; TLS, Sept. 14, 1940,
p. 475; B. A. Wright, RES, 16, 1940, 467-70; E. N. S.
T(hompson), PQ, 19, 1940, 414-15; A. M. Witherspoon,
SRL, Jan. 20, 1940, p. 7; NQ, 178, 1940, 449-50; Dora
N. Raymond, AHR, 46, 1940, 703-4; W. R. Parker, MLN,
56, 1941, 393; A. Barker, MLR, 36, 1941, 124-5; H. F.
Fletcher, JEGP, 40, 1941, 145-6.

1562 ------. Milton, Needham, and Mercurius Politicus. SP,
33, 1936, 236-52.
On Milton's participation.
Rev: L. C. Martin, YWES, 190.

1563 ------. Milton's Family Bible. PMLA, 53, 1938, 363-6.
On the underscorings in the Bible as a clue to Milton's
interests.

1564 ------. Milton's Homes and Investments. PQ, 28, 1949,
77-97.
Rev: L. C. Martin, YWES, 171.

1565 ------. Milton's Supplicats. HLQ, 5, 1942, 349-59.
Prints the supplicats for the BA and MA degrees.

1566 ------. Mr. Secretary Milton at Work. SAQ, 55, 1956, 313-21.

> "The purpose of this paper is to watch Milton in action as seen through the diary and letters of Mylius, from which Milton emerges as a brain among brawn, a scholar among mechanics."

1567 ------. Mute Inglorious John Miltons. MLQ, 1, 1940, 367-81.

> On the John Miltons who were contemporaries of the poet.

1568 ------. A New Letter by John Milton. PMLA, 49, 1934, 1069-70.

> Addressed to Sir Bulstrode Whitelocke.

1569 ------. The Powell-Milton Bond. Harvard Stud. and Notes, 29, 1938, 61-73.

> Rev: L. C. Martin, YWES, 179.

1570 ------. Two Notes on Milton and Wither. NQ, N. S., 1, 1954, 472-3.

> Opposes Kendall's views, ibid., 198, 1953, 473.

1571 FRYE, ROLAND MUSHAT. Milton's First Marriage. NQ, N. S., 3, 1956, 200-2.

> Contemporary opinion concerning Milton's courtship with Mary Powell.

1572 FULLER, EDMUND. John Milton. Pictures by Robert Ball. New York and London: Harper, 1944. 238pp.

> A fictional biography.

1573 GORDON, GEORGE S. The Youth of Milton. The Lives of Authors (London: Chatto and Windus, 1950), pp. 44-86.

> Remarks on Milton delivered at University College, London, Feb., 1926.
> Rev: Arnold Davenport, YWES, 174; TLS, June 9, 1950, p. 355; R. G. Cox, MGW, May 11, 1950, p. 11.

1574 GOULD, CHARLES. Milton and the Ghouls. SR, 150, 1930, 662-3.

> On a pamphlet describing the disinterment of Milton's remains in 1790.

1575 GRABILL, PAUL E. Milton's Residences and Real Estate Holdings. Doctoral diss., University of Illinois, 1954. Abs., DA, 14, 1954, 357-8.

1576 GRAVES, ROBERT. Wife to Mr. Milton: The Story of Marie Powell. London: Cassell, 1943; New York: Creative Age Press, 1944. viii, 372pp.

> A biased account as told by Mary herself.
> Rev: TLS, Jan. 30, 1943, p. 53; reply by Graves, ibid., Feb. 6, 1943, p. 67; Carlos Baker, NYTBR, No. 26, 1944, p. 5.

1577 GUIDI, AUGUSTO. John Milton. Brescia: Morcelleana, 1940. 195pp.
On Milton's life, pp. 7-42.

1578 HALLER, WILLIAM. Milton and the Levellers. Summarized in The Renaissance Conference at the Huntington Library. HLQ, 5, 1942, 155-201.

1579 HANFORD, JAMES H. Dr. Paget's Library. BMLA, 33, 1945, 91-9.
The auction sale catalogue of books of Dr. Nathan Paget, dated Oct. 24, 1681, reveals a close affinity of minds between Milton and Dr. Paget.

1580 ------. John Milton, Englishman. New York: Crown Publishers, 1949. 272pp.
An interpretation of Milton the man rather than a straightforward biography. Lengthy comments on the works.
Rev: W. Y. Tindall, NYTBR, Oct. 23, 1949, p. 6; S. C. Chew, NYHTBR, Oct. 30, 1949, p. 5; William Haller, SRL, 32, 1949, 22; Douglas Bush, NR, 121, 1949, 30; E. S. Gohn, MP, 48, 1950, 68-70; A. H. Gilbert, SAQ, 49, 1950, 409-11; TLS, Nov. 24, 1950, p. 739; T. B. Stroup, SCN, 8, 1950, 2; H. B. Charlton, MGW, Sept. 14, 1950, p. 12; R. Warner, Spect., Sept. 15, 1950, p. 295; Arnold Davenport, YWES, 31, 1950, 173-4; H. V. Routh, Eng., 8, 1951, 202.

1581 ------. John Milton Forswears Physic. BMLA, 32, 1944, 23-34.
Identifies Milton's Paris physician as Maistre Francois Thevenin and comments on the poet's own attitude toward his affliction.

1582 ------. The Marriage of Edward Phillips and Anne Milton. RES, 9, 1933, 58-60.
Rev: L. C. Martin, YWES, 250-1.

1583 ------. Pepys and the Skinner Family. RES, 7, 1931, 257-70.
Comments on Daniel Skinner, Milton's last amanuensis.

1584 HARKNESS, G. Eschatology in the Great Poets. Religion in Life, 22, 1952, 85-99.
Milton's views discussed, pp. 94-6.

1585 HAVENS, P. S. A Tract Long Attributed to Milton. HLB, 6, 1934, 109-14.
On the authorship of A Letter Written to A Gentleman in the Country. See Masson, Life, 4, 519-23.

1586 HENDRICKSON, G. L. Milton, Salmasius,—and Synizesis. PQ, 20, 1941, 597-600.

1587 HESSLER, L. B. Attributed to Milton. TLS, June 28, 1934, p. 460.

Submits a Latin poem, Julii Mazarini, Cardinalis, Epitaphium, found in Miscellany Poems upon several occasions...(1692), for expression of opinion as to its authenticity.

1588 HONE, RALPH E. Edward and John Phillips: Nephews and Pupils of John Milton. Doctoral diss., New York University, 1955.

1589 HOWARTH, R. G. Dramatists' Namesakes and Milton's Father. NQ, N. S., 1, 1954, 83.
Cites a document signed at the home of Milton's father between John Webster, a tallow-chandler, and William Rowley of Clavering.

1590 HOWE, ENA HAY. Blind Milton, a Dramatic Episode. London: S. French, 1947. 27pp.

1591 HUGHES, MERRITT Y. Milton as a Revolutionary. ELH, 10, 1943, 87-116.
Delivered as a lecture before the Tudor and Stuart Club of Johns Hopkins University.
Rev: L. C. Martin, YWES, 149-50.

1592 HUTCHINSON, FRANCIS E. Milton and the English Mind. Teach Yourself History Series. London: Hodder and Stoughton for the English Universities Press, 1946. vii, 197pp.
A sympathetic biographical account.
Rev: L. C. Martin, YWES, 28, 1947, 184; TLS, Mar. 29, 1947, p. 140; Charles Morgan, Sun. Times, Feb. 2, 1947, p. 4; A. N. Jeffares, ES, 28, 1947, 82-4; FR, 161, 1947, 311; H. N. Brailsford, NSN, Feb. 15, 1947, p. 138; Pierre Legouis, Les Langues modernes, 41, 1947, 443-4; B. A. Wright, RES, 24, 1948, 68-9; N. M., QQ, 55, 1948, 366; Lionel Stephenson, Pers., 30, 1949, 207-8.

1593 KELLEY, MAURICE. Addendum: The Later Career of Daniel Skinner. PMLA, 55, 1940, 116-18.

1594 - - - - - -. The Annotations in Milton's Family Bible. MLN, 63, 1948, 539-40.
Addenda to the Columbia notes.

1595 - - - - - -. Daniel Skinner, Lord Preston, and Milton's Commonplace Book. MLN, 64, 1949, 522-5.
Prints two letters from Skinner to Lord Preston.
Rev: L. C. Martin, YWES, 171.

1596 - - - - - -. Milton Autographs. TLS, Oct. 2, 1937, p. 715.

1597 - - - - - -. Milton and Machiavelli's Discorsi. Stud. in Bibliography, 4, 1951, 123-8.
Argues that Milton's notes on Machiavelli were made during 1651-2.

1598 - - - - - -. Milton and Mylius. TLS, June 17, 1949, p. 397.
On the discovery of two Milton autographs and a copy of Mylius' diary in the Niedersächsische Staatsarchiv at Oldenburg.
Rev: L. C. Martin, YWES, 164.

1599 - - - - - -. Milton and the Notes on Paul Best. Libr., 5th Ser., 5, 1950, 49-51.
Questions Milton's authorship.
Rev: Arnold Davenport, YWES, 177.

1600 - - - - - -. Milton's Commonplace Book, Folio 20. MLN, 62, 1947, 192-4.
Holds that the entry is in the handwriting of Lord Preston.
Rev: L. C. Martin, YWES, 193.

1601 - - - - - -. Milton's Library. TLS, Dec. 19, 1936, p. 1056.
Maintains that the signature discovered by Cameron is not genuine.

1602 - - - - - -. Robert Overton (1609-1668?), Friend of Milton. PULC, 4, 1943, 76-8.
Describes a recent acquisition by the Princeton Library, a notebook kept by Overton (370pp.) and compiled after 1665.

1603 KEMBLE, JAMES. John Milton and His Blindness. Idols and Invalids (London: Methuen, 1933; New York: Doubleday, 1936), pp. 247-92.
Argues that glaucoma was the cause of blindness and attempts to disprove other diagnoses.

1604 KENDALL, LYLE H., JR. A Letter from John Milton to George Wither? NQ, 198, 1953, 473.
Considers the probability of Milton's composition of a letter included in Wither's Se Defendendo (1643) and signed "J. M."

1605 KEYNES, GEOFFREY. John Donne's Sermons. TLS, May 28, 1954, p. 351.
Includes a transcription of a Latin letter written by Thomas Egerton to his father.

1606 KLIGER, SAMUEL. Milton in Italy and the Lost Malatesti Manuscript. SP, 51, 1954, 208-14.
Concerning Malatesti's collection of sonnets, La Tina, and an account of the MS which the poet gave to Milton.

1607 LAWRENCE, C. E. The Caged Eagle (a drama). Bookman (London), 84, 1933, 277-9.

1608 LE COMTE, EDWARD S. Milton Remembers The Praise of Folly. PMLA, 71, 1956, 840.
The fourth sentence of the Apology for Smectymnuus echoes a passage from Moriae Encomium and shows that Milton is "feeling doubts and strains that will shortly...impel him to marriage."

1609 LILJEGREN, S. B. Miltons italienische Reise. Ang. Bbl., 40, 1939, 377-8. Reprinted in UEIES, 16, 1956, xxvi-xxviii.
On Milton's alleged falsehoods concerning the journey.

1610 MABBOTT, THOMAS O. Archie Armstrong and Milton. NQ, 179, 1940, 14.
The young Milton and humorous verse.

1611 - - - - - -. Contemporary Evidence for Royal Favour to Milton. NQ, 169, 1935, 221.
Rev: L. C. Martin, YWES, 257.

1612 - - - - - -. Milton: Latin Inscription in a Bible. NQ, 159, 1930, 150.
From a Bible which belonged to Milton's wife.

1613 - - - - - -. Milton: A Marginal Note on Varchi. NQ, 163, 1932, 189.
Milton's note in a book found in the New York Public Library.

1614 - - - - - -. The Miltonic Epitaph on Mazarin. NQ, 167, 1934, 349-50.
Two texts in Miscellany Poems on Several Occasions (1692) may deserve inclusion in the Milton canon.

1615 - - - - - -. The Miltonic Epitaph on Mazarin: Cowper's Opinion. NQ, 172, 1937, 188.
Cowper considered the epitaph Milton's.

1616 - - - - - -. Milton, Leigh, and Dunkin. TLS, July 19, 1937, p. 512.
Perhaps the unpublished pamphlet mentioned by Edward Phillips refers to a religious controversy with Robert Dunkin, not Richard Leigh.

1617 - - - - - -. Milton to Mylius: Letter found at Oldenburg. NQ, 159, 1930, 208.
Reprint of a letter from Milton to Mylius.

1618 - - - - - -. Milton's Manuscript Notes. TLS, Jan. 30, 1937, p. 76.

1619 - - - - - -. Milton's "Overdaled sphears." NQ, 161, 1931, 459.
Query concerning B. M. MS. 36354.

1620 - - - - - -. Notes on Farnaby Ascribed to John Milton. NQ, 171, 1936, 152-4.
Reproduces the marginalia and an abridgment of the text of the Harvard copy of the Systema Grammaticum (1641) which bears the name "I. Miltoni."
Rev: L. C. Martin, YWES, 189-90.

1621 - - - - - -, and J. MILTON FRENCH. The Grand Case of Conscience Wrongly Attributed to Milton. NQ, 185, 1943, 302-3.
    Explains the decision not to include the work in the Columbia Edition.
    Rev: L. C. Martin, YWES, 154.

1622 - - - - - -. Milton: An Apocryphal Story. NQ, 181, 1941, 204.
    A query concerning the origin of the legend that Milton wrote Paradise Lost after marriage and Paradise Regained after Mary's death and that he locked her coffin.

1623 MACAULAY, ROSE. Milton. London: Duckworth, 1933. 141pp.
    A scholarly and concise biography.
    Rev: L. C. Martin, YWES, 15, 1934, 234; Clennell Wilkinson, Merc., 29, 1934, 477; Herbert Agar, ER, 58, 1934, 227-31; P. H., NYTBR, Mar. 10, 1934, p. 3; TLS, Jan. 11, 1934, p. 29; B. de Selincourt, Obs., Jan. 28, 1934; B. Dobrée, Spect., 152, 1934, 244; reply by Macaulay, ibid., 275-6, A. M. Witherspoon, SRL, 11, 1935, 646-7; Blanche Kelly, CW, 141, 1935, 368-70; E. Wagenknecht, VQR, 11, 1935, 601-6; R. S. Scholler, Unity, Oct. 7, 1935, pp. 56-7.

1624 McCOLLEY, GRANT. Milton's Lost Tragedy. PQ, 18, 1939, 73-83.
    Believes that after 1645 Milton designed a tragedy different from the drafts found in the Trinity MSS.

1625 Milton's Cottage. SRL, Apr. 6, 1957, p. 31.
    Pictures and describes briefly the cottage at Chalfont St. Giles.

1626 MORAND, PAUL P. The Effects of His Political Life upon John Milton (these complementaire). Paris: Didier, 1939. 126pp.
    Rev: E. M. W. Tillyard, MLN, 55, 1940, 635-6; E. N. S. T(hompson), PQ, 19, 1940, 223.

1627 MUIR, KENNETH. John Milton. Men and Books Series. London: Longmans, 1955. 196pp.
    A sympathetic biography containing attacks on the New Critics.
    Rev: Arnold Davenport, YWES, 158; B. Evan Owen, CR, 188, 1955, 132-3; Rex Warner, Lon. Mag., 2, No. 8, 1955, 74-6; NSN, May 14, 1955, p. 694; NQ, N. S., 2, 1955, 322; TLS, May 6, 1955, p. 238; Owen Chadwick, JEH, 7, 1956, 127; E. H. Emerson, JEGP, 51, 1956, 509-10.

1628 NAZÀRI, EMILIO. Problemi Miltoniani. Palermo: A Priulla, 1951. 250pp.
    Two chapters of interest in connection with Milton's biography: Il Viaggio di Milton in Italia e Ondeggiamenti Religiosi, pp. 7-43; Alcune Considerazioni Sulla Vita e Sulla Figura del Milton, pp. 218-47.

1629 NETHERCOT, ARTHUR H. Milton, Jonson, and Young Cowley. MLN, 49, 1934, 158-62.
Possibly the friendship between Jonson and Cowley aroused the envy of Milton.

1630 OCHI, FUMIO. Milton and Diodati. Stud. in Eng. Lit. (Eng. Lit. Soc. Japan), 18, 1938, 513-30.
Analyzes the friendship and observes that the severity of Milton's character was softened by Diodati's wit, humour, and laughter.

1631 Ormuz and Amurath. TLS, Mar. 30, 1933, pp. 205-6.
Milton's interest in contemporary exploration reflected in his works.
Rev: L. C. Martin, YWES, 253.

1632 PARKER, WILLIAM R. Above All Liberties: John Milton's Relations with His Earliest Publishers. PULC, 2, 1941, 512-15.

1633 ------. The Anonymous Life of Milton. TLS, Sept. 13, 1957, p. 547.
Cyriack Skinner. Replies by R. W. Hunt, ibid., Oct. 11, 1957, p. 609; and by Maurice Kelley, ibid., Dec. 27, 1957, p. 787.

1634 ------. Contributions toward a Milton Bibliography. Libr., 4th Ser., 16, 1936, 425-38.
On Milton and his early printers.

1635 ------. John Milton, Scrivener, 1590-1632. MLN, 59, 1944, 532-37.
An account of the elder Milton's career.

1636 ------. Milton and Edward Phillips. TLS, Feb. 28, 1942, p. 108.
Questions Milton's alleged part in the Theatrum Poetarum.

1637 ------. Milton and the News of Charles Diodati's Death. MLN, 72, 1957, 486-8.
On the poet's reaction.

1638 ------. Milton and the Marchioness of Winchester. MLR, 44, 1949, 547-50.
Rev: L. C. Martin, YWES, 162.

1639 ------. Milton and Thomas Young, 1602-1628. MLN, 53, 1938, 399-407.
Feels that Young's influence on Milton practically ended when the poet was eleven.
Rev: L. C. Martin, YWES, 177.

1640 ------. Milton as Secretary. NQ, N. S., 4, 1957, 441-2.
An attempt to clarify Milton's exact secretarial position at various times during the Interregnum.

A Bibliographical Supplement

1641 ------. Milton, Rothwell, and Simmons. Libr., 4th Ser., 18, 1938, 89-103.
On Milton and his printers.

1642 ------. Milton's Unknown Friend. TLS, May 16, 1936, p. 420.
Thomas Young.
Rev: L. C. Martin, YWES, 188.

1643 ------. On Milton's Early Literary Program. MP, 33, 1935, 49-53.
Rev: L. C. Martin, YWES, 254.

1644 ------. Thomas Myriell. NQ, 188, 1945, 103.
"Is the rector of St. Stephens, Walbrook, the church where Anne Milton was married, the Thomas Myriell who compiled the Tristitiae Remedium, MS collection of music containing ten compositions by Anne's father?"

1645 PARSONS, EDWARD S. The Authorship of the Anonymous Life of Milton. PMLA, 50, 1935, 1057-64.
Questions Darbishire's attribution to John Phillips.

1646 ------. Concerning The Earliest Life of Milton. ELH, 9, 1942, 106-15.
Opposes the view of Benham, ELH, 6, 1939, 245-55.

1647 PATTISON, MARK. Milton. English Men of Letters. London: Macmillan, 1932. vi, 227pp.
A reprint of Stevens' No. 1712.

1648 PHILLIPS, JOHN. A Satyr Against Hypocrites. Introd. by Leon Howard. The Augustan Reprint Society. Berkeley: University of California Press, 1953.
Phillips, the nephew of Milton.
Rev: Arnold Davenport, YWES, 199.

1649 RACINE, LOUIS. Life of Milton, together with Observations on Paradise Lost. Trans., with an Introd., by Katherine John. London: Hogarth Press, 1930. v, 158pp.
Rev: H. J. C. Grierson and A. Melville Clark, YWES, 223; Bookman, 79, 1930, 218; TLS, Oct. 23, 1930, p. 869; James Thornton, Nat. and Ath., 48, 1930, 197; ER, 52, 1931, 118; Oxf. Mag., May 14, 1931, p. 700; D. Saurat, RES, 7, 1931, 472-4; R. F. Russell, Merc., 23, 1932, 507.

1650 RAYMOND, DORA B. Oliver's Secretary: John Milton in an Era of Revolt. New York: Minton, Balch, 1932. 355pp.
Rev: L. C. Martin, YWES, 206; NR, 74, 1933, 289; A. M. Witherspoon, SRL, 9, 1933, 377; Nat., 134, 1933, 26; G. W. Whiting, MP, 31, 1933, 91-4; W. H. Coates, AHR, 38, 1933, 589-90; E. Hodder, JMH, 5, 1933, 230-1; G. Genzmer, CHR, 20, 1934, 106-7; TLS, Sept. 5, 1935, p. 554; G. D., EHR, 52, 1937, 163.

1651 READ, ALLEN W. The Disinterment of Milton's Remains. PMLA, 45, 1930, 1050-68.

1652 REBORA, PIERO. Milton a Firenze. Sei-Settecento (Firenze: Sansoni, 1956), pp. 251-70.

1653 RICKWORD, EDGELL. Milton: The Revolutionary Intellectual. The English Revolution 1640 (London: Lawrence and Wishart, 1940), pp. 101-132.
A stimulating account of Milton's political career.

1654 ROGERS, LAMBERT. John Milton's Blindness: A Suggested Diagnosis. Jour. Hist. Medicine and Allied Sciences, 4, 1949, 468-71.
The author, an M.D., suggests that the blindness was caused by a suprachiasmal cystic tumour.

1655 ROSEN, EDWARD. A Friend of John Milton: Valerio Chimentelli and His Copy of Viviani's De maximis et minimis. BNYPL, 57, 1953, 159-74. Printed also in pamphlet form by the New York Public Library, 1953. 18pp.

1656 ROWSE, ALFRED L. The Milton Country. The English Past, Evocations of Persons and Places (New York: Macmillan, 1952), pp. 85-112.
Concerning Milton's ancestors, the countryside around Milton (the town), the Powell house, etc.

1657 RUHE, EDWARD L. Milton and the Duke of York. NQ, 198, 1953, 524-5.
Quotes the story of Milton and the Duke from Joseph Towers' British Biography (1769).

1658 SCHNITTKIND, HENRY T. and DANA A. John Milton. Living Biographies of Great Poets (New York: Garden City Pub. Co., 1941), pp. 47-59.

1659 SCHOLFIELD, A. F. Notes by Milton. TLS, July 17, 1937, p. 528.
The author is trying to locate a certain copy of Harrington's translation of Orlando Furioso, said to contain marginal notes in the handwriting of Milton.

1660 SCHRÖDER, A. Milton als Schullektüre. Neuphilologische Mschr., 1, 1930, 177-96.

1661 SEATON, ETHEL. Literary Relations of England and Scandinavia in the Seventeenth Century. Oxford: Clarendon Press, 1935. 384pp.
Milton, passim.
Rev: L. C. Martin, YWES, 249-50; TLS, Mar. 28, 1936, p. 262; J. Nordström, Lychnos, 1, 1936, 353; J. Kruuse, RLC, July, 1936, 608-12; E. Eckhardt, Ang. Bbl., 47, 1936, 365-7; A. B., Archiv, 169, 1936, 135-6.

1662 SENIOR, H. L. John Milton, the Supreme Englishman. London: W. H. Allen, 1944. 38pp.
Senior, a Communist, emphasizes the "freedom element" in Milton's writings.

1663 SENSABAUGH, GEORGE F. A Milton Ascription. NQ, 194, 1949, 337.
In a copy of The King's Cabinet opened (1645).

1664 ------. Milton Bejesuited. SP, 47, 1950, 224-42.
On the origin of the idea that Milton died a papist.
Rev: Arnold Davenport, YWES, 175.

1665 SORSBY, ARNOLD. On the Nature of Milton's Blindness. British Jour. of Ophthalmology, 14, 1930, 339-54.
Suggests myopia.

1666 SPEARS, JEWEL. Milton's Literary Records of His Personal Relationships. Master's thesis, University of Alabama, 1939.

1667 STOYE, J. W. English Travellers Abroad 1604-1667. London: Cape, 1952. 479pp.
Invaluable background study. Milton's Italian journey, passim.
Rev: TLS, July 11, 1952, p. 454.

1668 STUART, DOROTHY MARGARET. Milton and Prynne: Some New Light on the Secret History of the Commonwealth. NSN, N. S., 1, 1931, 15-6.
On Milton's part in Prynne's arrest.

1669 THOMPSON, KARL F. Milton's Eighteenth Century Biographers. Doctoral diss., Yale University, 1950.

1670 TILLYARD, E. M. W. Milton. London: Chatto and Windus; New York: Dial Press, 1930. viii, 396pp.
Contains sections on the early poems, the period of the prose, Milton's beliefs, and the later poems. Appendices, i. a., on Thomas Young, the dating of the sonnets, and Spenser's influence on Milton.
Rev: H. J. C. Grierson and A. Melville Clark, YWES, 219-22; TLS, May 22, 1930, p. 431; H. Read, Crit., 10, 1930, 192-5; M. Nicolson, MP, 28, 1930, 239-41; G. R. Potter, University of California Chron., 32, 1930, 504-7; G. Saintsbury, Bookman, 78, 1930, 161-2; O. Burdett, Merc., 22, 1930, 466-8; K. M. L., Oxf. Mag., Oct. 16, 1930, p. 34; Spect., May 3, 1930, p. 745; O. Burdett, Sat. Rev., 169, 1930, 591; T. E. Welby, WER, 1, 1930, 235-6; C. H. H., MGW, 23, 1930, 112; Edmund Blunden, Nat. and Ath., 47, 1930, 113; E. N. S. Thompson, PQ, 10, 1931, 223-4; H. F. Fletcher, JEGP, 30, 1931, 592-4; W. P. Mustard, AJP, 52, 1931, 92-3; E. Greenlaw, MLN, 46, 1931, 527-8; Paul Chauvet, RA-A, 8, 1931, 256-7; J. J. Reilly, CW, 134, 1931, 244-5; F. Delatte, Rev. belge. Philol. et d'hist., 12, 1933, 309-12.

1671 TURNBULL, GEORGE H. Hartlib, Dury, and Comenius. Cleanings from Hartlib's Papers. London: Hodder and Stoughton; Liverpool: University Press of Liverpool, 1947. xi, 447pp.
Milton, passim.
Rev: TLS, Apr. 3, 1948, p. 192; J. M. Batten, Jour. Religion, 28, 1948, 147-8; Dorothy Stimson, Isis, 39, 1948, 181-2.

1672 ------. Notes on John Durie's Reformed Librarie-Keeper. Libr., 5th Ser., 1, 1946, 64-7.
Argues that Milton did not instigate the writing of the work.

1673 ------. Samuel Hartlib's Connection with Sir Francis Kynaston's Musaeum Minervae. NQ, 197, 1952, 33-7.

1674 TURNER, W. ARTHUR. Cromwell and the Piedmont Massacres. NQ, 193, 1948, 135-6.

1675 ------. John Winthrop, F. R. S. TLS, Nov. 1, 1947, p. 563.
Letters from Milton to Winthrop may exist.

1676 ------. The Known English Acquaintances of John Milton. Doctoral diss., Ohio State University, 1947. Abs., Ohio State University, Abstracts of Doctoral Diss., No. 53, 1947, pp. 161-7.

1677 ------. Masson's Identification of Milton's Pupil Richard Heath. NQ, 193, 1948, 383.
Questions Masson's identification of Heath as the Richard Heath who assisted Brian Walton with the Polyglott Bible.

1678 ------. Milton and Spenser's Grandson. NQ, 192, 1947, 547.
William Spenser, grandson of the poet, may have been the "Spencer" aided by Milton.

1679 ------. Milton, Marvell, and Dradon at Cromwell's Funeral. PQ, 28, 1949, 320-3.
Calls attention to Br. Mus. MS Lansdowne 95, No. 2, p. 11v, which connects Milton, Marvell, and possibly Dryden with Cromwell's funeral.
Rev: L. C. Martin, YWES, 164-5.

1680 ------. Milton's Aid to Davenant. MLN, 63, 1948, 538-9.
In 1650-4.
Rev: L. C. Martin, YWES, 196.

1681 ------. Milton's Aid to the Polyglott Bible. MLN, 64, 1949, 345.
Rev: L. C. Martin, YWES, 164.

1682 ------. Milton's Friendship with Cromwell's Grand-daughter. NQ, N. S., 1, 1954, 199.
On the possible friendship between Milton and Bridget Bendish.

A *Bibliographical Supplement*

1683 VISIAK, E. H. A Miltonian Puzzle. NQ, 176, 1939, 200-1.
Holds that the verses sent to Queen Christina with Cromwell's picture are the collaboration of Milton and Marvell.

1684 VISSER, MARTINUS. Het leven van Milton. Amsterdam: H. J. Spruyt's Uitgevers-Mij., 1940. 147pp.

1685 WHITING, GEORGE W. Milton and the "Postscript."
MLR, 30, 1935, 506-8.
Declares that Milton did not write the postscript to An
Answer to A Book Entituled An Humble Remonstrance...
(1641).
Rev: L. C. Martin, YWES, 254.

1686 - - - - - -. Milton a Jesuit. NQ, 168, 1935, 150-1.
Concerning the ridiculousness of Pelling's charge (1680).

1687 WILLOUGHBY, EDWIN E. Milton's Taxes (1641-2?).
MLR, 26, 1931, 178-9.
Rev: F. S. Boas, YWES, 209.

1688 WILMER, W. H. The Blindness of Milton. JEGP, 32,
1933, 301-15.
Diagnoses glaucoma.
Rev: L. C. Martin, YWES, 252.

1689 - - - - - -. The Blindness of Milton. BHM, 1, 1933, 85-106.

1690 WITHERSPOON, A. M. Milton as a Statesman. SRL, 9,
1933, 377.
A review article of Raymond's study.

1691 - - - - - -. Milton is Still Timely. SRL, 11, 1935, 646.
Reviews studies by Macaulay and Belloc and concludes that
Roman Catholics and women have been Milton's severest
critics.

1692 WOLFE, DON M. Lilburne's Note on Milton. MLN, 56,
1941, 360-3.

1693 WRIGHT, B. A. The Alleged Falsehoods in Milton's
Account of His Continental Tour. MLR, 28, 1933,
308-14.
Rev: L. C. Martin, YWES, 251-2.

1694 - - - - - -. Milton's First Marriage. MLR, 26, 1931, 383-
400; 27, 1932, 6-23.
Rev: F. S. Boas, YWES, 208-9.

1695 YOUNG, R. F. Comenius in England, as Described in
Contemporary Documents. London: Oxford University
Press, 1932. 100pp.
Comenius possibly influenced Milton through Hartlib.
Rev: F. S. Boas, YWES, 220-1.

1696 ZANGORIN, P. The Authorship of Mans Mortallitie. Libr., 5th Ser., 5, 1951, 179-83.
Attributes the tract to Richard Overton the Leveller, not Robert Overton the friend of Milton.

STYLE AND VERSIFICATION

1697 BANKS, THEODORE H. Milton's Imagery. New York: Columbia University Press, 1950. xiv, 260pp.
Rev: Arnold Davenport, YWES, 175; A. H. Gilbert, SAQ, 50, 1951, 151-2; F. Michael Krouse, MLN, 67, 1952, 474-8; A. E. Barker, MLR, 47, 1952, 579-80; B. A. Wright, RES, 3, 1952, 390-2.

1698 BINYON, LAURENCE. A Note on Milton's Imagery and Rhythm. Seventeenth Century Studies Presented to Sir Herbert Grierson (Oxford: Clarendon Press, 1938), pp. 184-91.

1699 BORDELON, ROMA BOLOLT. The Use of Verbal Repetition as a Structural Device in the Poetry of Milton. Master's thesis, Louisiana State University, 1939.

1700 BOTTRALL, MARGARET. The Baroque Element in Milton. English Miscellany: A Symposium of History, Literature and the Arts. Ed. by Mario Praz et al (Rome: Edizioni di Storia e Letteratura, 1950), 1, 31-42.

1701 BROWN, JAMES. Eight Types of Pun. PMLA, 71, 1956, 14-26.
Draws several examples from Milton.

1702 CANDY, HUGH C. H. Milton—the Individualist in Metre. NQ, 159, 1930, 165-67, 189-92. Reprinted, London: Nisbet, 1934, in an expanded version.
Finds Milton's metrical hand in the Ovid stanzas, formerly attributed to Milton on other grounds.
Rev: H. J. C. Grierson and A. Melville Clark, YWES, 222; TLS, June 21, 1934, p. 447; B. A. W(right), MLR, 30, 1935, 413.

1703 CLARK, DONALD L. John Milton and 'the fitted stile or lofty, mean, or lowly.' SCN, 11, 1953, suppl., 5-9.
An expanded version of a paper delivered in December, 1952, to the Modern Language Association.

1704 DARBISHIRE, HELEN. Milton's Poetic Language. E&S, 10, 1957, 31-52.
Feels that Milton "holds to the idiom and vocabulary of our common speech as the groundwork of his diction."

1705 DIEKHOFF, JOHN S. Milton's Prosody in the Poems of the Trinity Manuscript. PMLA, 54, 1939, 153-83.

1706 ------. Rhyme in Paradise Lost. PMLA, 49, 1934, 539-43.

1707 ------. Terminal Pause in Milton's Verse. SP, 32, 1935, 235-39.

1703 ELLEDGE, SCOTT B. Milton's Imagery. Doctoral diss., Cornell University, 1941. Abs., Cornell Abstracts of Theses...1941, pp. 32-35.

1709 ELVIN, LIONEL. Milton and the Artificial Style. Introduction to the Study of Literature (London: Sylvan Press, 1949), I, 49-90. Also passim.

1710 EVANS, ROBERT O. A Study of Milton's Theory and Practice of Elision. Master's thesis, University of Florida, 1950.

1711 ------. The Theory and Practice of Poetic Elision from Chaucer to Milton with Special Emphasis on Milton. Doctoral diss., University of Florida, 1954. Abs., DA, 14, 1954, 2056-7.

1712 FLETCHER, HARRIS F. A Possible Origin of Milton's Counterpoint or Double Rhythm. JEGP, 54, 1955, 521-25.
Latin and Hebrew prosody.

1713 FRICKER, ROBERT. Eigenart und Grenzen von Milton's Bildersprache. Ang., 71, 1953, 331-45.
Milton's similes both arabesque and functional.
Rev: Arnold Davenport, YWES, 208.

1714 GROOM, BERNARD. Milton. The Diction of Poetry from Spenser to Bridges (Toronto: University of Toronto Press, 1956), pp. 74-94.
Concerned mainly with the diction of Paradise Lost.

1715 HAMER, MRS. ENID. The Meters of English Poetry London: Methuen, 1930. 326pp.
Lengthy discussions of Milton's poems, passim.
Rev: TLS, Aug. 21, 1930, p. 671; N. R. Tempest, RES, 7, 1931, 493-4; M. W. Croll, MLN, 46, 1931, 338; A. Brandl, DL, 52, 1931, 357-9; R. Spindler, ESt., 67, 1932, 258-9; B. E. C. D(avis), MLR, 27, 1932, 113; A. Eichler, Ang. Bbl., 44, 1933, 291-4.

1716 HARWOOD, ALMA MERLE. Milton's Similes. Master's thesis, McMaster University, 1935. 24pp.

1717 HOWE, M. L. Anapestic Feet in Paradise Lost. MLN, 45, 1930, 311-12.
Rev: H. J. C. Grierson and A. Melville Clark, YWES, 222.

1718 HUNTER, WILLIAM B., JR. The Sources of Milton's Prosody. PQ, 28, 1949, 125-44.
Sylvester and the metrical psalters.
Rev: L. C. Martin, YWES, 169-70.

1719 KELLOGG, GEORGE A. Bridges' Milton's Prosody and Renaissance Metrical Theory. PMLA, 68, 1953, 268-85.
Milton's prosody based on Italian and classical procedents.
Rev: Arnold Davenport, YWES, 200-1.

1720 LEATHES, SIR STANLEY. Rhythm in English Poetry. London: Heinemann, 1935. vi, 154pp.
Passim.
Rev: B. Ifor Evans, YWES, 15-16.

1721 LERNER, L. D. The Miltonic Simile. EIC, 4, 1954, 297-308.
Similes remind us of the world of humanity of which the poem itself is a part.
Rev: Arnold Davenport, YWES, 143.

1722 MACKENZIE, BARBARA K. The Similes of John Milton. Master's thesis, McMaster University, 1935. 20pp.

1723 MILES, JOSEPHINE. The Continuity of Poetic Language: Studies in English Poetry from the 1540's to the 1940's. University of California Pubs. in Eng., 19. Berkeley: University of California Press, 1951. 542pp.
Passim. Concerned with the vocabulary of poetry.
Rev: Siegfried Mandel, SRL, Oct. 13, 1951, p. 46; S. H. Monk, JEGP, 51, 1952, 426-8.

1724 - - - - - -. Major Adjectives in English Poetry from Wyatt to Auden. University of California Pubs. in Eng., 12, 3. Berkeley: University of California Press, 1946.
Finds "heaven" the most frequently recurring word in Milton's poetry. Also passim.
Rev: H. W. Wells, AL, 18, 1946, 267-8.

1725 - - - - - -. The Primary Language of Poetry in the 1640's. Part One of The Continuity of Poetic Language. Berkeley: University of California Press, 1948. 160pp.
Rev: James Sledd, MP, 47, 1949, 140-3; C. T. Harrison, SR, 57, 1949, 709-14.

1726 - - - - - -. The Vocabulary of Poetry. Berkeley: University of California Press, 1946.
Passim.
Rev: Ethel Seaton, YWES, 16-17.

1727 MOLONEY, M. F. Donne's Metrical Practice. PMLA, 65, 1950, 232-9.
Considers the possible critical reconciliation of Donne and Milton.

1728 MOUNG, DAPHNE AYE. Controversy on Miltonic Inversions. NQ, 180, 1941, 210.
After the 1887 publication of Bridges' Milton's Prosody.

1729 NELSON, LOWRY, JR. Góngora and Milton: Toward a Definition of the Baroque. CL, 6, 1954, 53-63.
Using Góngora's Polifemo and Milton's Nativity Ode, sets forth an analysis of style in terms of the time structure of the lyric.
Rev: Arnold Davenport, YWES, 139.

1730 P(ARKER), W(ILLIAM) R. Milton's Meter: A Note. SCN, 2, No. 1, 1943.

1731 PETIT, HERBERT H. Milton, Aristotle, and the Modern Critics. Class. Bull., 25, Nov., 1948, 8-10.
Aristotle's Poetics (xx-xxii) and Rhetoric (iii, 2-19) contain the basis of Milton's style.

1732 ROSE, NORMA V. Milton's Nature Images. Master's thesis, University of North Carolina, 1937.

1733 SEIGLER, MILLEDGE BROADUS. Milton's Prosody. Doctoral diss., Duke University, 1942.

1734 SITWELL, EDITH, comp. The Pleasures of Poetry. A Critical Anthology. First Series. Milton and the Augustan Age. London: Duckworth, 1930. 236pp.
Lengthy discussion of Milton's versification in the Introduction, pp. 3-80.
Rev: TLS, Dec. 18, 1930, pp. 918, 1083, and ibid., May 28, 1931, p. 422; Oxf. Mag., Mar. 12, 1931, p. 606; Sat. Rev., 151, 1931, 804; A. Fremantle, Merc., 24, 1931, 378; F. T. Wood, ESt., 66, 1932, 429-32; M. R. R., Oxf. Mag., May 18, 1933, 687; B. de Selincourt, Obs., Sept 23, 1934; K. Hare, ER, 59, 1934, 755-8; E. Blunden, FR, 142, 1934, 628-30; AM, 33, 1934; NB, 18, 1934, 82; E. L. Walton, Nat., 139, 1934, 307.

1735 SMITH, CORA LEE. Milton's Use of Similes. Master's thesis, McMaster University, 1935. 39pp.

1736 SMITH, J. C. Feminine Endings in Milton's Blank Verse. TLS, Dec. 5, 1936, p. 1016.
Rev: L. C. Martin, YWES, 189.

1737 SPROTT, S. ERNEST. Milton's Art of Prosody. Oxford: Blackwell, 1953. xi, 147pp.
Contains a special chapter on the prosody of Samson Agonistes.
Rev: Arnold Davenport, YWES, 201; TLS, May 15, 1953, p. 318; Ants Oras, SCN, 11, 1953, 30; Wilhelmina Gordon, QQ, 61, 1954, 139-41; F. T. Prince, RES, 5, 1954, 292-4; Edgar Mertner, Ang., 63, 1955, 229-39.

1738 STEIN, ARNOLD. Answerable Style. Answerable Style: Essays on Paradise Lost (Minneapolis: University of Minnesota Press, 1953), pp. 119-62.

1739 ------. A Note on Meter. KR, 18, 1956, 451-60.
Comment by John Crowe Ransom, ibid., pp. 473-6.

1740 ------. Structures of Sound in Milton's Verse. KR, 15, 1953, 266-77.

1741 SYPHER, WYLIE. Four Stages of Renaissance Style. Transformation in Art and Literature 1400-1700. Anchor Books Original. Garden City: Doubleday, 1955. 312pp. Passim.

1742 THOMPSON, E. N. S. Milton's Prose Style. PQ, 14, 1935, 38-53.

1743 TILLYARD, E. M. W. A Note on Milton's Style. The Miltonic Setting (Cambridge: Cambridge University Press, 1947), pp. 105-40.

1744 TUVE, ROSEMOND. Elizabethan and Metaphysical Imagery. Chicago: University of Chicago Press, 1947. xii, 442pp.
Passim.
Rev: V. B. Heltzel, PQ, 26, 1947, 382-4; W. K. Wimsatt, JAAC, 6, 1948, 277-9; TLS, Jan. 17, 1948, p. 39; T. H. Jones, LL, 58, 1948, 247-9; G. R. Potter, MLQ, 9, 1948, 359-60; S. G. Putt, Eng., 7, 1948, 136-8; Rosemary Freeman, RES, 24, 1948, 331-2; Kenneth Burke, Accent, 8, 1948, 125-7; Josephine Miles, SR, 56, 1948, 312-15; Helen C. White, CE, 10, 1948, 53-4; NQ, 193, 1948, 484.

1745 WEISMILLER, E. R. The Versification of Paradise Lost and Paradise Regained. A Study of Movement and Structure in Milton's Non-Dramatic Blank Verse. Doctoral diss., Merton College, Oxford, 1951.

1746 WHALER, JAMES. Animal Simile in Paradise Lost, PMLA, 47, 1932, 534-53.
Rev: L. C. Martin, YWES, 210-11.

1747 ------. The Compounding and Distribution of Similes in Paradise Lost. MP, 28, 1931, 313-27.

1748 ------. Counterpoint and Symbol. An Inquiry into the Rhythm of Milton's Epic Style. Anglistica, 6. Copenhagen: Rosenkilde and Bagger, 1956. 225pp.
Rev: E. R. Weismiller, MLN, 72, 1957, 612-18; R. O. Evans, JEGP, 56, 1957, 487-90; V. de S. Pinto, NQ, N. S., 4, 1957, 273-4.

1749 ------. Grammatical Nexus of the Miltonic Simile. JEGP, 30, 1931, 327-34.

1750 ------. The Miltonic Simile. PMLA, 46, 1931, 1034-74.
Rev: F. S. Boas, YWES, 208.

1751 WILLIAMSON, GEORGE. The Senecan Amble. A Study
in Prose from Bacon to Collier. London: Faber, 1951.
377pp.
Milton's ideas concerning style, passim.
Rev: Arnold Davenport, YWES, 171-2.

1752 WYLD, H. C. Some Aspects of the Diction of English
Poetry. Oxford: Basil Blackwell, 1933. 72pp.
Passim.

EDITORS, EDITIONS, AND ILLUSTRATORS

1753 ARNOLD, E. J. Edward Hill, M. D. (1741-1830), Editor of Milton. Bull. of the Friends of the Library of Trinity College, Dublin, 1951, pp. 11-15.

1754 BAKER, C. H. COLLINS. Some Illustrators of Milton's Paradise Lost (1688-1850). Libr., 5th Ser., 3, 1948, 1-21, 101-19.

1755 BALSTON, THOMAS. Some Illustrators of Milton's Paradise Lost. Libr., 5th Ser., 4, 1949, 146-7.
Corrects Baker in some instances.

1756 BATTLE, GUY A. The Box Rule Pattern in the First Edition of Paradise Lost. PBSA, 42, 1948, 315-21.

1757 BRADNER, LEICESTER. Milton's Epitaphium Damonis. TLS, Aug. 18, 1932, p. 581.
Describes an edition in the British Museum.
Rev: L. C. Martin, YWES, 208.

1758 DARBISHIRE, HELEN. The Columbia Edition of Milton. RES, 9, 1933, 61-2, 319.
Criticizes the editors' handling of the text.

1759 - - - - - -. The Printing of the First Edition of Paradise Lost. RES, 17, 1941, 415-27.

1760 FLETCHER, HARRIS F. The First Edition of Milton's History of Britain. JEGP, 35, 1936, 405-14.
A description of the various states in which the first edition exists and suggestions for an accurate text.
Rev: L. C. Martin, YWES, 190.

1761 - - - - - -. A Second (?) Title-Page of the Second Edition of Paradise Lost. PBSA, 43, 1949, 173-8.
Describes a title page different from that of other copies of the second edition.

1762 FRENCH, J. MILTON. That Late Villain Milton; History of the Publications of Milton's Letters of State. PMLA, 55, 1940, 102-18.
A supplement to Vol. 13 of the Columbia Edition.

1763 - - - - - -. An Unrecorded Edition of Milton's Defensio Secunda (1654). PBSA, 49, 1955, 262-8.
Variants between two editions published by Vlacq at the Hague.

1764 - - - - - -, MAURICE KELLEY, and THOMAS O. MAB-BOTT. The Columbia Milton: Fifth Supplement, NQ, 197, 1952, 376-8.

1765 GARDNER, HELEN. Milton's First Illustrator. E&S, 9, 1956, 27-38.
John Baptist Medina, illustrator of the 4th edition of Paradise Lost (1688).

1766 GASELEE, S. Milton's Asclepiadean Verses. NQ, 163, 1932, 249.
Praises the Columbia Edition.

1767 GOODE, JAMES. The Bohn Edition of Milton's Prose. TLS, Aug. 1, 1929, p. 608.
Corrects three textual errors.
Rev: F. S. Boas, YWES, 206-7.

1768 GRIERSON, H. J. C. The Columbia Milton. RES, 9, 1933, 316-19.
Feels that Darbishire has been "unduly censorious."

1767 HANFORD, JAMES H. Milton Among the Book Collectors. NLB, 4, 1957, 97-109.

1770 HARASZTI, ZOLTAN. First Editions of Milton. MB, 7, 1932, 323-35, 375-90.
Comments on the first editions in the Boston Public Library.

1771 HARKNESS, BRUCE. The Precedence of the 1676 Editions of Milton's Literae Pseudo-Senatus Anglicani. Stud. in Bibliography, Papers of the Bibliographical Society of the University of Virginia, 7, 1955, 181-5.

1772 HAVILAND, THOMAS P. Three Early Milton Editions. University of Pennsylvania Libr. Chron., 9, 1941, 78-82.
Addenda to Howard.

1773 HOWARD, LEON. Early American Copies of Milton. HLB, 7, 1935, 169-79.

1774 HUGHES, MERRITT Y. Milton's Poems. TLS, Dec. 31, 1954, p. 853.
Announces the plans for the variorum commentary.

1775 KELLEY, MAURICE. A Note on Milton's Pro Populo Anglicano Defensio. Libr., 4th Ser., 17, 1937, 466-7.
Addenda to editions listed by Madan (Stevens' No. 76).

1776 KUETHE, J. LOUIS. Paradise Lost: Fourteenth and Fifteenth Editions. NQ, 172, 1937, 136.
Argues that the "15th" edition was incorectly dated 1738.

1777 LEWIS, CLARISSA O. A Further Note on Milton's Pro Populo Anglicano Defensio. Libr., 4th Ser., 23, 1943, 45-7.
On textual variants in the editions of 1651-2.

A Bibliographical Supplement

1778 LUTAUD, OLIVIER. Milton le Lutteur: Études et Éditions Récentes de la Prose Miltonienne. EA, 8, 1955, 233-48.
On the rise of scholarly interest in the prose.

1779 MABBOTT, THOMAS O. Milton's Asclepiadean Verses. NQ, 162, 1932, 263-4; 163, 1932, 170.
Defends the reading of the Columbia Edition.

1780 ------. Notes by Milton. TLS, Nov. 17, 1932, p. 859.
Desires to locate the copy of William Browne's Britannia's Pastorals (1613-16) which contains the marginal notes attributed to Milton.

1781 ------, and J. MILTON FRENCH. The Columbia Milton. Third Supplement. NQ, 181, 1941, 16-17.
Addenda.

1782 ------. First Supplement to the Columbia Milton. NQ, 177, 1939, 329-30.

1783 ------. Milton's Proposalls of Certain Expedients, 1659. NQ, 173, 1937, 66.
Asks for information on the Proposalls.

1784 ------, and MAURICE KELLEY. The Columbia Milton: Second Supplement. NQ, 178, 1940, 20-1.
Three additional items.

1785 ------. The Columbia Milton, Fourth Supplement. NQ, 195, 1950, 244-6.
Lists eleven items discovered since the third supplement.

1786 MACKAIL, J. W. Bentley's Milton. Studies in Humanism (London: Longmans, 1938), pp. 186-209.
A reprint of Stevens' No. 2691. Analysis of the edition and remarks on the early rise of Milton's reputation.

1787 MADAN, F. F. A Revised Bibliography of Salmasius's Defensio Regia and Milton's Pro populo Anglicano Defensio. Libr., 5th Ser., 9, 1954, 101-21.
A revision of an earlier article, ibid., N. S., 4, 1923, 119-45.

1788 McC., H. Milton's First Prose Work. MB, 12, 1937, 311.
Describes a copy of the first edition of Of Reformation, recently asquired by the Boston Public Library.

1789 McCAIN, JOHN WALKER, JR. Further Notes on Milton's Artis Logicae. NQ, 165, 1933, 56-9.
The apparent identity of the 1672 and 1673 editions.

1790 ------. Milton's Artis Logicae. NQ, 164, 1933, 149-50.
Rev: L. C. Martin, YWES, 253.

184

1791 MILLER, SONIA. The Text of the Second Edition of Milton's Eikonoklastes. JEGP, 52, 1953, 214-20.
Defends Haller's work on the Columbia Edition.

1792 MOLIN, SVEN ERIC. John Wesley's Techniques in Revising Literary Masterpieces for His Methodist Audience, with Special Reference to Paradise Lost. Doctoral diss., University of Pennsylvania, 1956. Abs., DA, 16, 1956, 957-8.

1793 MYERS, ROBERT MANSON. Handel, Dryden, and Milton: Being a Series of Observations on the Poems of Dryden and Milton, as alter'd and adapted by Various Hands, and Set to Musick by Mr. Handel, to which are added Authentick Texts of Several of Mr. Handel's Oratorios. Cambridge: Bowes and Bowes, 1956.

1794 ORAS, ANTS. Milton's Editors and Commentators from Patrick Hume to Henry John Todd (1695-1801). A Study in Critical Views and Methods. London: Oxford University Press; Tartu: University of Tartu (Dorpat), 1931. 381pp.
Rev: TLS, Aug. 6, 1931, p. 611; S. B. Liljegren, Ang. Bbl., 43, 1932, 365-9; R. D. Havens, JEGP, 31, 1932, 299-300; B. A. W(right), MLR, 27, 1932, 364; H. Read, Crit. 11, 1932, 746-7; A. B(randl), Archiv, 161, 1932, 305-6; A. Bosker, MLN, 48, 1933, 204-5; M. Schutt, Literaturblatt, 55, 1933, 27-8.

1795 PARKER, WILLIAM R. Flecher's Milton: A First Appraisal. PBSA, 41, 1947, 33-52.
An examination of the text and critical apparatus of Fletcher's fascimile edition.

1796 (PATRICK, J. MAX). American Scholars and Scotch Reviewers. SCN, 13, 1955, 32-3.
Objects to a review of Vol. 1 of the Yale prose edition by J. George, Aberdeen University Rev., 36, 1955, 55-8.

1797 - - - - - -. Milton and the Crystal-Gazer. SCN, 14, 1956, 5-6.
A defence of the Yale prose edition.

1798 - - - - - -. Should the Project for a Milton Variorum Be Completely Reconsidered? SCN, 10, 1952, 10.
Suggests a less expensive edition then the one planned.

1799 PERSHING, JAMES H. The Different States of the First Edition of Paradise Lost. Libr., 4th Ser., 22, 1941, 34-66.
Rev: John Southgate, YWES, 231.

1800 R., V. Milton's Asclepiadean Verses. NQ, 163, 1932, 209, 371.
Feels that the editors of the Columbia Edition should not correct the errors in Milton's Latin poems.

1801 ROBERTSON, D. S. A Copy of Milton's Eikonoklastes. TLS, June 15 and 22, 1951, pp. 380, 396.
Textual problems in editing the prose tract.

1802 SHERWIN, OSCAR. Milton for the Masses: John Wesley's Edition of Paradise Lost. MLQ, 12, 1951, 267-85.

1803 SIRLUCK, ERNEST. Certain Editorial Tendencies Exemplified: A New Edition of Milton's An Apology. MP, 50, 1953, 201-5.
A review article of Jochums' edition.

1804 SMUTS, HENRY Q. More Errata in the Introduction to (the) Complete Prose Works of John Milton. SCN, 13, 1955, suppl., 5.

1805 THORPE, JAMES. The Presentation Paradise Lost. New Colophon, 1, 1948, 357-65.
Questions the authenticity of the presentation inscription in the copy in the Princeton library.

1806 TODD, WILLIAM B. The Issues and States of the Second Folio and Milton's Epitaph on Shakespeare. Stud. in Bibliography, Papers of the Bibliographical Society of the University of Virginia, 5, 1952, 81-108.

1807 TURNER, W. ARTHUR. The Yale Milton. TLS, Sept. 24, 1954, p. 609.
Replies to adverse reviews of the Yale prose edition.

1808 WHITING, GEORGE W. James Thomson, Editor of Areopagitica. NQ, 164, 1933, 457.

1809 WITHERSPOON, ALEXANDER M. A New Milton Gift. Yale University Libr. Gazette, 20, 1945, 33-5.
A first edition of Of Education.

1810 WURTSBAUGH, JEWEL. John Hughes. TLS, Feb. 22, 1934, p. 126.
Hughes' participation in Tickell's Milton.

FAME AND INFLUENCE

1811 ADLER, JACOB H. A Milton-Bryant Parallel. NEQ, 24, 1951, 377-80.
Notes similarities between On the Late Massacre at Piedmont and The Massacre at Scio.

1812 ALBERT, FRANCIS L. Dryden's Debt to Milton. Master's thesis, University of North Carolina, 1951.

1813 ALBRECHT, MILTON C. Sixty Years of Miltonic Criticism: from Aiken to Masson. Doctoral diss. University of California (Berkeley), 1938.

1814 ALSPACH, RUSSELL K. A Dublin Milton Enthusiast. MLN, 56, 1941, 284-6.
Samuel Whyte (1733-1811).

1815 AUBIN, ROBERT A. Nathanael Salmon on Milton, 1728. MLN, 56, 1941, 214-15.
Comments on Milton from Salmon's History of Hertfordshire.

1816 BACKUS, EDYTHE N. The MS. Play, Anna Bullen. PMLA, 47, 1932, 741-52.
A Restoration piece having repeated echoes of Paradise Lost.

1817 BAIRD, J. R. Milton and Edward Ecclestone's Noah's Flood. MLN, 55, 1940, 183-7.
Noah's Flood, an opera (1679), exhibits influence of Paradise Lost.

1818 BAKER, CARLOS. A Note on Shelley and Milton. MLN, 55, 1940, 585-9.
Milton's influence on Shelley more pronounced than admitted by Havens.

1819 BECK, RICHARD. Jon Porlaksson—Icelandic Translator of Pope and Milton. JEGP, 32, 1933, 572-85.
An eighteenth-century translator.

1820 BOGORAD, SAMUEL N. Milton's Paradise Lost and Gay's Trivia: a Borrowing. NQ, 195, 1950, 98-9.
On Paradise Lost, 4, 814-19 and Gay's Trivia, 3, 382-6.

1821 BOYCE, BENJAMIN. Milton and Thomas Brown's Translation of Gelli. NQ, 171, 1936, 328-9.
1702.

1822 BROADBENT, J. B. Milton and Arnold. EIC, 6, 1956, 404-17.

1823 BURKE, CHARLES B. Coleridge and Milton. NQ, 176, 1939, 42.

187

1824 BUSH, DOUGLAS. Seventeenth-Century Poets and the Twentieth Century. MHRA Bull., No. 27, 1955, pp. 16-28.
The Presidential Address. Milton "appears to sit more securely than ever on a throne that has partly new and even more solid foundations."

1825 CHAN, SHAN WING. Nineteenth Century Criticism of Paradise Lost, Paradise Regained, and Samson Agonistes. Doctoral diss., Stanford University, 1937. Abs., Abstracts of Diss., Stanford University, 12, 1937, 37-9.

1826 COLGATE, WILLIAM. Horace Walpole on Milton. A Summary of His Annotations on the Work of Thomas Warton Concerning the Poems of John Milton, from the London Edition of James Dodsley, 1785. Toronto: Printed privately, 1953. 18pp.

1827 CORDASCO, FRANCESCO. Junius and Milton. NQ, 195, 1950, 250-1.

1828 DENNY, MARGARET. The Literary Hero in a Sentimental Age: An Unlisted Reference to Milton. MLN, 63, 1948, 259-61.
An allusion in a poem by Henry Pickering.

1829 DILTHEY, WILHELM. Milton und Klopstock. Die Grosse Phantasiedichtung und andere Studien zur vergleichenden Literaturgeschichte (Gottingen: Vanderhoek und Ruprecht, 1954), pp. 122-8.

1830 DODDS, M. H. Chaucer: Spenser: Milton in Drama and Fiction. NQ, 176, 1939, 69.
See letter by T. O. M(abbott), ibid., 89.

1831 DORGAN, RUTH. Milton and Two of His Eighteenth-Century Critics, John Dennis and Joseph Addison. Master's thesis, Lousiana State University, 1955.

1832 ECKMAN, FREDERICK. Karl Shapiro's Adam and Eve. UTSE, 35, 1956, 1-10.
Points out that Shapiro occasionally follows Paradise Lost.

1833 ERSTLING, JULIUS H. Thomas Wolfe's Knowledge and Use of Milton, Master's thesis, University of Florida, 1941.

1834 EVANS, G. BLAKEMORE. Addison's Early Knowledge of Milton. JEGP, 49, 1950, 204-7.

1835 - - - - - -. Milton and Lee's The Rival Queens (1677). MLN, 64, 1949, 527-8.
Milton's Satan reflected in Lee's villain.

1836 FAROOQUI, M. A. The Influence of Milton on the Romantic Poets. Thesis, Lucknow University, 1946.

1837 FARRELL, ALFRED. Joshua Poole and Milton's Minor Poems. MLN, 58, 1943, 198-200.
Milton's poems quoted in Poole's The English Parnassus, 1657.

1838 FLETCHER, EDWARD G. Defoe on Milton. MLN, 50, 1935, 31-2.
Rev: L. C. Martin, YWES, 257.

1839 FLETCHER, HARRIS F. Nathaniel Lee and Milton. MLN, 44, 1929, 173-5.
Verses contributed by Lee to Dryden's The State of Innocence.

1840 FOGLE, FRENCH. Milton Lost and Regained. HLQ, 15, 1952, 351-69.
A discussion of the history of Milton criticism.

1841 FREEDMAN, MORRIS. All for Love and Samson Agonistes. NQ, N. S., 3, 1956, 514-17.

1842 - - - - - -. Milton and Dryden. Doctoral diss., Columbia University, 1953. Abs., DA, 14, 1954, 109.

1843 FRENCH, J. MILTON. "Blind Milton" Ridiculed in Poor Robin, 1664-1674. NQ, 196, 1951, 470-1.
Rev: Arnold Davenport, YWES, 192.

1844 - - - - - -. Lamb and Milton. SP, 31, 1934, 92-103.

1845 GORDON, R. K. Keats and Milton. MLR, 42, 1947, 434-46.

1846 GOSSMAN, ANN. Harmonius Jones and Milton's Invocations. NQ, N. S., 1, 1954, 527-9.
Sir William Jones' debt to Milton.

1847 - - - - - -. Milton Trickt and Frounc't. NQ, N. S., 2, 1955, 100-2.
Paraphrases and adaptations.

1848 GRUSHKIN, A. Pushkin in the Thirties of the Nineteenth Century on the Creative Independence of the Artist (Voltaire, Milton, Chateaubriand). Zwiesda (USSR), 9, 1939, 136-59.

1849 GUIDI, AUGUSTO. Milton e Hopkins. English Miscellany, 6, 1955, 31-43.

1850 HALLER, WILLIAM O. Milton's Reputation and Influence, 1643-1647. Tracts on Liberty in the Puritan Revolution (New York: Columbia University Press, 1935), 1, 128-42.

1851 HANFORD, JAMES HOLLY. Milton among the Book Collectors. NLB, 4, 1956, 97-109.

1852 HARDY, BARRABA. Coleridge and Milton. TLS, Nov. 9, 1951, p. 711.

1853 HAVENS, RAYMOND D. The Influence of Milton on English Poetry. Cambridge: Harvard University Press, 1922.
Rev: R. Spindler, ESt., 45, 1931, 283-90.

1854 ------. Milton's Influence on Wordsworth's Early Sonnets. PMLA, 63, 1948, 751-2.
Disagrees with McNulty.

1855 HAVILAND, THOMAS P. How Well Did Poe Know Milton? PMLA, 69, 1954, 841-60.

1856 ------. A Measure for the Early Freneau's Debt to Milton. PMLA, 55, 1940, 1033-40.

1857 ------. The Miltonic Quality of Brackenridge's Poem on Divine Revelation. PMLA, 56, 1941, 588-92.

1858 HEALY, SISTER M. AQUINAS, R. S. M. Milton and Hopkins. UTQ, 22, 1952, 18-25.

1859 HELSZTYNSKI, STANISLAS. Milton in Poland. SP, 26, 1929, 145-54.
An account of Milton's reputation in Poland.

1860 HEWELL, ONYCE OLIVE. The Relation of Carlyle to Milton. Master's thesis, Duke University, 1937.

1861 HIBERNICUS. Benlowes and Milton. TLS, Aug. 22, 1929, p. 652.
On Benlowes' borrowings.

1862 HOLLOWAY, JOHN. Milton and Arnold. EIC, 7, 1957, 226-8.

1863 HORTON, KENNETH J. The Influence of John Milton on the Connecticut Wits. Master's thesis, University of Florida, 1940.

1864 HOWARD, LEON. Early American Copies of Milton. HLB, 7, 1935, 169-79.
Rev: L. C. Martin, YWES, 257.

1865 ------. The Influence of Milton on Colonial American Poetry. HLB, 9, 1936, 63-89.
Rev: L. C. Martin, YWES, 190.

1866 HUCKABAY, CALVIN. Milton's Literary Reputation During the Victorian Era. Doctoral diss., Louisiana State University, 1955.

1867 (HUNTER, WILLIAM B.) The Study of Milton in the Southeastern United States. SCN, 8, No. 4, 1950, 6.
During the academic year 1949-50.

1868 JENKINS, HAROLD. Benlowes and Milton. MLR, 43, 1948, 186-95.
Benlowes borrowed from Milton.
Rev: L. C. Martin, YWES, 186.

1869 JOHNSON, W. G. Skriften om Paradis and Milton. JEGP, 64, 1945, 263-9.
On the relationship of Spegel's poems (1705) to Paradise Lost.

1870 JONES, FREDERICK L. Shelley and Milton. SP, ⁴⁹, 1952, 488-519.

1871 KATO, R. S. T. Coleridge and His Criticism of Milton. Stud. in Eng. Lit. (Eng. Lit. Soc. Japan), 13, 1933, 482-93.

1872 KELLEY, GRACIE LEE. Milton's Reputation in the Eighteenth Century as Reflected in the Gentleman's Magazine and the Monthly Review. Master's thesis, University of Georgia, 1940.

1873 KITTREDGE, PAUL M. Macaulay's Essay on Milton: A Literary, Historical, and Political Evaluation. Master's thesis, University of Florida, 1951.

1874 KURZ, MYRTIS T. Milton and Shelley: A Study in Similarities and Parallels. Master's thesis, Florida State College for Women, 1940.

1875 LARSEN, T. Swinburne on Milton. TLS, June 17, 1937, pp. 357-8.

1876 LILL, JAMES V. Dryden's Adaptation from Milton, Shakespeare, and Chaucer. Doctoral diss., University of Minnesota, 1954.

1877 LOANE, GEORGE G. Shakespeare, Milton, and Pope. TLS, Jan. 23, 1937, p. 60.
Dalila, Millamant, and Pope's treatment of Donne.

1878 LOEWENSON, LEO. E. G. von Berge, Translator of Milton and Russian Interpreter (1649-1722). SEER, 34, 1956, 281-91.

A Bibliographical Supplement

1879 MABBOTT, THOMAS O. Chatterton and Milton: a Question of Forgery. NQ, 177, 1939, 314.
Cf. Columbia Edition, 18, 562, 599.

1880 ------, and J. MILTON FRENCH. A Satyr Against J. M. 1655. NQ, 173, 1937, 45.
Prints short poem preserved in the notebook of Thomas Stringer.

1881 MALE, R. R., JR. Dual Aspects of Evil in Rappaccini's Daughter, PMLA, 69, 1954, 99-109.
Consideration of Milton's influence, pp. 107-8.

1882 MANNING, C. A. Milton et Njegos. Revue des Etudes Slaves, 18, 1938, 63-72.
Paradise Lost and Njegos' The Torch of the Microcosm (1845).

1883 MANUEL, M. The Seventeenth-Century Critics and Biographers of Milton. Doctoral diss., University of Wisconsin, 1956. Abs., DA, 16, 1956, 2166-7.

1884 McNULTY, JOHN B. Milton, and Wordsworth's Bucer, Erasmus, and Melancthon. NQ, 197, 1952, 61.
Wordsworth's reference to the three Renaissance scholars (Prelude, 3, 479-81) found in Milton's divorce pamphlets.

1885 ------. Milton's Influence on Wordsworth's Early Sonnets. PMLA, 62, 1947, 745-51.
Wordsworth acknowledged a greater debt than he owed.

1886 MEGAFFIN, BLANCHE ISABEL. The Warton Brothers: Their Relation to Romanticism and Milton. Master's thesis, Manitoba University, 1931.

1887 MILLIGAN, BURTON. An Early American Imitator of Milton. AL, 11, 1939, 200-206.
Nathaniel Evans, Poems on Several Occasions (1772).

1888 MONK, S. H. Wordsworth's "unimaginable touch of time." MLN, 52, 1937, 503-4.
Borrowed from Of Education.

1889 MOORE, JOHN R. Milton among the Augustans: the Infernal Council. SP, 48, 1951, 15-25.

1890 MYERS, ROBERT M. Handel and Milton. Tulane Stud. in Eng., 3, 1952, 93-124.
Milton and the eighteenth-century librettists and composers, especially Handel.
Rev: Arnold Davenport, YWES, 178.

1891 NANES, LAURA MAY. John Milton's Ideas on Civil and Religious Liberty and Their Acceptance During the Interregnum. Master's thesis, State University of Iowa, 1933.

1892 ORAS, ANTS. Miltonic Elements in Shelley. SCN, 13, 1955, 22.
The Chariot of Paternal Deity appears in Prometheus Bound, 4.

1893 ------. The Multitudinous Orb: Some Miltonic Elements in Shelley. MLQ, 16, 1955, 247-57.
Considers Prometheus Bound.

1894 OREL, HAROLD. The Dynasts and Paradise Lost. SAQ, 52, 1953, 355-60.

1895 PARKER, WILLIAM R. Milton on King James the Second. MLQ, 3, 1942, 41-44.
The pamphlet Pro Populo Adversus Tyrannos (1689) mostly a reprint of The Tenure of Kings and Magistrates.

1896 ------. Milton's Contemporary Reputation, an Essay, together with a Tentative List of Printed Allusions to Milton, 1641-1674, and Facsimile Reproductions of Five Contemporary Pamphlets Written in Answer to Milton. Columbus: Ohio State University Press, 1940. xii, 229pp.
Rev: L. C. Martin, YWES, 172-3; A Barker, MLR, 36, 1941, 529-30; W. Haller, MLQ, 2, 1941, 322-7; E. N. S. Thompson, PQ, 20, 1941, 191-2; TLS, Mar. 22, 1941, p. 143; J. S. Diekhoff, MLN, 57, 1942, 403-4; J. H. Hanford, JEGP, 41, 1942, 236-8; B. A. Wright, RES, 18, 1942, 232-5.

1897 ------. Milton's Harapha. TLS, Jan. 2, 1937, p. 12.
Replies by E. N. Allen, ibid., Jan. 16, 1937, p. 44; by Jacob Leveen and H. Loewe, ibid., Jan. 23, 1937, p. 60. A discussion of the reference to Milton's poetry in Edward Phillips' New World of Words (1671 ed.).
Rev: L. C. Martin, YWES, 186.

1898 PETTET, E. C. Milton and the Modern Reader. Orion. Ed. by C. Day Lewis et al (London: Nicholson and Watson, 1945), pp. 3, 68-81.
Argues that Milton has been dislodged because "his language and rhythm are extravagantly artificial and narrowly restricted."

1899 PETTIGREW, RICHARD C. Emerson and Milton. AL, 3, 1931, 45-59.

1900 ------. Lowell's Criticism of Milton. AL, 3, 1932, 457-64.

1901 PLUNKETT, FRANK W. The Miltonic Tradition in One of Its Phases. The Criticism of Milton as Found in Leading British Magazines of the Pre-Romantic and Romantic Periods (1779-1832). Doctoral diss., Indiana University, 1931. Printed in summary form, State College, Arkansas: Arkansas State College Press, 1934. 15pp.

A Bibliographical Supplement

1902 POLLITT, JOE DONALD. Ralph Waldo Emerson's Debt to John Milton. Marshall Rev. (Huntington, West Virginia), 3, Dec., 1939, 13-21.

1903 POMMER, HENRY F. Milton and Melville. Doctoral diss., Yale University, 1946. Pittsburgh: University of Pittsburgh Press, 1950. 172pp.
Rev· R. E. Spiller, AL, 23, 1951, 384-5; Sherman Paul, NEQ, 24, 1951, 550-2.

1904 PORTER, HELEN ELIZABTH. Milton's Influence on Tennyson. Master's thesis, Duke University, 1938.

1905 POTTS, ABBIE F. Spenserian and Miltonic Influence in Wordsworth's Ode and Rainbow. SP, 29, 1932, 607-16.

1906 RACINE, LOUIS. Life of Milton. Trans. with an Introd. by Katherine John. London: Hogarth Press, 1930.
The Introd., pp. 9-94, contains a history of Milton's reputation in France.

1907 SAMARIN, R. M. Tvorchestvo Dzh. Mil'tona v otsenke Pushkina. Doklady i soobsheheniia filol. Fakul'tetov, Moscow, Universitet. Soobsheheniia, 6, 1948, 62-70.
On the genius and influence of Milton according to Pushkin.

1908 SANDERLIN, GEORGE. The Influence of Milton and Wordsworth on the Early Victorian Sonnet. ELH, 5, 1938, 225-51.
Part of a doctoral dissertation, The Sonnet in English Literature, 1800-1850, Johns Hopkins University, 1938. Printed in pamphlet form by the Johns Hopkins University Press, 1938.

1909 SATO, KIYOSHI. Samuel Johnson on Milton and Shakespeare. Stud. in Eng. Lit. (Eng. Lit. Soc. Japan), 19, 1939, 339-50.

1910 SAURAT, DENIS. Blake and Milton. London: Stanley Nott, 1935. 159pp.
Rev: London Merc., 33, 1935, 262; Charles Madge, Crit., 15, 1936, 527-9.

1911 SCHAUPP, ROSCOE F. Blake's "Correction" of Milton in Poem and Picture. Doctoral diss., Ohio State University, 1934.

1912 SCHERPBIER, H. Milton in Holland: A Study of Literary Relations of England and Holland before 1730. Doctoral diss., Amsterdam. Amsterdam: H. J. Paris, 1933. 220pp.
Rev: Thomas Weevers, ES, 16, 1934, 69-72.

1913 SCHICK, GEORGE B. Appreciation of Milton as a Criterion of Eighteenth-Century Taste. NQ, N. S., 4, 1957, 113-14.
On Joseph Warton's belief that an appreciation of Milton was a criterion of true literary taste.

1914 SCHULZE, HANS GEORG. Miltons Verlorenes Paradies im deutschen Gewand. Doctoral diss., Bonn, 1928. 103pp.

1915 SENSABAUGH, GEORGE F. Adaptations of Areopagitica. HLQ, 13, 1950, 201-5.
In 1679 and 1681, in connection with attempts to regulate the press.

1916 - - - - - -. Areopagitica Adapted. MLN, 61, 1946, 166-69.
In 1681.
Rev: L. C. Martin, YWES, 175.

1917 - - - - - -. Jefferson's Use of Milton in the Ecclesiastical Controversies of 1776. AL, 26, 1955, 552-9.
Jefferson used The Reason of Church Government and Of Reformation.

1918 - - - - - -. Milton and the Attempted Whig Revolution. The Seventeenth Century (Stanford: Stanford University Press, 1951), pp. 291-305.
Milton's influence on Lord Russell.
Rev: Arnold Davenport, YWES, 192.

1919 - - - - - -. Milton and the Doctrine of Passive Obedience. HLQ, 13, 1949, 19-54.
A study of Milton's influence on Rev. Samuel Johnson and other Whig writers; argues that Milton played an important role "in shaping events which accompanied the Whig rise to power."
Rev: L. C. Martin, YWES, 171.

1920 - - - - - -. Milton at the Trial of Thomas Paine. NQ, N. S., 2, 1955, 212-13.
The Areopagitica quoted by Thomas Erskine, Paine's defense attorney, at the trial in 1792.

1921 - - - - - -. Milton in Early American Schools. HLQ, 19, 1956, 353-83.
From the Revolution through the first quarter of the nineteenth century.

1922 - - - - - -. Milton in the Revolution Settlement. HLQ, 9, 1946, 175-208.
The influence of Pro Populo Adversus Tyrannos.
Rev: L. C. Martin, YWES, 175.

1923 - - - - - -. That Grand Whig, Milton. Stanford University Pubs., University Ser., Lang. and Lit., 11. Stanford: Stanford University Press, 1952. ix, 213pp.

The study "purposes to trace the impact of Milton's arguments in the battle of ideas which led to the acceptance of the Settlement and the Bill of Rights...."
Rev: Arnold Davenport, YWES, 178; J. W. Gough, EHR, 68, 1953, 478-9.

1924 SHUDOFSKY, M. MAURICE. An Early Eighteenth-Century Rhymed Paraphrase of Paradise Lost, II, 1-225. MLN, 56, 1941, 133-4.
In Reflections...on the Vices and Follies of the Age (1707-9).

1925 SMITH, J. H. Shelley and Milton's Chariot of Paternal Deity. MLN, 51, 1936, 215-17.

1926 STARR, HERBERT. An Echo of L'Allegro in Gray's Bard. MLN, 57, 1942, 676.

1927 STAVROU, C. N. Milton, Byron, and the Devil. University of Kansas City Rev., 21, 1955, 153-9.
Argues that Cain is a refutation of Milton's theological position in Paradise Lost.

1928 STEVENS, ALBERT K. Milton and Chartism. PQ, 12, 1933, 377-88.
Rev: L. C. Martin, YWES, 253.

1929 STROUP, THOMAS B. Gay's Mohocks and Milton. JEGP, 46, 1947, 165-7.
Echoes of Milton in Gay's play.

1930 SUMMERS, JOSEPH H. Milton and the Cult of Conformity. YR, 46, 1957, 511-27.
Appreciative analysis of Milton's position in the twentieth century.

1931 SUTHERLAND, W. O. S. Addison's Paradise Lost Criticisms in the Spectator. Master's thesis, University of North Carolina, 1947.

1932 TAYLOR, GEORGE C. Why Read Milton Now? Twentieth Century English (New York: Philosophical Library, 1946), pp. 453-60.
"Amidst the babel of voices...his voice...would give carrying power to all emotional and intellectual forces which serve to elevate rather than degrade us in the scale of being."

1933 THOMPSON, E. N. S. The Rebel Angel in Later Poetry. PQ, 27, 1948, 1-16.
Against the background of Milton's treatment.

1934 THOMPSON, KARL F. Milton's Eighteenth Century Biographers. Doctoral diss., Yale University, 1950.

A Bibliographical Supplement

1935 THORPE, JAMES E., JR. The Decline of the Miltonic Tradition. Doctoral diss., Harvard University, 1941. Abs., Harvard University, Summaries of Theses, 1941, pp. 347-50.

1936 ------, ed. Milton Criticism: Selections from Four Centuries. New York: Rinehart, 1950. 376 pp.
A brief history of Milton criticism, pp. 3-22.

1937 ------. A Note on Coleridge's Gutch Commonplace Book. MLN, 63, 1948, 130-1.
A passage on Milton copied from Jonathan Richardson.

1938 TILLYARD, E. M. W. Matthew Arnold on Milton. Church Quar. Rev., 148, 1949, 153-60. Reprinted in Studies in Milton (London: Chatto and Windus, 1951), pp. 1-7.

1939 VAHID, S. A. Iqbal and Milton. Pakistan Quar., 8, Summer, 1957, 52-5.
Considers Milton's influence on the Persian poet.

1940 VALLESE, TARQUINIO. Un presunto plagio di Milton. Naples: R. Pironti, 1949. 35pp.

1941 VISIAK, E. H. The Arcturan Shadow (A Complement to Milton's Satan). NQ, 178, 1940, 225-7.
Satan and David Lindsay's A Voyage to Arcturus (1920).

1942 V(ISIAK), E. H. A Curious Double Parallel Between Milton and Fielding. NQ, 176, 1939, 260.

1943 WALZ, JOHN. Miltonic Words in the German Poetic Vocabulary: Empyreum, Hyazinthene Locken. Monat. f. dt. Unt., 37, 1946, 192-200.

1944 WASSERMAN, EARL R. Early Evidence of Milton's Influence. MLN, 58, 1943, 293-5.
Addenda to Havens' list.
Rev: L. C. Martin, YWES, 158.

1945 ------. The Source of Motherwell's Melancholye. MLN, 55, 1940, 296.
Il Penseroso.

1946 WHITING, GEORGE W. Colley Cibber and Paradise Lost. NQ, 164, 1933, 171-2.
Quotations from Paradise Lost in Cibber's The Refusal (1721) were intended to ridicule the idealism of Milton's conception of love.

1947 ------. A Late Seventeenth Century Milton Plagiarism. SP, 31, 1934, 37-50.
A Letter from General Ludlow borrows from Eikonoklastes.

1948 - - - - - -. Milton and Lord Brooke on the Church. MLN, 51, 1936, 161-6.
Borrowings from Of Prelatical Episcopacy.
Rev: L. C. Martin, YWES, 189.

1949 - - - - - -. Mrs. M—and Milton. NQ, N. S., 2, 1955, 200-1.
An unidentified Mrs. M. gives Milton special praise in a poem, The Progress of Poetry (1759).

1950 - - - - - -. Mrs. M—and M. M. NQ, N. S., 4, 1957, 446-7.
Identifies the author of The Progress of Poetry as Mrs. Madan.

1951 - - - - - -. Ode on Milton. TLS, July 26, 1957, p. 457.
A poem by J. Lawes (1793).

1952 - - - - - -. Rowe's Debt to Paradise Lost. MP, 32, 1935, 271-80.

1953 - - - - - -. A Whig Reference to Paradise Lost, 1682. TLS, June 7, 1934, p. 408.
In A Pleasant Conference upon the Observator....

1954 - - - - - -. Woodward's Debt to Milton in 1644. SP, 33, 1936, 228-35.
Woodward's A Dialogue contains borrowed passages from the anti-episcopal pamphlets.

1955 WIEGEL, JOHN A. The Miltonic Tradition in the First Half of the Nineteenth Century. Doctoral diss., Western Reserve University, 1939.

1956 WILCOX, STEWART C., and JOHN M. RAINES. Lycidas and Adonais. MLN, 67, 1952, 19-21.
Parallels.

1957 WILSON, EDMUND. T. S. Eliot. The New Republic, 60, 1929, 341-49.
Believes that Milton's poetic reputation has declined with the ascendancy of Eliot.

1958 WOLFE, DON M. Milton and Mirabeau. PMLA, 49, 1934, 116-28.

1959 WORDSWORTH, JOHN and WILLIAM. Milton and Wordsworth. TLS, Oct. 4, 1947, p. 507.
Call attention to a copy of Milton owned by Wordsworth during his Cambridge days.

1960 ZIMMERMAN, LESTER F. Some Aspects of Milton's American Reputation to 1900. Doctoral diss., University of Wisconsin, 1950. Abs., Summaries of Doctoral Diss., University of Wisconsin, 11, 1951, 358-60.

ADDENDA

116a BROADBENT, J. B. The Rhetoric of Paradise Lost. Doctoral diss., St. Catharine's College, Oxford, 1956.

1322a O'BRIEN, GORDON W. Renaissance Poetics and the Problem of Power. Chicago: Institute of Elizabethan Studies, 1956. xxvi, 127pp.

Milton given a prominent place, for "...he was the last of these for whom the Renaissance concept of the dignity of man and of the aims of human knowledge went far toward creating the form and theme of his discourse."

1336a PATRIDES, C. A. Milton and the Christian Faith: a Study of His Orthodoxy. Doctoral diss., Wadham College, Oxford, 1957.

1889a MUSGROVE, T. J. John Milton's Influence on French Poetry in the Romantic Period (1800-1850). Master's thesis, University College, London, 1957.

INDEX OF AUTHORS

Reference figures are to item numbers.

Coolidge, Lowell W., 639, 876, 1530.
Cooper, Lane, 1120.
Cope, Jackson I., 141.
Corcoran, Sister Mary Irma, 142.
Cordasco, Francesco, 1827.
Cormican, L. A., 1121.
Cowling, George, 143.
Cox, Robert, 877.
Craig, Hardin, 878, 1122.
Cramer, Marjorie Lee, 1123.
Crino, Anna Maria, 1124.
Crundell, H. W., 144.
Curgenven, J. P., 640.
Curious, 641.
Curry, Walter C., 145-9, 1125-6.

Dahlberg, Charles, 150.
Daiches, David, 642, 1531.
Dambrin, M., 1127.
Dane, Nathan, 1128.
Daniels, Edgar F., 151.
Danniells, Roy, 152, 1129.
Darbishire, Helen, 59, 65, 153, 1532-3, 1704, 1758-9.
Daube, David, 466.
Davenport, Arnold, 8, 879, 11300.
Davis, Godfrey, 920, 1534.
Dawson, Grace G., 1131.
Day, Mabel, 643.
Day-Lewis, Cecil, 154.
De Beer, E. S., 644-5, 1535.
De Filippis, Michele, 646.
De Maisères, Cecil, 154.
Dennis, Leah, 156.
Denny, Margaret, 1828.
De Pilato, S., 157.
De Selincourt, Ernest, 1132.
De Soet, F. D., 1133.
Deutch, Alfred H., 158.
Dickson, David W. D., 159, 1134.
Diekhoff, John S., 160-3, 647-51, 1135-6, 1536, 1705-7.
Dillard, Kathryn, 652.
Dilthey, Wilhelm, 1829.
Dobrée, Bonamy, 1137.

Dodds, M. H., 1830.
Dorgan, Ruth, 1831.
Dorian, Donald C., 653-8, 1537-8.
Dos Passos, John R., 1539.
Douglas, Norman, 164.
Drew, Helen L., 881.
Dubbell, S. Earl, 1138.
Duhamel, P. Albert, 882.
Duncan, Edgar H., 165-7.
Duncan-Jones, E. E., 659.
Duncan-Jones, Elsie, 883, 1540.
Durling, Dwight, 516.
Durr, Robert A., 168.
Durrett, R. W., 1139.
Dustoor, P. E., 169.
Dworsky, Besa R., 1140.
Dyson, A. E., 660.

Eargle, Mayre Wall, 884.
Eastland, Elizabeth W., 1141.
Eastman, Fred, 1142.
Eckman, Frederick, 1832
Egle, A., 1143.
Eisenring, J. Th., 885.
Eisig, K. T., 1144.
Ekfelt, Fred E., 886-8.
Eliot, T. S., 1145-7.
Elledge, Scott, 661, 1708.
Elliott, G. R., 1148-50.
Ellis-Fermor, Una, 517.
Ellwood, Thomas, 1541.
Elton, William, 170, 662.
Elvin, Lionel, 1709.
Emerson, Everett H., 171-2.
Emerson, Francis W., 663.
Empson, William, 173, 1151.
England, Sylvia L., 1542.
Erskine, John, 174.
Erstling, Julius H., 1833.
Ethel, Garland, 175.
Evans, B. Ifor, 889-90.
Evans, G. Blakemore, 664-6, 1834-5.
Evans, Robert O., 176-7, 1710-11.
Evans, Willa McClung, 667, 1543.

Maas, P., 736.
Mabbott, Thomas O., 95, 269, 737-41, 1610-22, 1779-85, 1879-80.
Macaulay, Rose, 1623.
MacDonald, Angus, 24.
Mackail, J. W., 1786.
Mackellar, Walter, 270, 569, 1274.
Mackenzie, Barbara K., 1722.
Mackenzie, Phyllis, 1275.
Mackinnon, Malcolm H. M., 1276.
Macklem, Michael, 1277.
Maclean, Hugh N., 742.
Macmillan, D., 3.
Madan, Francis F., 943, 1787.
Madsen, William G., 1278.
Magealson, Viola, 944.
Mahood, M. M., 271.
Male, R. R., Jr., 1881.
Malone, Kemp, 272.
Manning, Clarence A., 273, 1882.
Manuel, M., 1279, 1883.
Marilla, Esmond L., 274-6, 480, 537, 743, 1280.
Marks, Emerson R., 744.
Martin, L. C., 8, 745, 945.
Martin, Patricia, 1281.
Martz, Louis L., 746.
Mason, M. G., 946.
Mathies Geb. Dorner, Maria Elizabeth, 538.
Maxey, Chester C., 1282.
Maxwell, I. R., 277.
Maxwell, J. C., 278-9, 539-40, 747, 947.
Mayerson, Caroline W., 748.
Mayoux, Jean-Jacques, 948.
McC., H., 1788.
McCain, John Walker, 1789-90.
McCall, Lois G., 541.
McCarthy, Thomas J., 280.
McColley, Grant, 281-92, 749, 1283-5, 1624.
McCoy, Patricia, 234.
McDavid, Raven I., 542, 1286.
McDill, Joseph M., 1287.

McKenzie, J., 750-2.
McKerahan, Annabelle L., 293.
McLachlan, H., 1288.
McLeod, Frances R., 1289.
McManaway, James G., 543.
McNulty, John B., 1884-5.
Megaffin, Blanche Isabel, 1886.
Megroz, Rodolphe L., 1290.
Menzies, W., 1291.
Merrill, Harry G., 949.
Mertner, Edgar, 1292.
Meyerstein, E. H. W., 294.
Miles, Josephine, 1723-6.
Miller, Milton, 295, 1293.
Miller, Sonia, 950, 1791.
Miller, Virginia, 1294.
Milligan, Burton, 1887.
Milton, John, Areopagitica, translations of, 1038-45; collected works, editions of, 37-45; collected poems, editions of, 46-63; collected prose works and individual prose selections, editions of, 847-63; minor poems and selected minor poems, editions of, 566-91; Paradise Lost, editions of, 64-77; Paradise Lost, translations of, 1010-24; Paradise Regained, editions of, 454-7; Samson Agonistes, editions of, 500-8; shorter poems, translations of, 1025-37.
Mims, Edwin, 1299-1300.
Mineka, Francis E., 951.
Mirsky, Prince D. S., 848.
Mitchell, Charles B., 753.
Mody, Jehangir R. P., 296.
Mohl, Ruth, 297.
Molin, Sven, Eric, 1792.
Möller, Alfred, 1301.
Moloney, Michael F., 754, 1727.
Monk, S. H., 1888.
Montgomery, Sara Drake, 1302.
Montgomery, Walter A., 755.
Moody, Lester Deane, 862.
Moore, John R., 1889.
Morand, Paul Phelps, 1303, 1626.

More, Paul Elmer, 756.
Morse, J. Mitchell, 298.
Moung, Daphne Aye, 1728.
Mounts, Charles E., 1304.
Muir, Kenneth, 1627.
Muir, Lynette R., 300.
Mullen, Cecil, 1305.
Müller, Ursula, 299.
Mummendey, Richard, 25.
Munsterberg, M., 301.
Murdoch, Walter, 1306.
Murray, John F., 1307.
Murry, John Middleton, 1308-9.
Musgrove, S., 302.
Musgrove, T. J., 1889a.
Mutschmann, H., 303-4, 757-8, 1310.
Myers, Robert Manson, 1793, 1890.
Myhr, Ivar L., 759, 1311.

Nanes, Laura May, 1891.
Nash, Ralph, 952.
Nazàri, Emilio, 305, 1312, 1628.
Neilson, William A., 1313.
Neiman, Fraser, 760.
Nelson, Lawrence E., 306.
Nelson, Lowry, Jr., 1729.
Nethercot, Arthur H., 1629.
Neumann, Joshua H., 953.
Newell, Samuel William, Jr., 481.
Nicholas, Constance, 954, 1314-15.
Nicolson, Marjorie Hope, 307, 1316-19.
Nott, Kathleen, 1320.
Noyes, Alfred, 1321.

O'Brien, Gordon W., 1322a.
O'Connor, John J., 1323.
Ochi, Fumio, 1630.
Ogden, H. S. V., 308, 1324.
Oldfather, W. A., 955.
Oman, Sir Charles, 761.
Oras, Ants, 309-11, 762-4, 1325-6, 1794, 1892-3.
Orel, Harold, 1894.
Orsini, Napoleone, 1327-8.

Osborne, Lawrence, 1329.
Osgood, Charles G., 51, 956, 1330-2.
Ould, Herman, 957.
Owen, Eivion, 958.

Pakenham, Thomas, 312.
Parish, John E., 313.
Parker, William Riley, 544-50, 765-72, 880, 959, 1333, 1632-44, 1730, 1795, 1895-7.
Parkinson, Mabel B., 1334.
Parks, George B., 960-1.
Parsons, Edward S., 1335, 1645-6.
Partrides, C. A., 314, 1336a.
Patrick, John M., 315-16.
Patrick, J. Max, 962, 1336, 1796-8.
Patterson, Frank A., 37-9, 46-7, 573.
Pattison, Mark, 1647.
Peple, Edward C., 773.
Percival, A. M., 503.
Pershing, James H., 1799.
Peter, John, 1337.
Petersen, Vict. Juul, 963.
Petit, Herbert H., 1338, 1731.
Pettet, E. C., 1898.
Pettigrew, Richard C., 1899-1900.
Pettit, Henry J., Jr., 24.
Phillips, John, 1648.
Pilato, S. De, 317.
Pinto, Vivian de Sola, 26.
Pitts, Dessie D., 482.
Pollitt, Joe Donald, 1902.
Pommer, Henry F., 1903.
Pope, Elizabeth M., 483.
Porter, Helen Elizabeth, 1904.
Post, Martin M., 774.
Potter, James L., 775.
Potts, Abbie F., 1905.
Powell, F. Townshend, 318.
Powys, John C., 1339.
Praz, Mario, 319, 1340-3.
Price, Allan F., 964.
Priest, Harold M., 1344.
Prince, F. T., 508, 1345-6.